# ON NAUSICAÄ
## By Hayao Miyazaki

Nausicaä was a Phaecian princess in *The Odyssey*. I have been fascinated by her ever since I first read about her in Bernard Evslin's Japanese translation of a small dictionary of Greek mythology. Later, when I actually read *The Odyssey*, I was disappointed not to find the same splendor in her there as I had found in Evslin's book. So, as far as I am concerned, Nausicaä is still the girl Evslin described at length in his paperback. I can tell that he was particularly fond of Nausicaä as he devoted three pages to her in his small dictionary, but gave only one page to both Zeus and Achilles.

As Evslin described her, Nausicaä was a beautiful and fanciful girl, quick on her feet. She loved playing the harp and singing more than the attentions of her suitors or pursuing earthly comforts. She took delight in nature and had an especially sensitive personality. It was she who, unafraid, saved Odysseus and nursed his wounds when he drifted ashore covered with blood. Nausicaä soothed his spirit by improvising a song for him.

Nausicaä's parents worried that she might fall in love with Odysseus and pressured him to set sail. Nausicaä watched his ship until it was out of sight. According to legend, she never married, but traveled from court to court as the first female minstrel, singing about Odysseus and his adventures on his voyage.

Evslin concludes, "This girl occupied a special place in the weather-beaten heart of the great voyager Odysseus."

Nausicaä reminded me of a Japanese heroine — I think I read about her in *The Tales of the Past and Present*. She was the daughter of an aristocratic family and was called the "princess that loved insects." She was regarded as an eccentric because even after reaching a marriageable age, she still loved to play in the fields and would be enchanted by the transformation of a pupa into a butterfly. Her eyebrows were dark and her teeth white — unlike the other girls of her era, she did not follow the custom of shaving off her eyebrows and blackening her teeth. According to the *Tales*, she looked very strange!

Today she wouldn't be perceived as an eccentric. Even though she might be considered a little peculiar, she would be able to fit into society easily, accepted as a nature lover, or just as someone with individualistic interests. In the era of *The Tale of Genji* and *The Pillow Book* [early eleventh century], however, an aristocrat's daughter who loved insects and would not shave her eyebrows would have been shunned. Even as a child, I couldn't help but worry about the princess's fate.

This princess was not daunted by social restrictions; she ran about as she pleased in the mountains and fields, moved by the plants and trees and the floating clouds... I've always wondered how the princess survived as an adult. Today she would be able to find someone who would understand and love her. What was her fate then, in the Heian period [794-1185], with all its conventions and taboos?

Unfortunately, unlike Nausicaä, the "princess that loved insects" never had an Odysseus wash up on her shores, nor songs to sing, nor foreign lands to wander in, to escape society's restrictions. If she had met the great voyager, however, I'm sure she would have experienced the same illumination from "the man covered with blood."

Unconsciously, Nausicaä and this Japanese princess became one person in my mind.

The people at *Animage* [a premiere Japanese animation magazine] encouraged me to do comics, so I went ahead and set down my own concept of Nausicaä. Now I am "doomed" and have to learn the hard way again why, a long time ago, I concluded that I had no talent for comics and gave them up [Miyazaki is being overly modest here]. Now I just want this girl to attain freedom and happiness.

This article appeared in volume one of the original Japanese version of *Nausicaä of the Valley of the Wind*.

# NAUSICAÄ
## Of The Valley Of The Wind

I

# HAYAO MIYAZAKI

# Nausicaä of the Valley of the Wind
## Volume 1

## STORY & ART BY HAYAO MIYAZAKI

Translation/David Lewis and Toren Smith [Studio Proteus]
Translation Assist — Studio Ghibli Library Edition/Kaori Inoue, Joe Yamazaki
Touch-up Art & Lettering/Walden Wong
Design/Izumi Evers
Editor — 1st Edition/Annette Roman
Editor — Studio Ghibli Library Edition/Elizabeth Kawasaki

Kaze no Tani no Nausicaä [Nausicaä of the Valley of the Wind]
Illustrations and Story by Hayao Miyazaki
© 1983 Studio Ghibli - H. All rights reserved.
First published in Japan by Tokuma Shoten Co., Ltd.

Printed in Canada

Published by VIZ Media, LLC
P.O. Box 77010
San Francisco, CA 94107

Studio Ghibli Library Edition

13

First printing, February 2004
Thirteenth printing, August 2018
First English edition, May 1995

www.viz.com

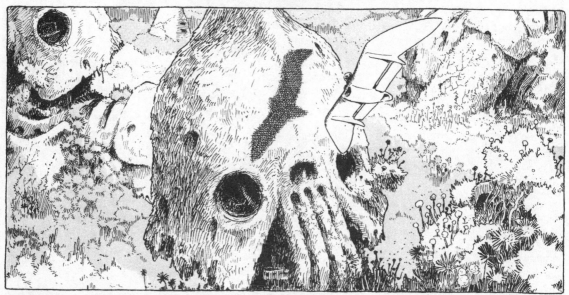

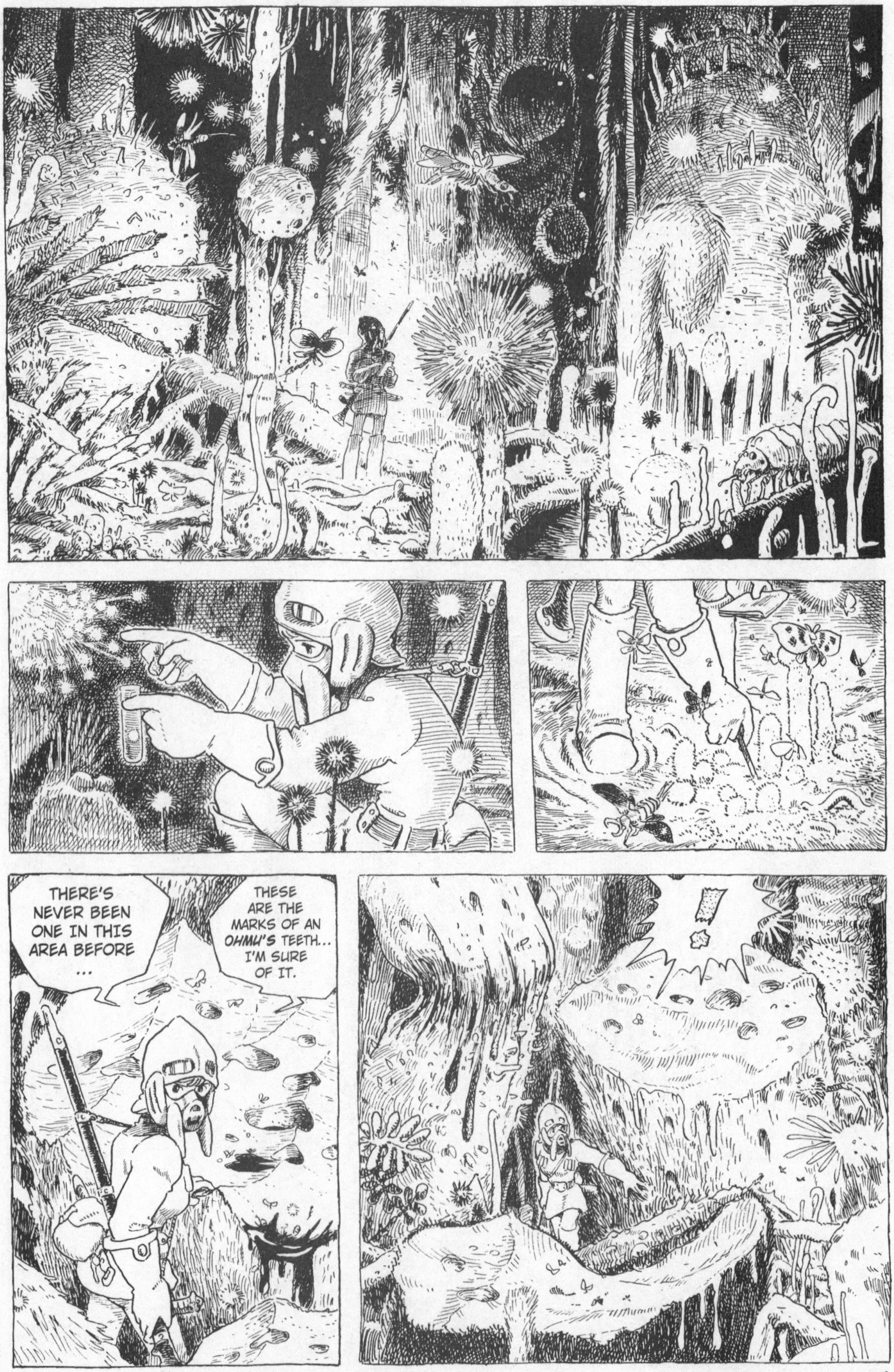
!
THESE ARE THE MARKS OF AN OHMU'S TEETH... I'M SURE OF IT.
THERE'S NEVER BEEN ONE IN THIS AREA BEFORE ...

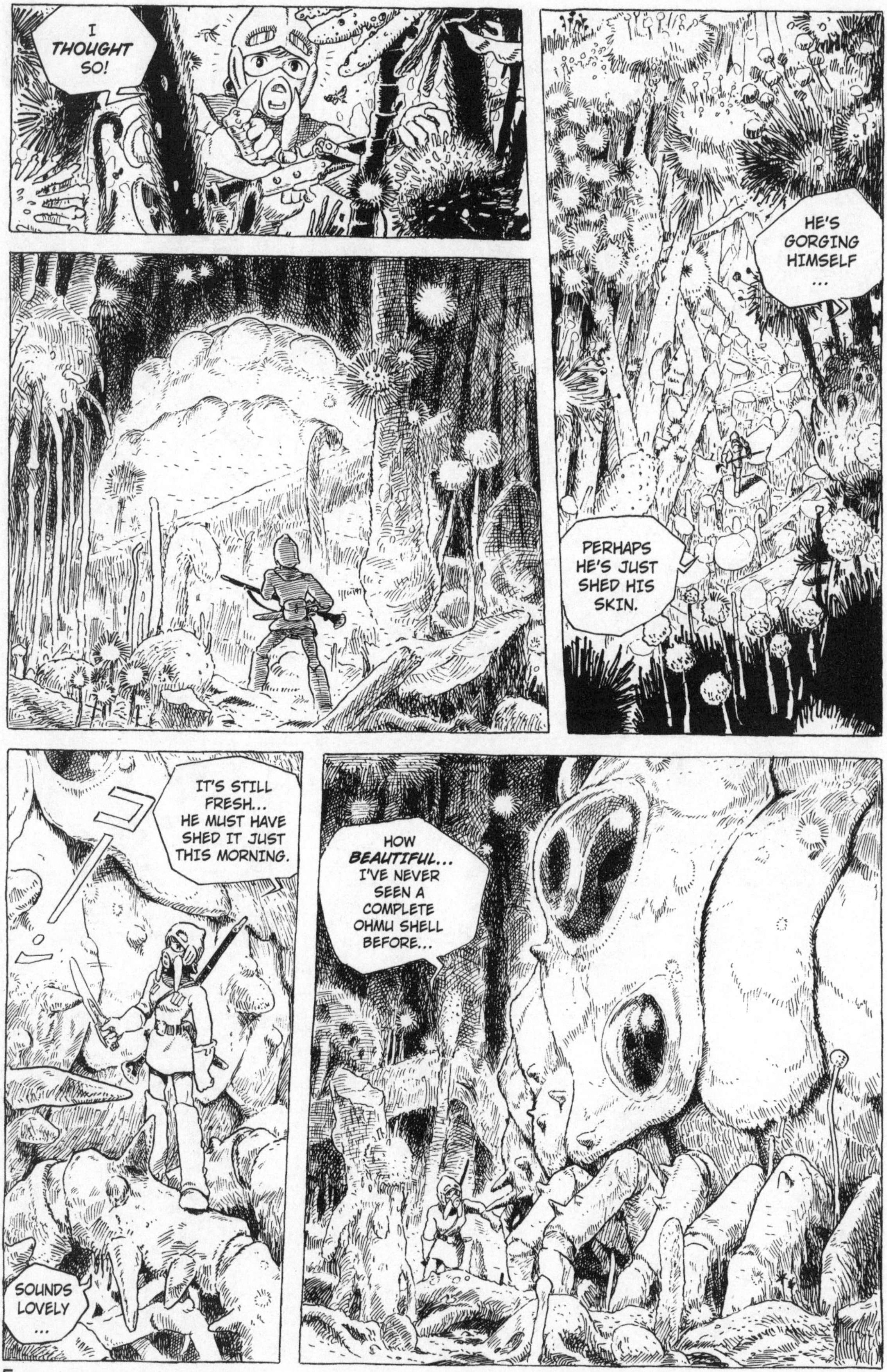
HE'S GORGING HIMSELF ...
PERHAPS HE'S JUST SHED HIS SKIN.
I *THOUGHT* SO!
HOW *BEAUTIFUL...* I'VE NEVER SEEN A COMPLETE OHMU SHELL BEFORE...
IT'S STILL FRESH... HE MUST HAVE SHED IT JUST THIS MORNING.
SOUNDS LOVELY ...

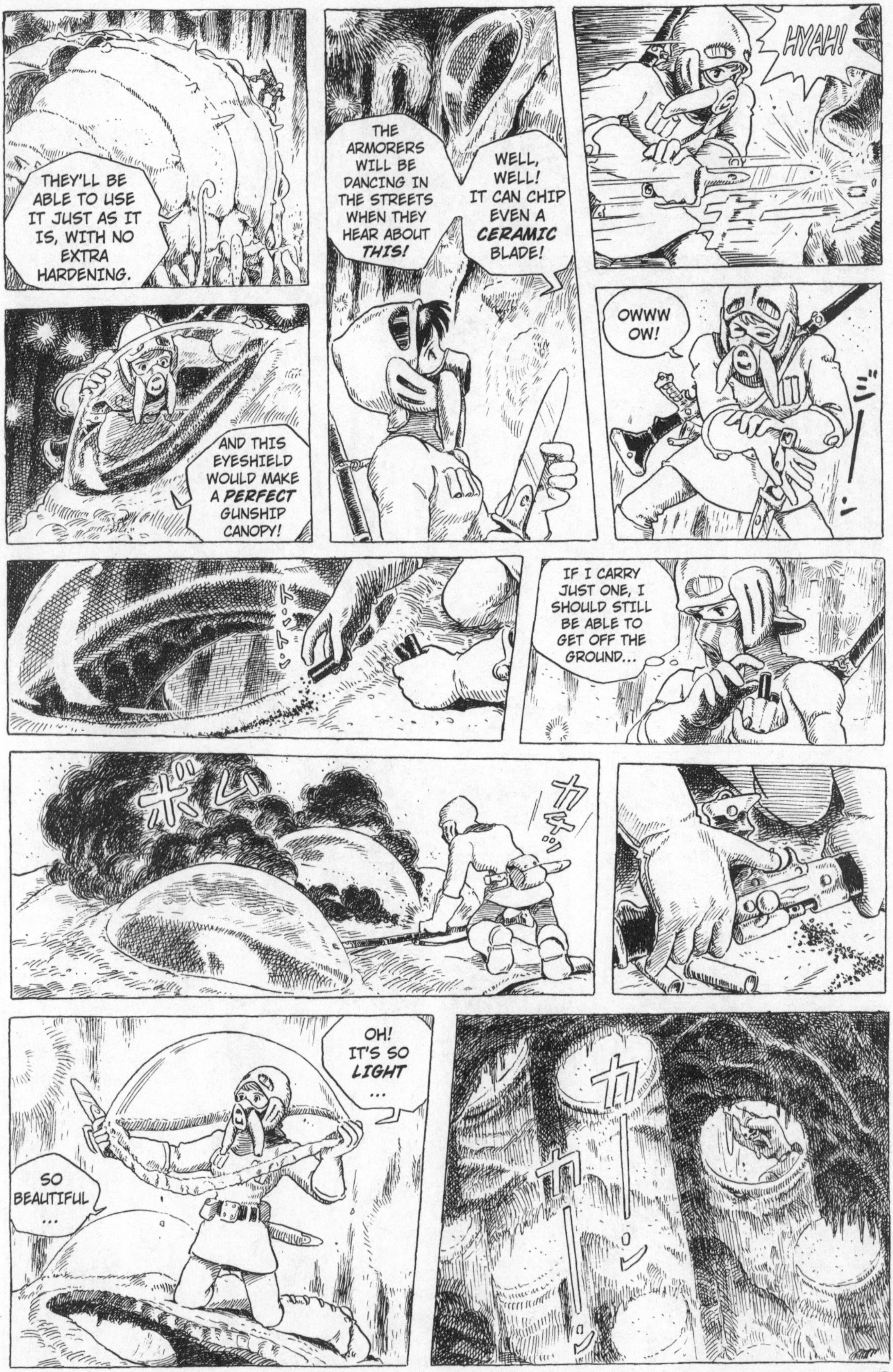
HYAH!
OWWW OW!
WELL, WELL! IT CAN CHIP EVEN A CERAMIC BLADE!
THE ARMORERS WILL BE DANCING IN THE STREETS WHEN THEY HEAR ABOUT THIS!
THEY'LL BE ABLE TO USE IT JUST AS IT IS, WITH NO EXTRA HARDENING.
AND THIS EYESHIELD WOULD MAKE A PERFECT GUNSHIP CANOPY!
IF I CARRY JUST ONE, I SHOULD STILL BE ABLE TO GET OFF THE GROUND...
OH! IT'S SO LIGHT...
SO BEAUTIFUL...

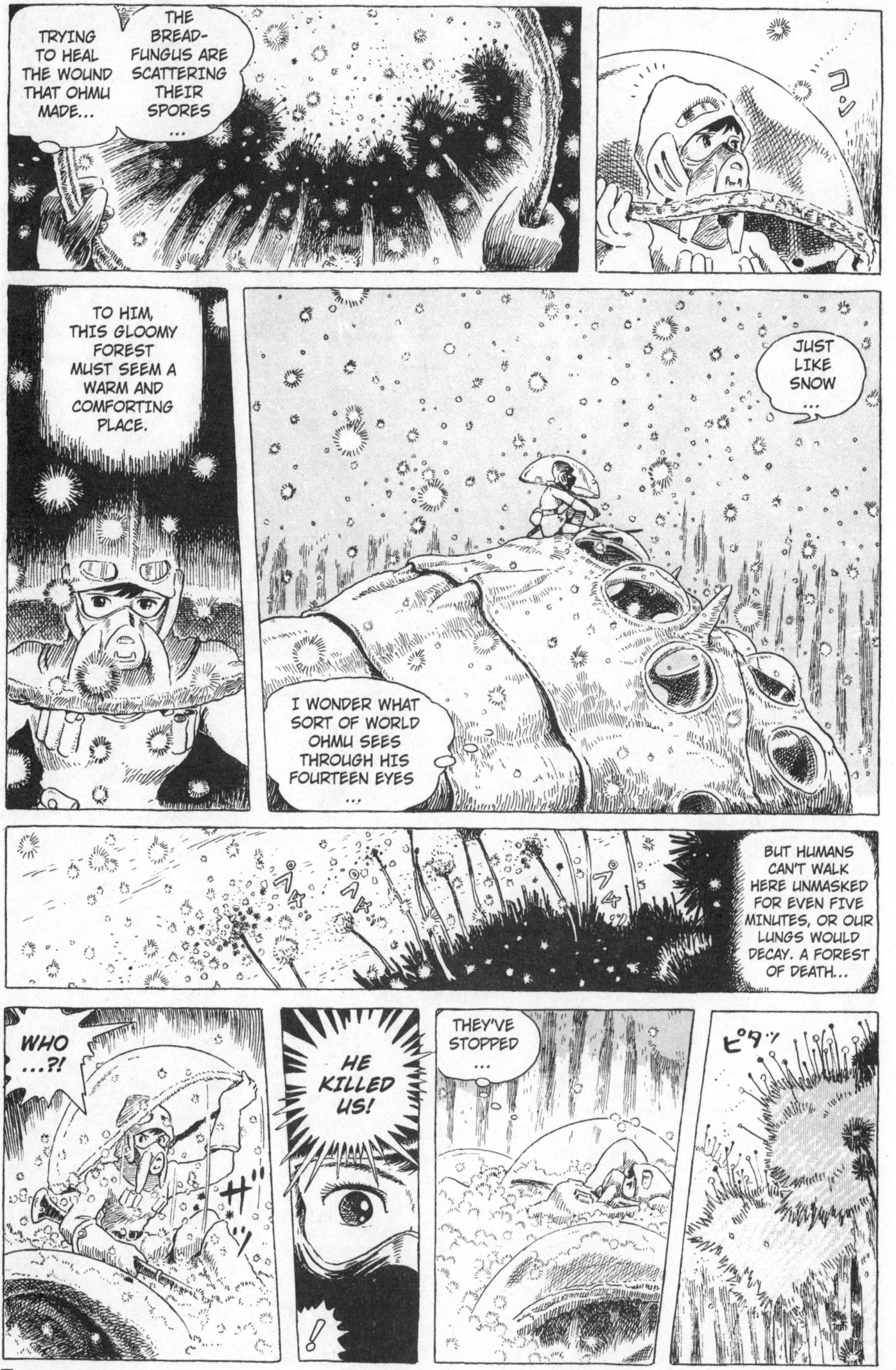

コン
THE BREAD-FUNGUS ARE SCATTERING THEIR SPORES ...
TRYING TO HEAL THE WOUND THAT OHMU MADE...
JUST LIKE SNOW ...
I WONDER WHAT SORT OF WORLD OHMU SEES THROUGH HIS FOURTEEN EYES ...
TO HIM, THIS GLOOMY FOREST MUST SEEM A WARM AND COMFORTING PLACE.
BUT HUMANS CAN'T WALK HERE UNMASKED FOR EVEN FIVE MINUTES, OR OUR LUNGS WOULD DECAY. A FOREST OF DEATH...
ピタッ
THEY'VE STOPPED ...
HE KILLED US!
!
WHO ...?!
ザッ

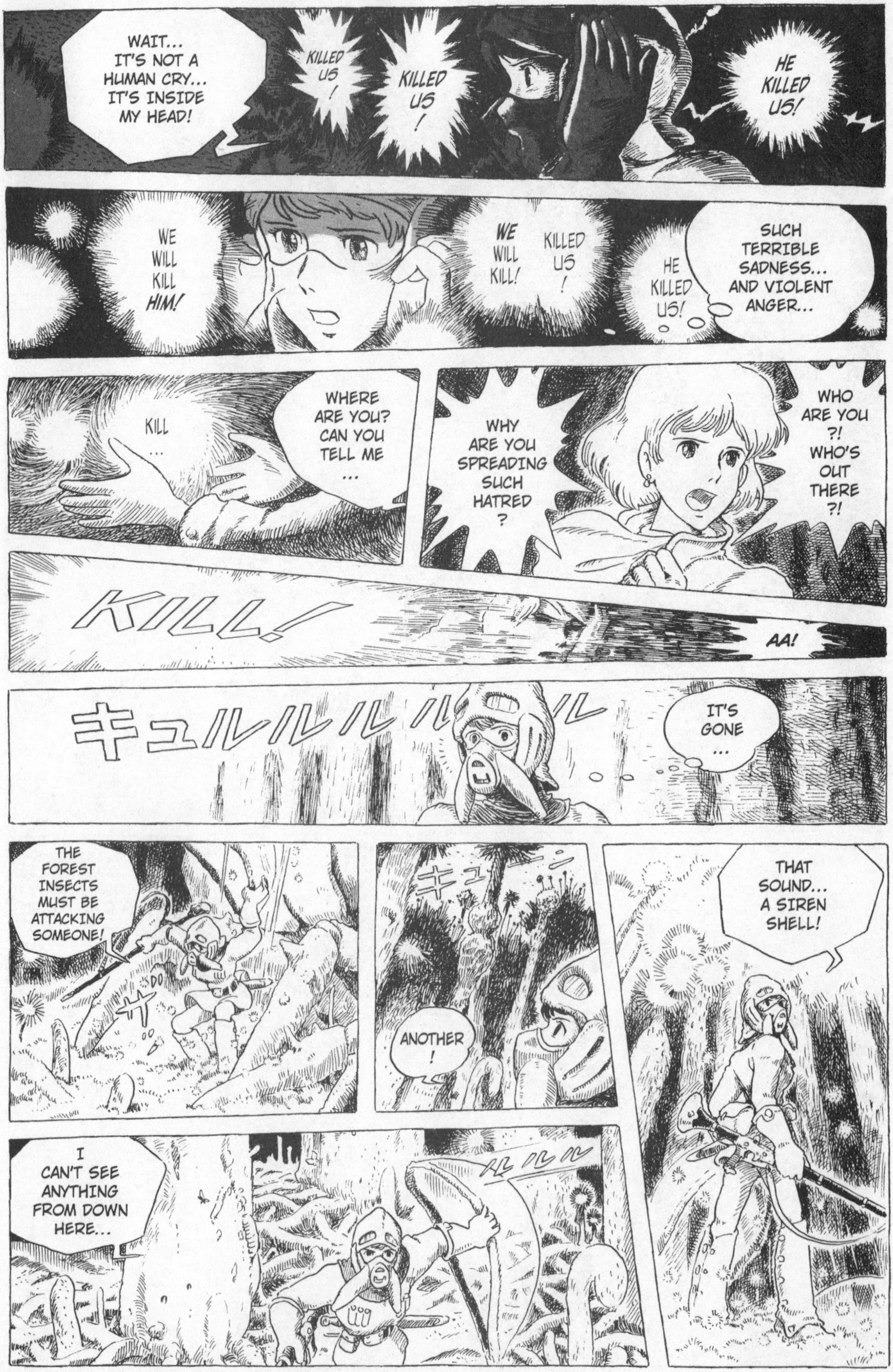

HE KILLED US!
KILLED US!
KILLED US!
WAIT... IT'S NOT A HUMAN CRY... IT'S INSIDE MY HEAD!
SUCH TERRIBLE SADNESS... AND VIOLENT ANGER...
HE KILLED US!
KILLED US!
WE WILL KILL!
WE WILL KILL HIM!
WHO ARE YOU?! WHO'S OUT THERE?!
WHY ARE YOU SPREADING SUCH HATRED?
WHERE ARE YOU? CAN YOU TELL ME...
KILL...
AA!
KILL!
IT'S GONE...
キュルルルルル
THAT SOUND... A SIREN SHELL!
キュー
ANOTHER!
THE FOREST INSECTS MUST BE ATTACKING SOMEONE!
DO
ルルル
I CAN'T SEE ANYTHING FROM DOWN HERE...

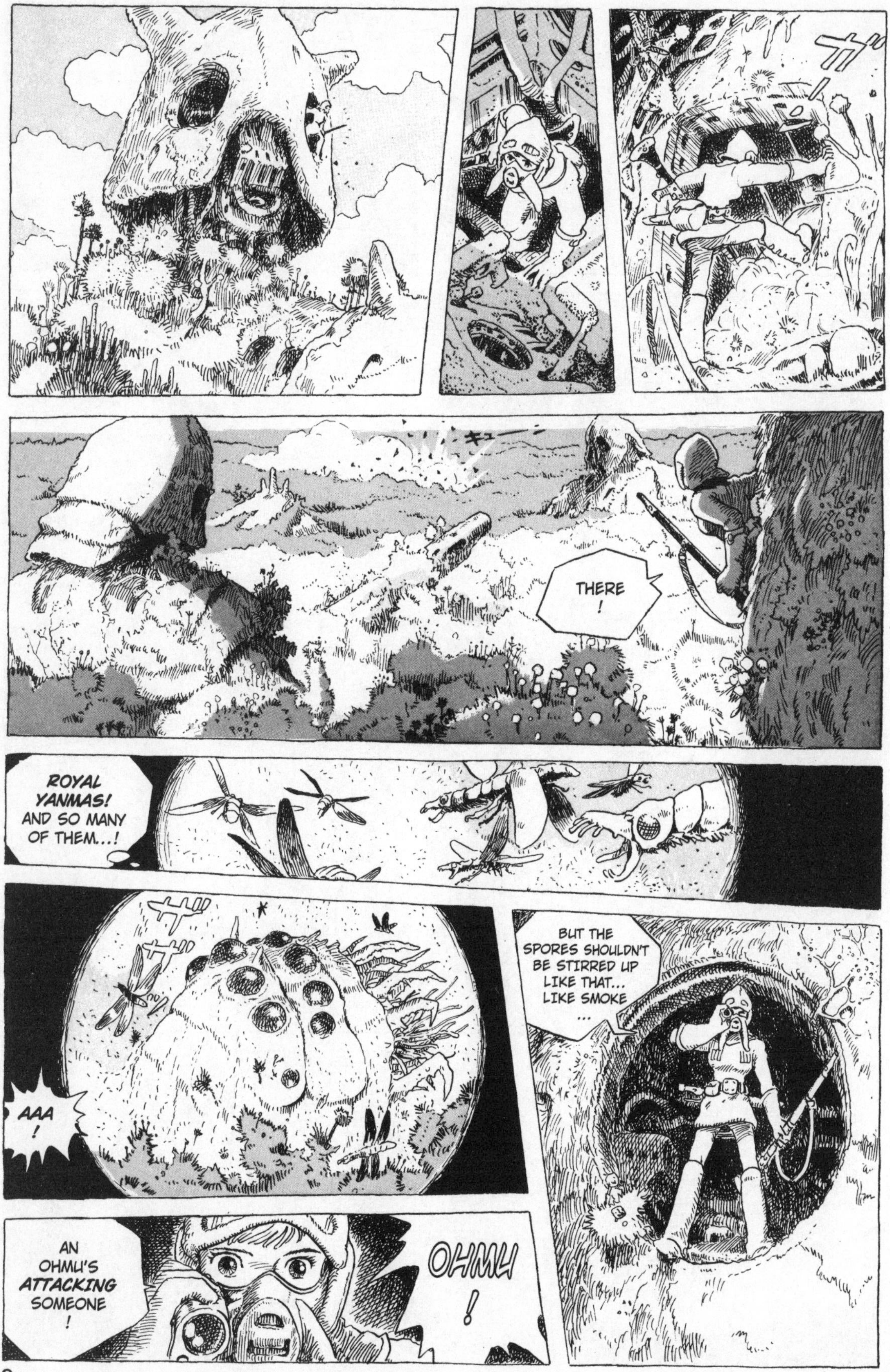
THERE !
ROYAL YANMAS! AND SO MANY OF THEM...!
BUT THE SPORES SHOULDN'T BE STIRRED UP LIKE THAT... LIKE SMOKE ...
AAA !
OHMU !
AN OHMU'S ATTACKING SOMEONE !

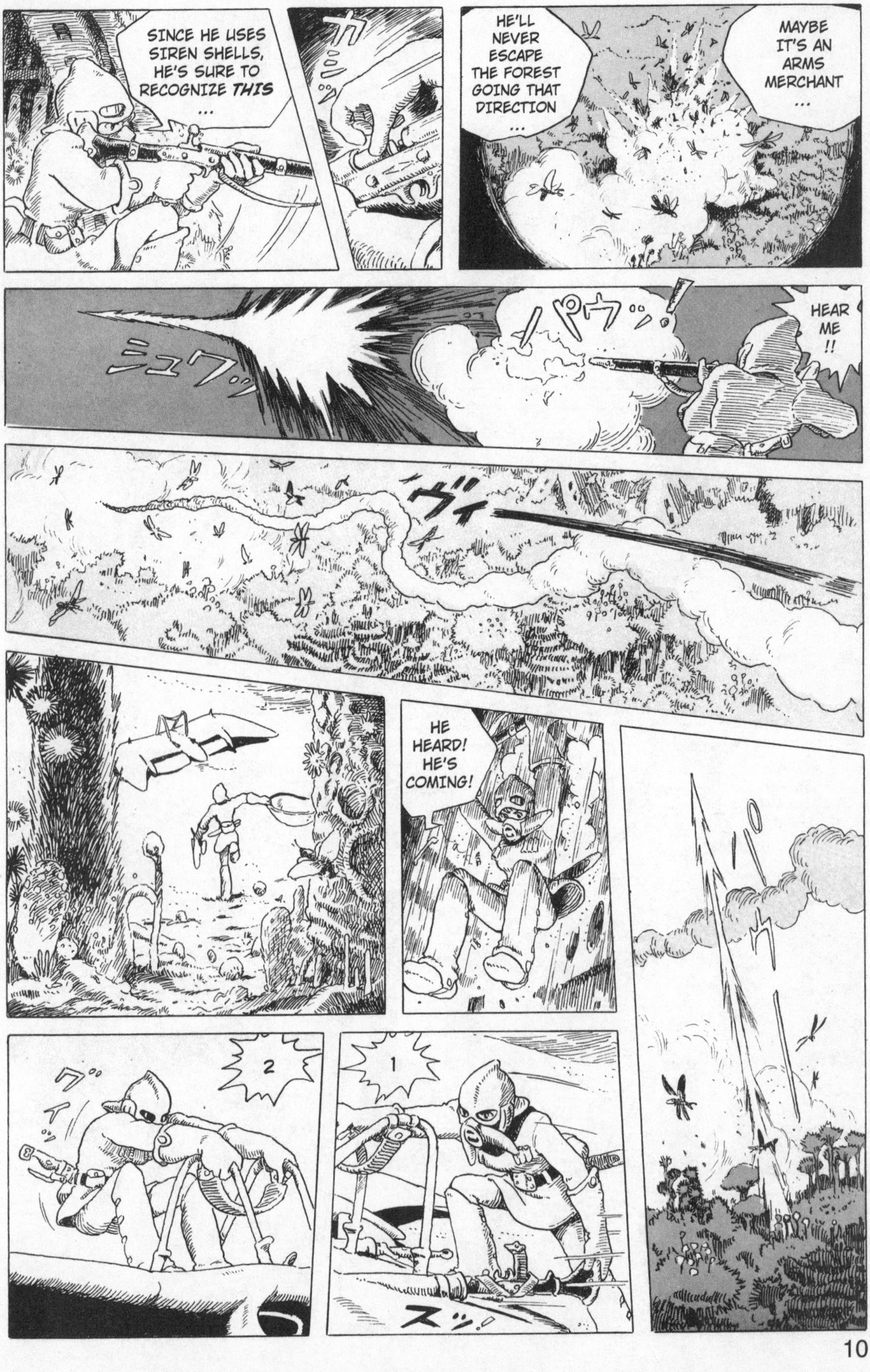
MAYBE IT'S AN ARMS MERCHANT ...
HE'LL NEVER ESCAPE THE FOREST GOING THAT DIRECTION ...
カシッ
SINCE HE USES SIREN SHELLS, HE'S SURE TO RECOGNIZE ***THIS*** ...
HEAR ME !!
パウッ!
シュワッ
ヴィ
パッ
HE HEARD! HE'S COMING!
1
スッ
2
グイッ

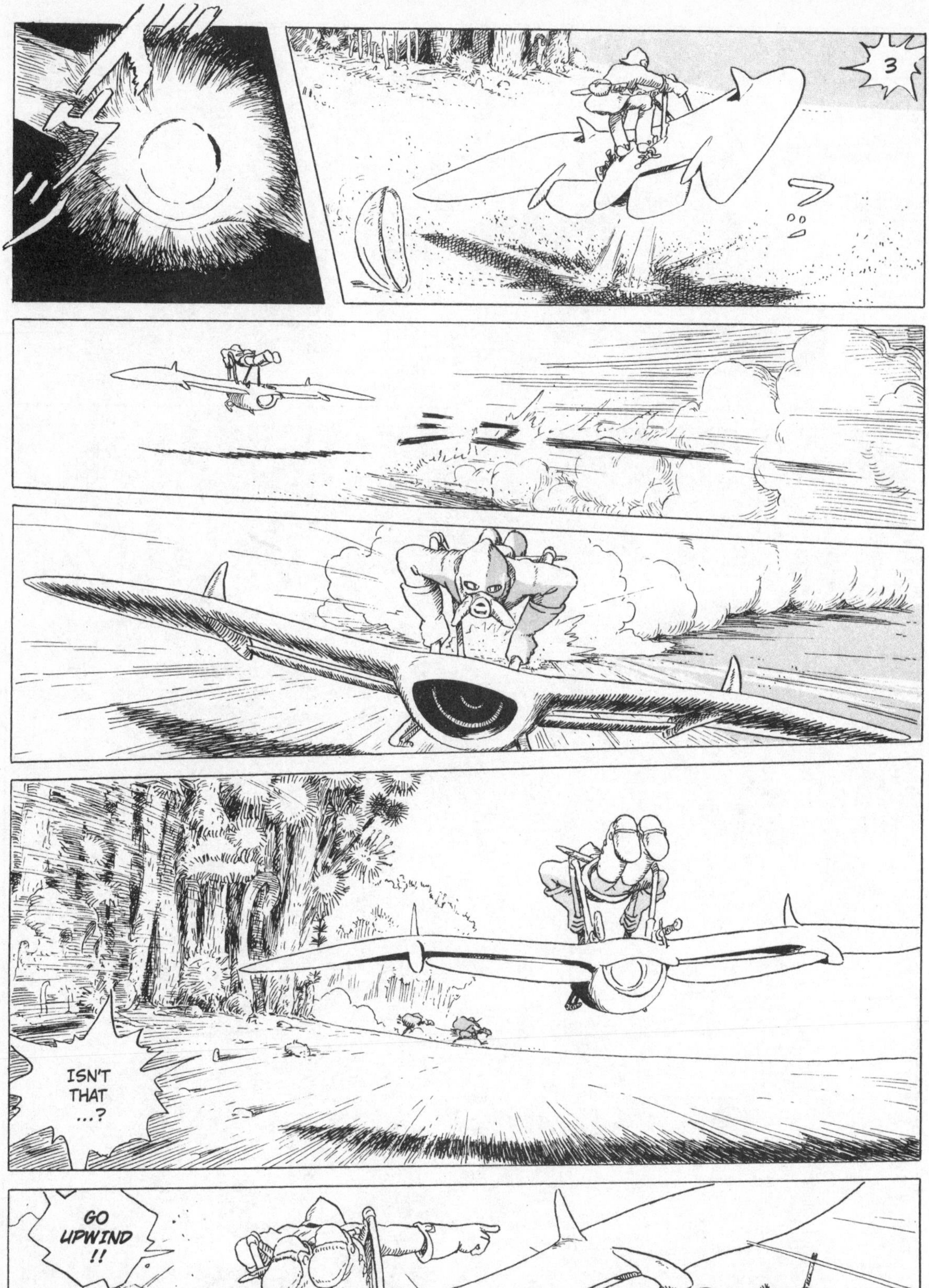

ISN'T THAT ...?
GO UPWIND !!

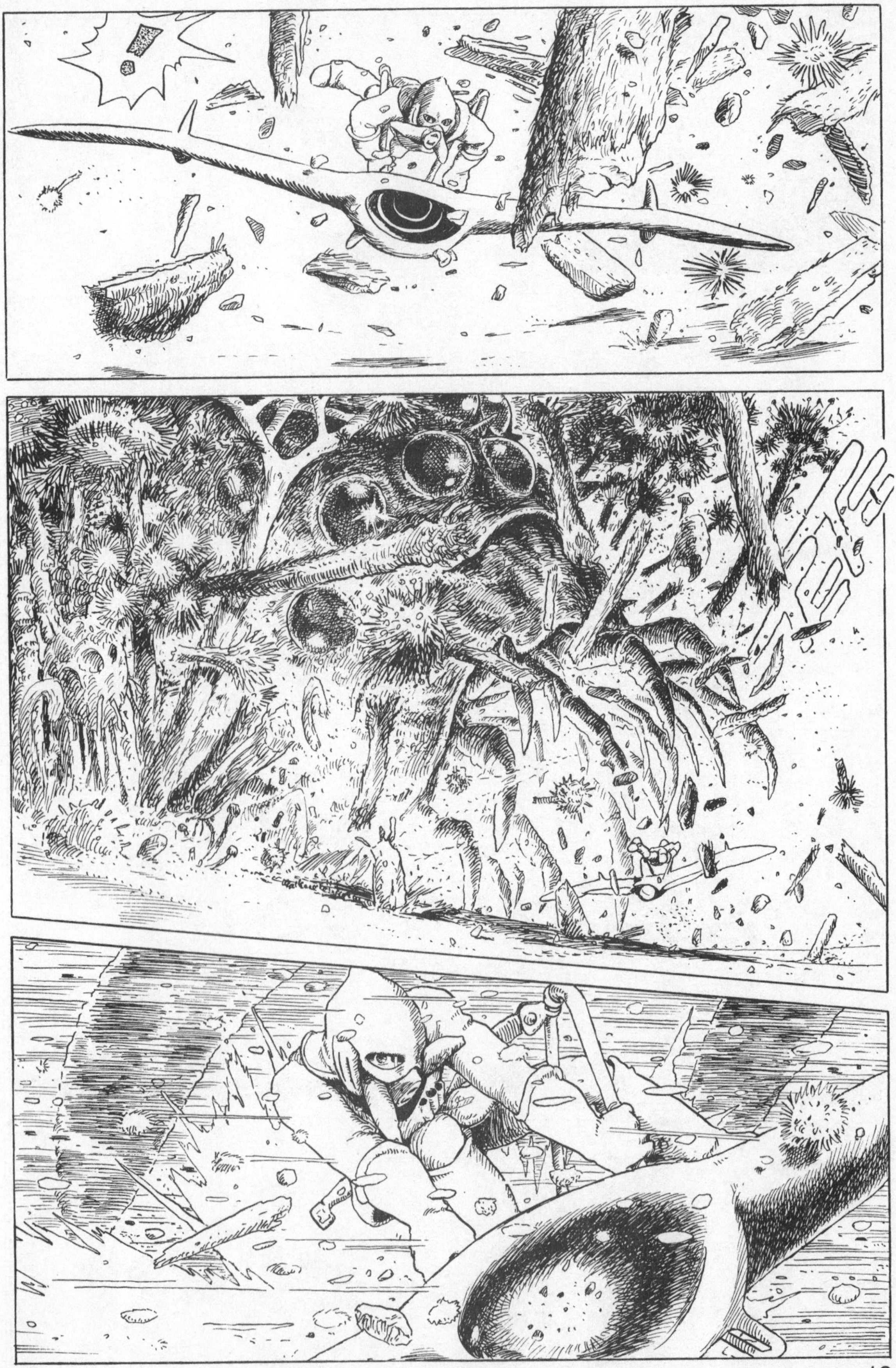
!

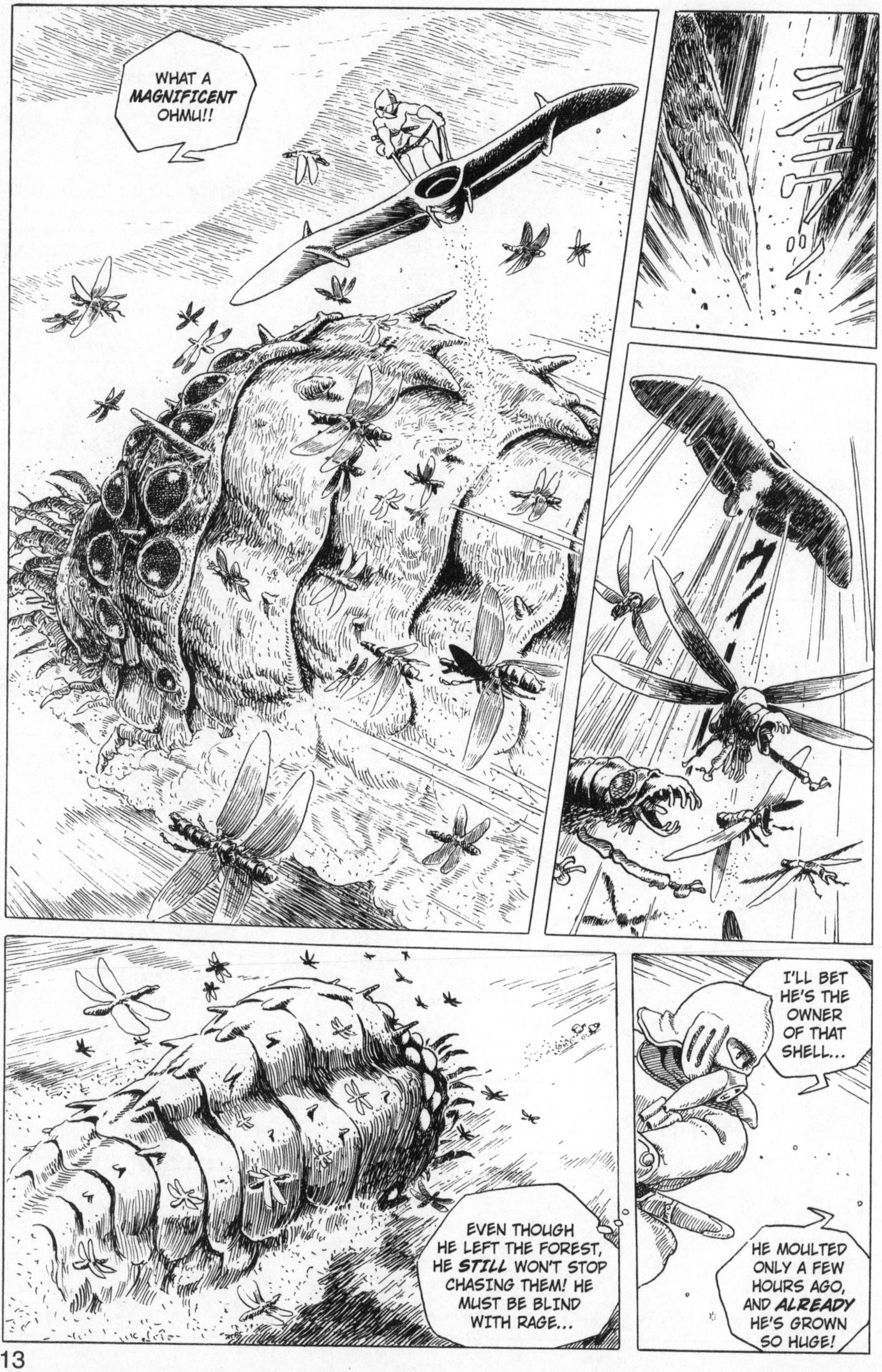
WHAT A MAGNIFICENT OHMU!!
I'LL BET HE'S THE OWNER OF THAT SHELL...
HE MOULTED ONLY A FEW HOURS AGO, AND ALREADY HE'S GROWN SO HUGE!
EVEN THOUGH HE LEFT THE FOREST, HE STILL WON'T STOP CHASING THEM! HE MUST BE BLIND WITH RAGE...

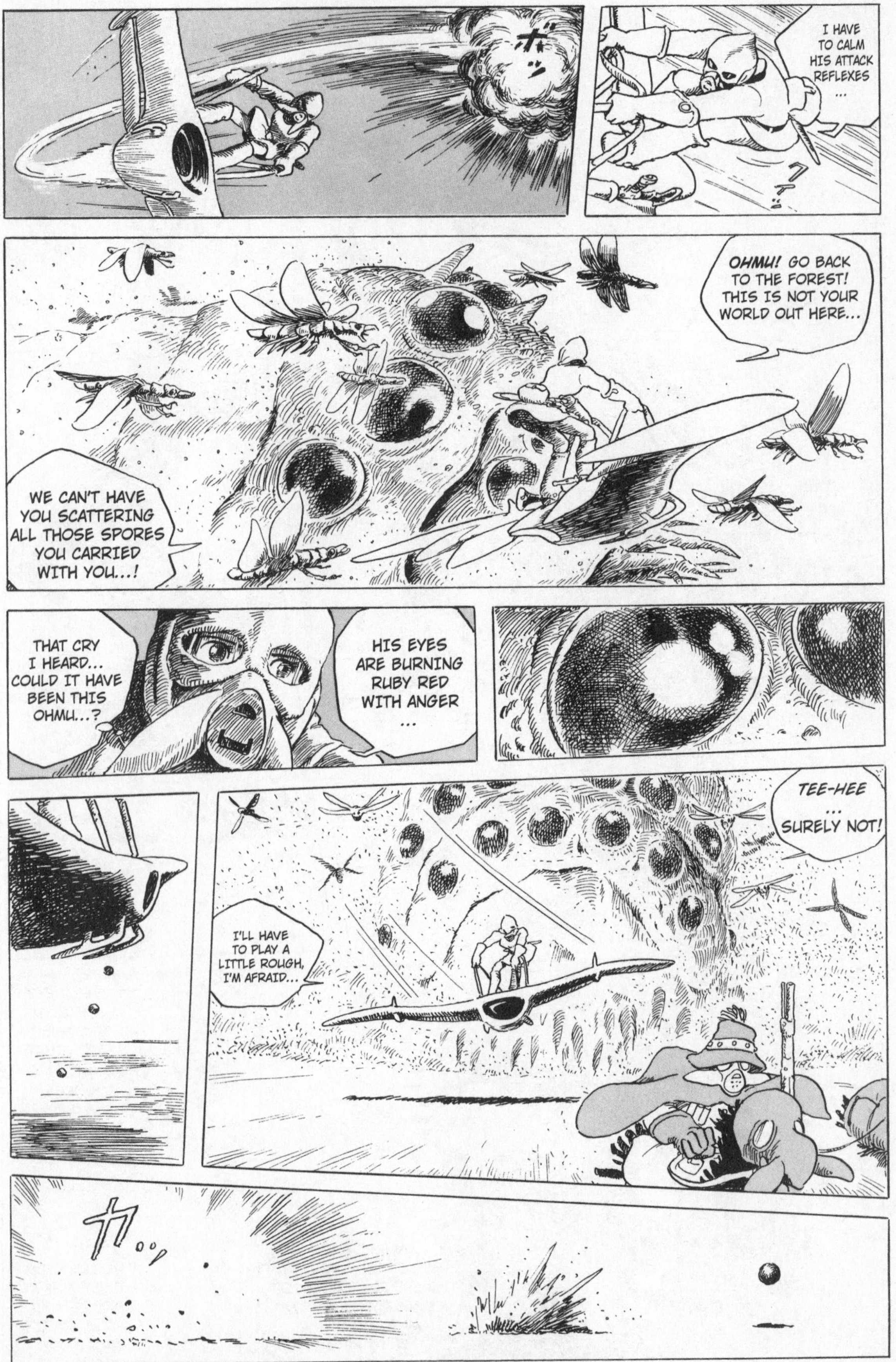
I HAVE TO CALM HIS ATTACK REFLEXES ...
ボッ
OHMU! GO BACK TO THE FOREST! THIS IS NOT YOUR WORLD OUT HERE...
WE CAN'T HAVE YOU SCATTERING ALL THOSE SPORES YOU CARRIED WITH YOU...!
HIS EYES ARE BURNING RUBY RED WITH ANGER ...
THAT CRY I HEARD... COULD IT HAVE BEEN THIS OHMU...?
TEE-HEE ... SURELY NOT!
I'LL HAVE TO PLAY A LITTLE ROUGH, I'M AFRAID...

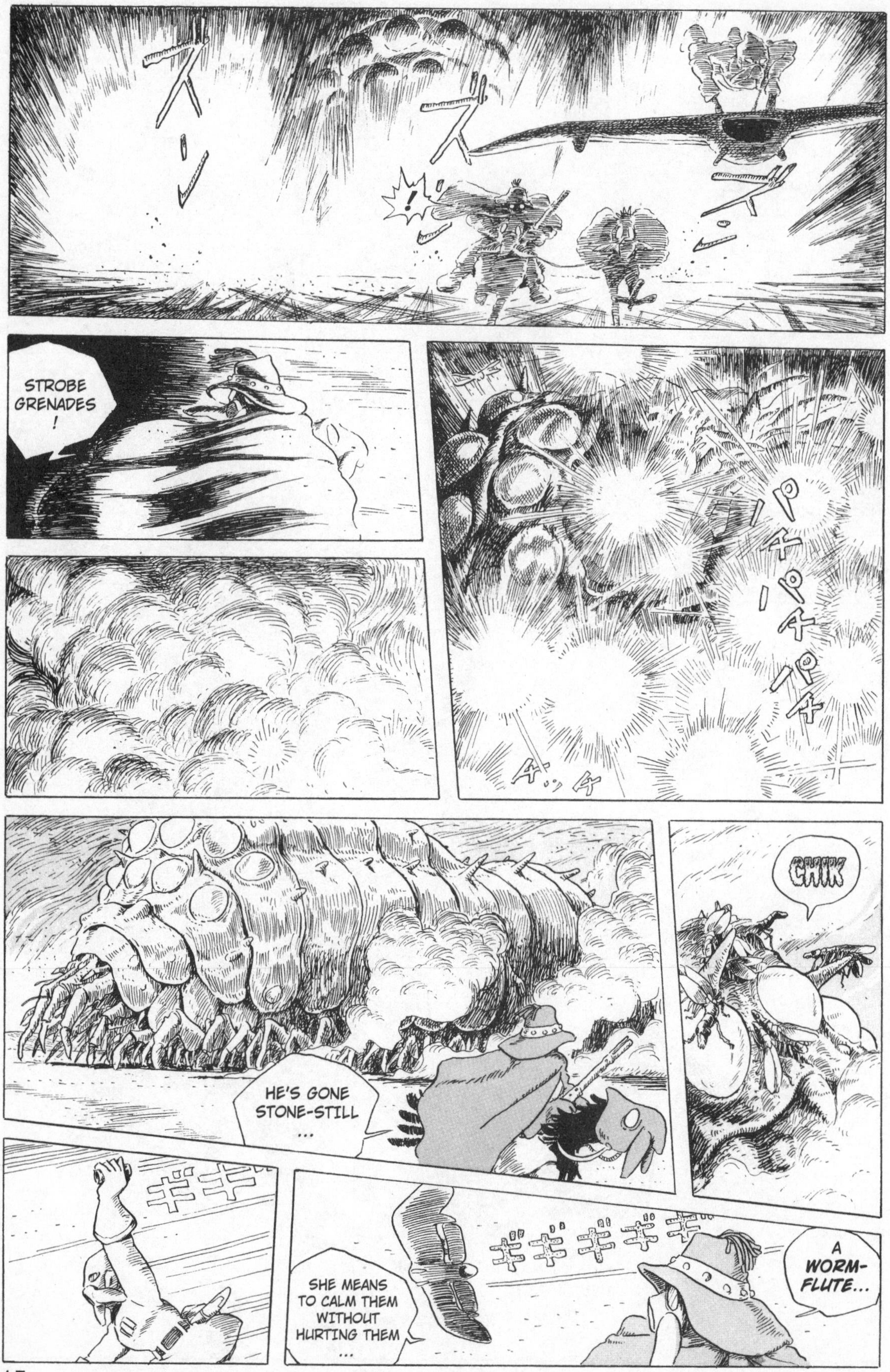
STROBE GRENADES !
CHIIK
HE'S GONE STONE-STILL ...
A WORM-FLUTE...
SHE MEANS TO CALM THEM WITHOUT HURTING THEM ...

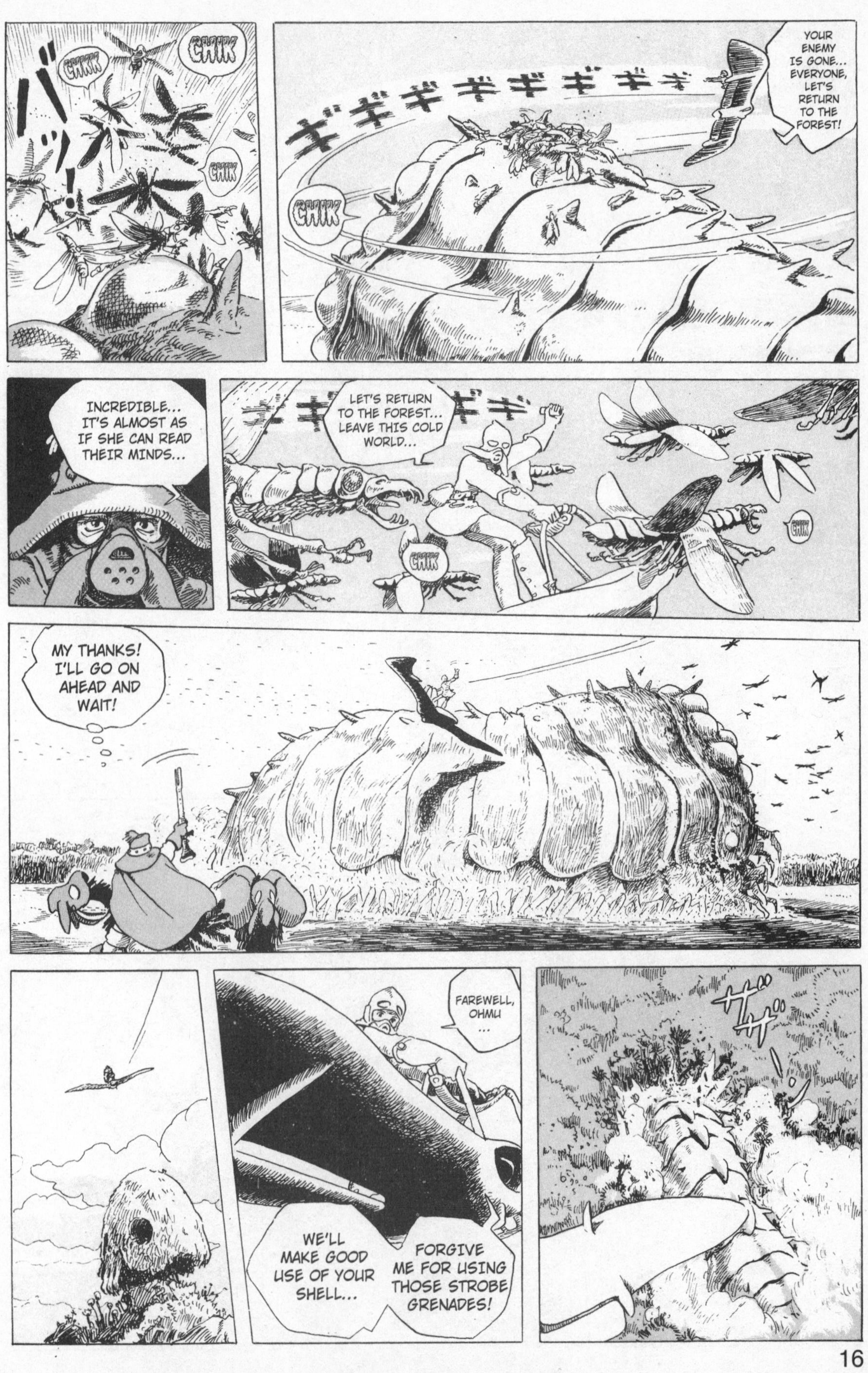
YOUR ENEMY IS GONE... EVERYONE, LET'S RETURN TO THE FOREST!
CHIK
CHIK
CHRRK
CHIK
バッ!
LET'S RETURN TO THE FOREST... LEAVE THIS COLD WORLD...
CHIK
CHIK
INCREDIBLE... IT'S ALMOST AS IF SHE CAN READ THEIR MINDS...
MY THANKS! I'LL GO ON AHEAD AND WAIT!
FAREWELL, OHMU ...
FORGIVE ME FOR USING THOSE STROBE GRENADES!
WE'LL MAKE GOOD USE OF YOUR SHELL...

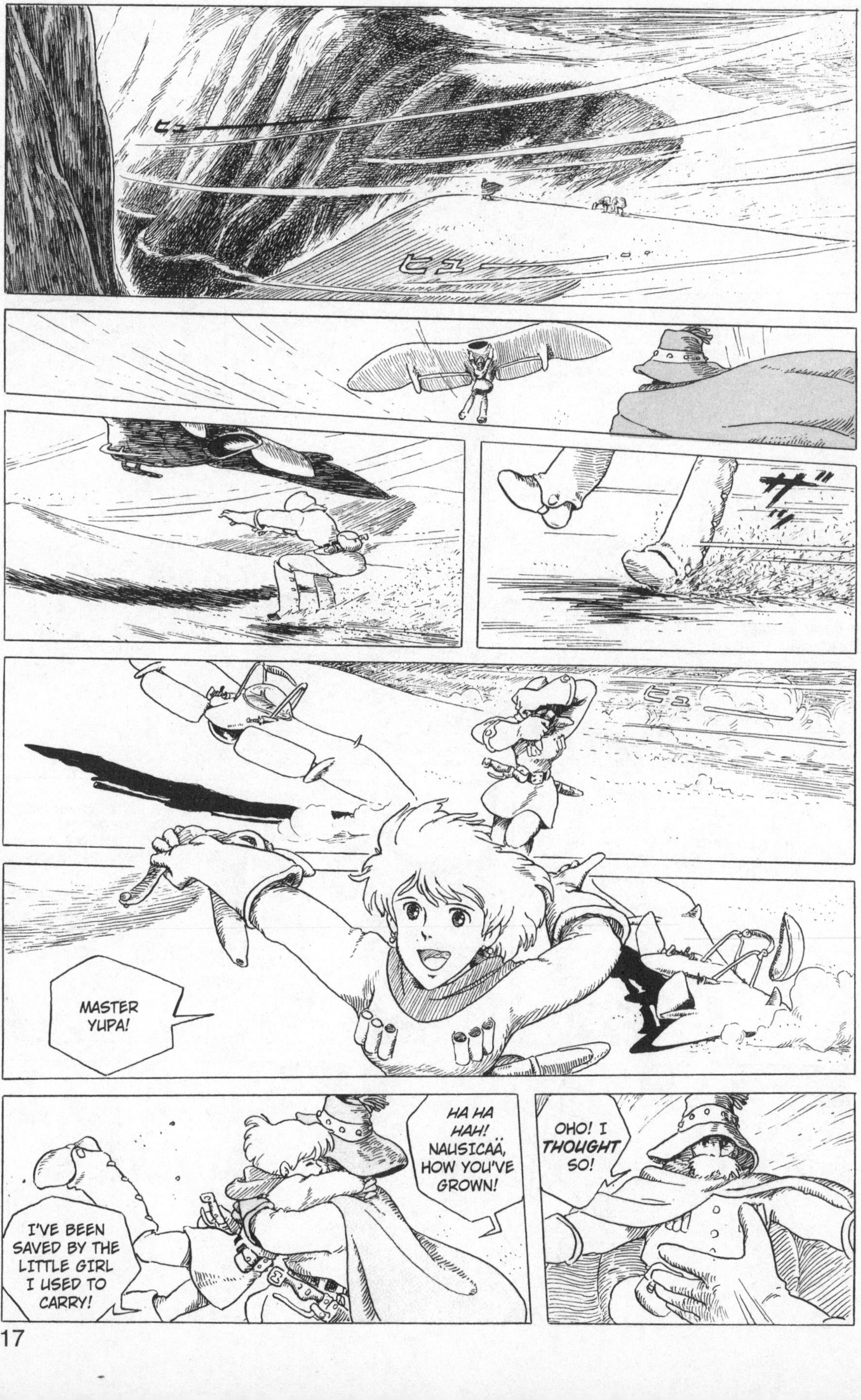

ヒュー
ヒュー
ザッ
ヒュー
MASTER YUPA!
OHO! I *THOUGHT* SO!
HA HA HAH! NAUSICAÄ, HOW YOU'VE GROWN!
I'VE BEEN SAVED BY THE LITTLE GIRL I USED TO CARRY!

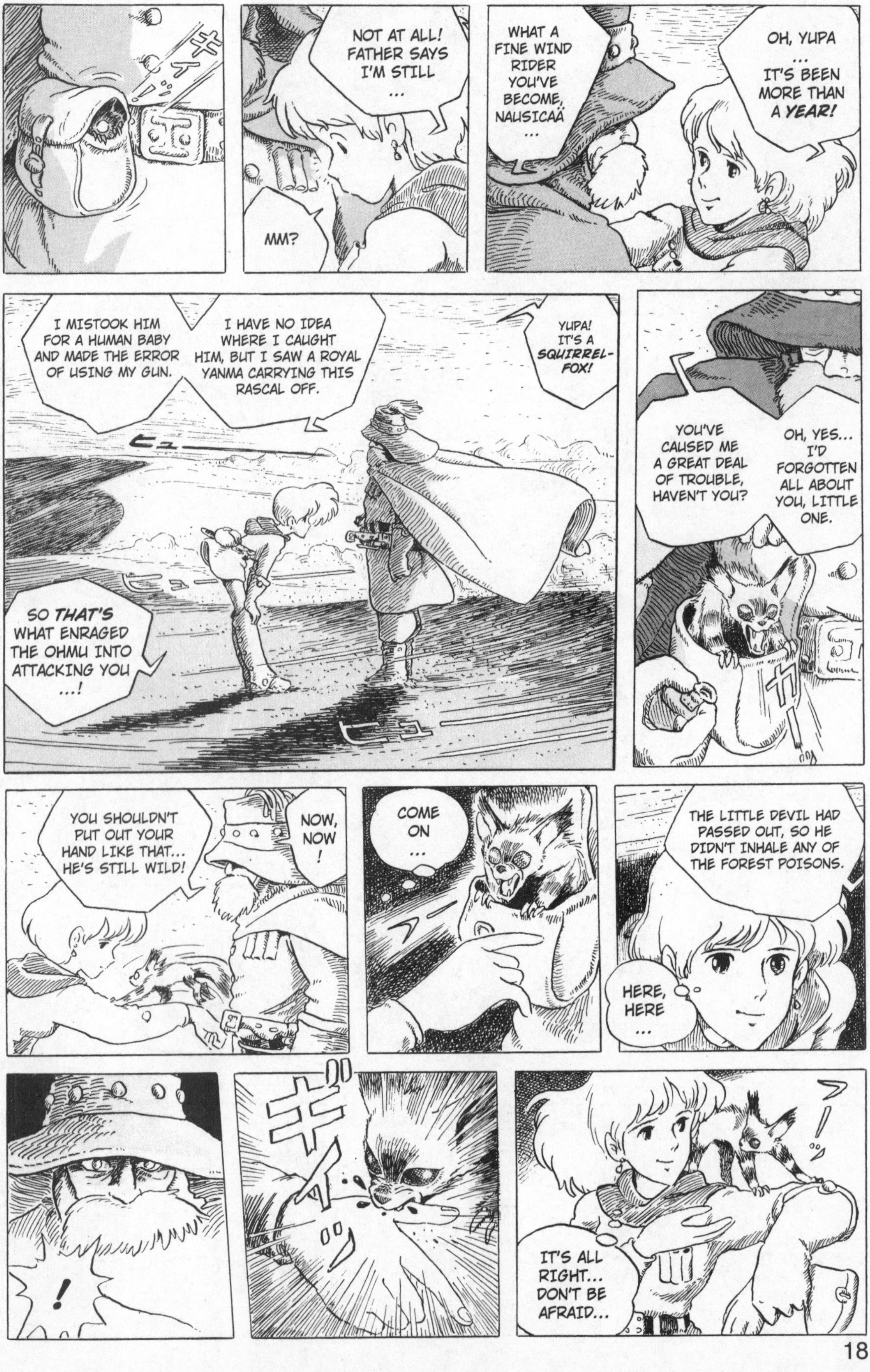
OH, YUPA ... IT'S BEEN MORE THAN A ***YEAR!***
WHAT A FINE WIND RIDER YOU'VE BECOME, NAUSICAÄ ...
NOT AT ALL! FATHER SAYS I'M STILL ...
MM?
OH, YES... I'D FORGOTTEN ALL ABOUT YOU, LITTLE ONE.
YOU'VE CAUSED ME A GREAT DEAL OF TROUBLE, HAVEN'T YOU?
YUPA! IT'S A ***SQUIRREL-FOX!***
I HAVE NO IDEA WHERE I CAUGHT HIM, BUT I SAW A ROYAL YANMA CARRYING THIS RASCAL OFF.
I MISTOOK HIM FOR A HUMAN BABY AND MADE THE ERROR OF USING MY GUN.
SO ***THAT'S*** WHAT ENRAGED THE OHMU INTO ATTACKING YOU ...!
THE LITTLE DEVIL HAD PASSED OUT, SO HE DIDN'T INHALE ANY OF THE FOREST POISONS.
HERE, HERE ...
COME ON ...
NOW, NOW !
YOU SHOULDN'T PUT OUT YOUR HAND LIKE THAT... HE'S STILL WILD!
IT'S ALL RIGHT... DON'T BE AFRAID...
!

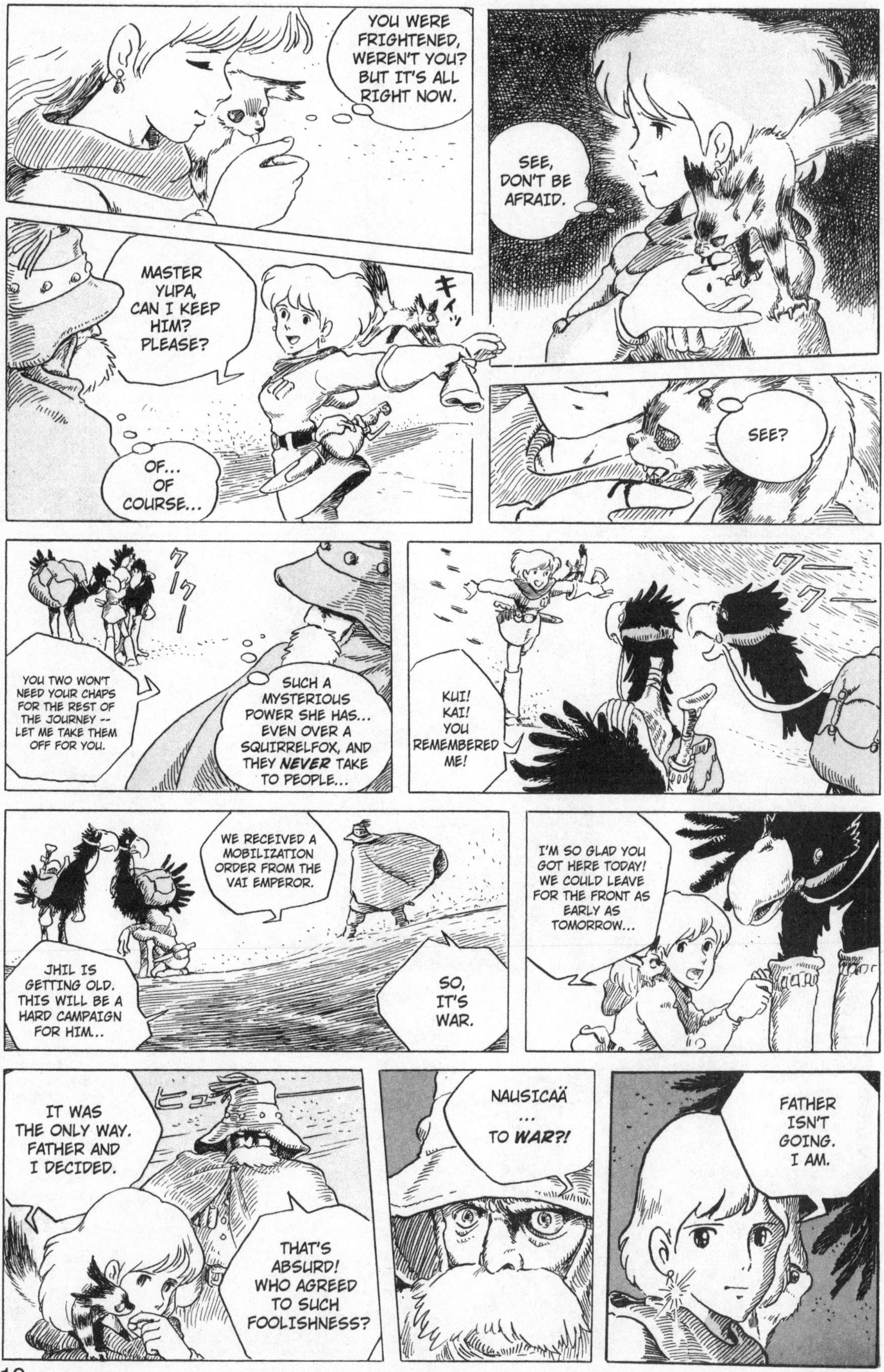
SEE, DON'T BE AFRAID.
SEE?
YOU WERE FRIGHTENED, WEREN'T YOU? BUT IT'S ALL RIGHT NOW.
MASTER YUPA, CAN I KEEP HIM? PLEASE?
キィッ
OF... OF COURSE...
クー クー
KUI! KAI! YOU REMEMBERED ME!
クークー
SUCH A MYSTERIOUS POWER SHE HAS... EVEN OVER A SQUIRRELFOX, AND THEY ***NEVER*** TAKE TO PEOPLE...
YOU TWO WON'T NEED YOUR CHAPS FOR THE REST OF THE JOURNEY -- LET ME TAKE THEM OFF FOR YOU.
I'M SO GLAD YOU GOT HERE TODAY! WE COULD LEAVE FOR THE FRONT AS EARLY AS TOMORROW...
WE RECEIVED A MOBILIZATION ORDER FROM THE VAI EMPEROR.
SO, IT'S WAR.
JHIL IS GETTING OLD. THIS WILL BE A HARD CAMPAIGN FOR HIM...
FATHER ISN'T GOING. I AM.
NAUSICAÄ ... TO ***WAR?!***
IT WAS THE ONLY WAY. FATHER AND I DECIDED.
ヒュー
THAT'S ABSURD! WHO AGREED TO SUCH FOOLISHNESS?

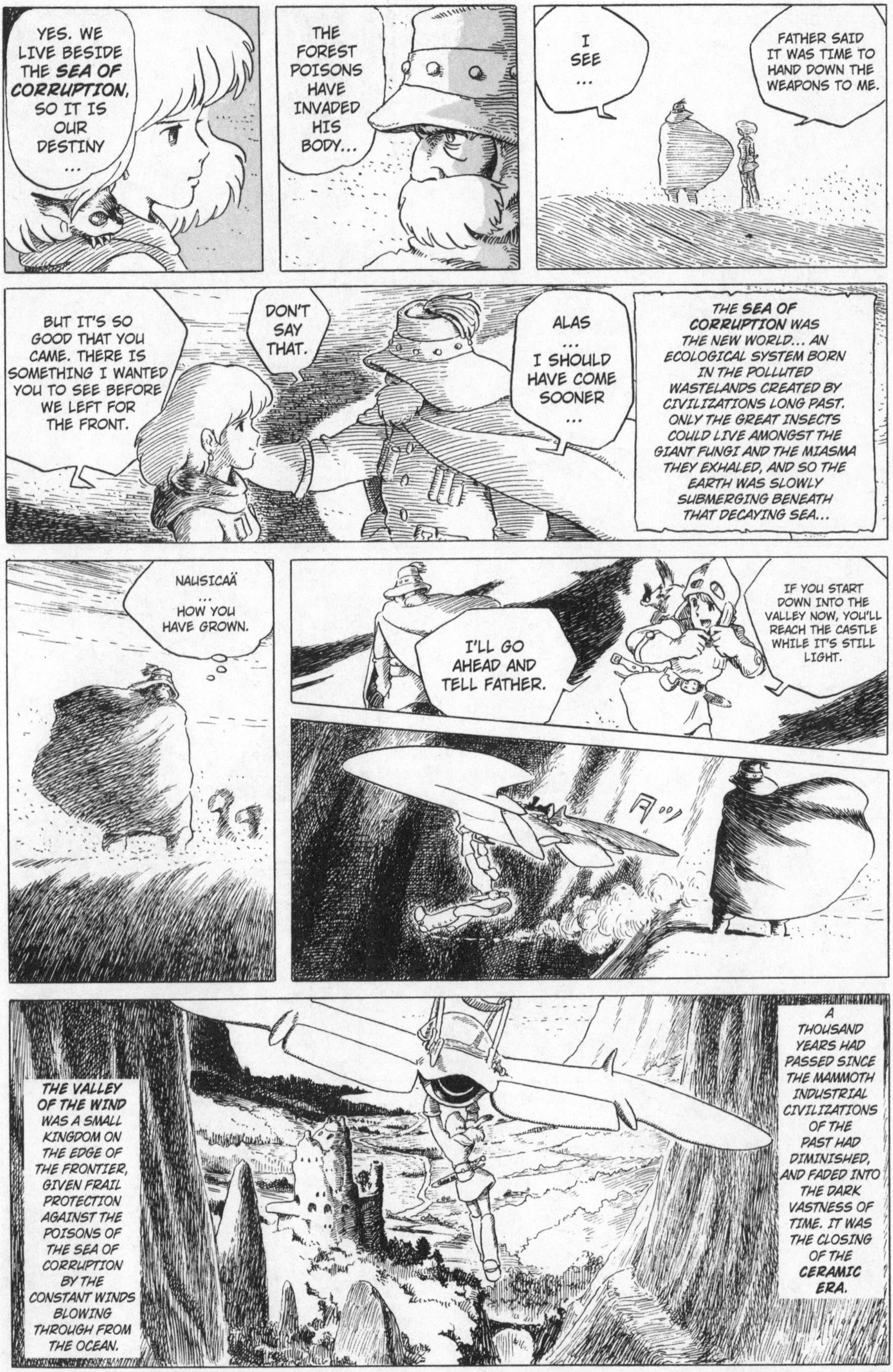
FATHER SAID IT WAS TIME TO HAND DOWN THE WEAPONS TO ME.
I SEE ...
THE FOREST POISONS HAVE INVADED HIS BODY...
YES. WE LIVE BESIDE THE SEA OF CORRUPTION, SO IT IS OUR DESTINY ...
THE SEA OF CORRUPTION WAS THE NEW WORLD... AN ECOLOGICAL SYSTEM BORN IN THE POLLUTED WASTELANDS CREATED BY CIVILIZATIONS LONG PAST. ONLY THE GREAT INSECTS COULD LIVE AMONGST THE GIANT FUNGI AND THE MIASMA THEY EXHALED, AND SO THE EARTH WAS SLOWLY SUBMERGING BENEATH THAT DECAYING SEA...
ALAS ... I SHOULD HAVE COME SOONER ...
DON'T SAY THAT.
BUT IT'S SO GOOD THAT YOU CAME. THERE IS SOMETHING I WANTED YOU TO SEE BEFORE WE LEFT FOR THE FRONT.
IF YOU START DOWN INTO THE VALLEY NOW, YOU'LL REACH THE CASTLE WHILE IT'S STILL LIGHT.
I'LL GO AHEAD AND TELL FATHER.
NAUSICAÄ ... HOW YOU HAVE GROWN.
A THOUSAND YEARS HAD PASSED SINCE THE MAMMOTH INDUSTRIAL CIVILIZATIONS OF THE PAST HAD DIMINISHED, AND FADED INTO THE DARK VASTNESS OF TIME. IT WAS THE CLOSING OF THE CERAMIC ERA.
THE VALLEY OF THE WIND WAS A SMALL KINGDOM ON THE EDGE OF THE FRONTIER, GIVEN FRAIL PROTECTION AGAINST THE POISONS OF THE SEA OF CORRUPTION BY THE CONSTANT WINDS BLOWING THROUGH FROM THE OCEAN.

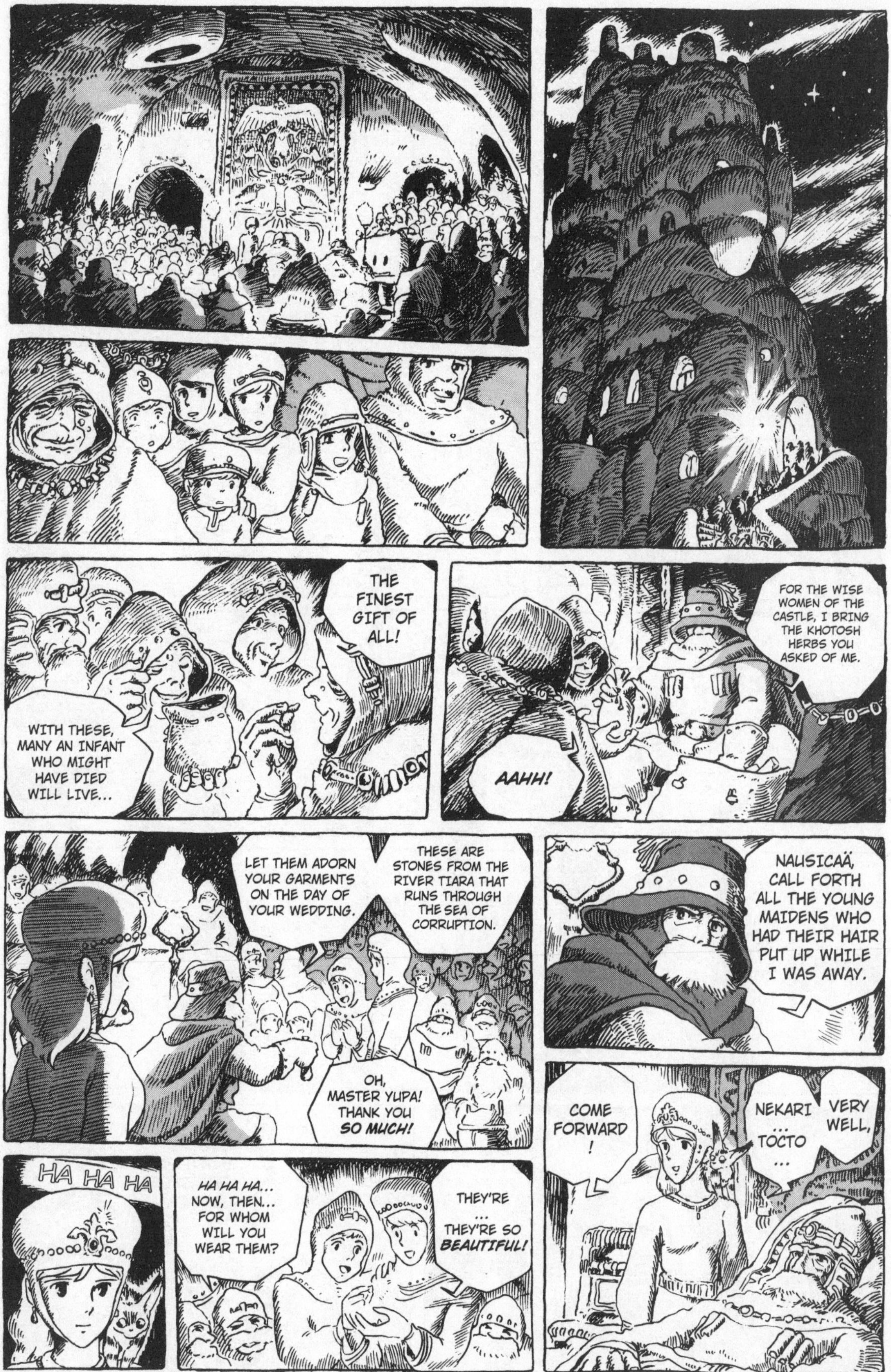

FOR THE WISE WOMEN OF THE CASTLE, I BRING THE KHOTOSH HERBS YOU ASKED OF ME.
AAHH!
THE FINEST GIFT OF ALL!
WITH THESE, MANY AN INFANT WHO MIGHT HAVE DIED WILL LIVE...
NAUSICAÄ, CALL FORTH ALL THE YOUNG MAIDENS WHO HAD THEIR HAIR PUT UP WHILE I WAS AWAY.
VERY WELL,
NEKARI ... TOCTO ...
COME FORWARD!
THESE ARE STONES FROM THE RIVER TIARA THAT RUNS THROUGH THE SEA OF CORRUPTION.
LET THEM ADORN YOUR GARMENTS ON THE DAY OF YOUR WEDDING.
OH, MASTER YUPA! THANK YOU *SO MUCH!*
THEY'RE ... THEY'RE SO *BEAUTIFUL!*
*HA HA HA...* NOW, THEN... FOR WHOM WILL YOU WEAR THEM?
HA HA HA

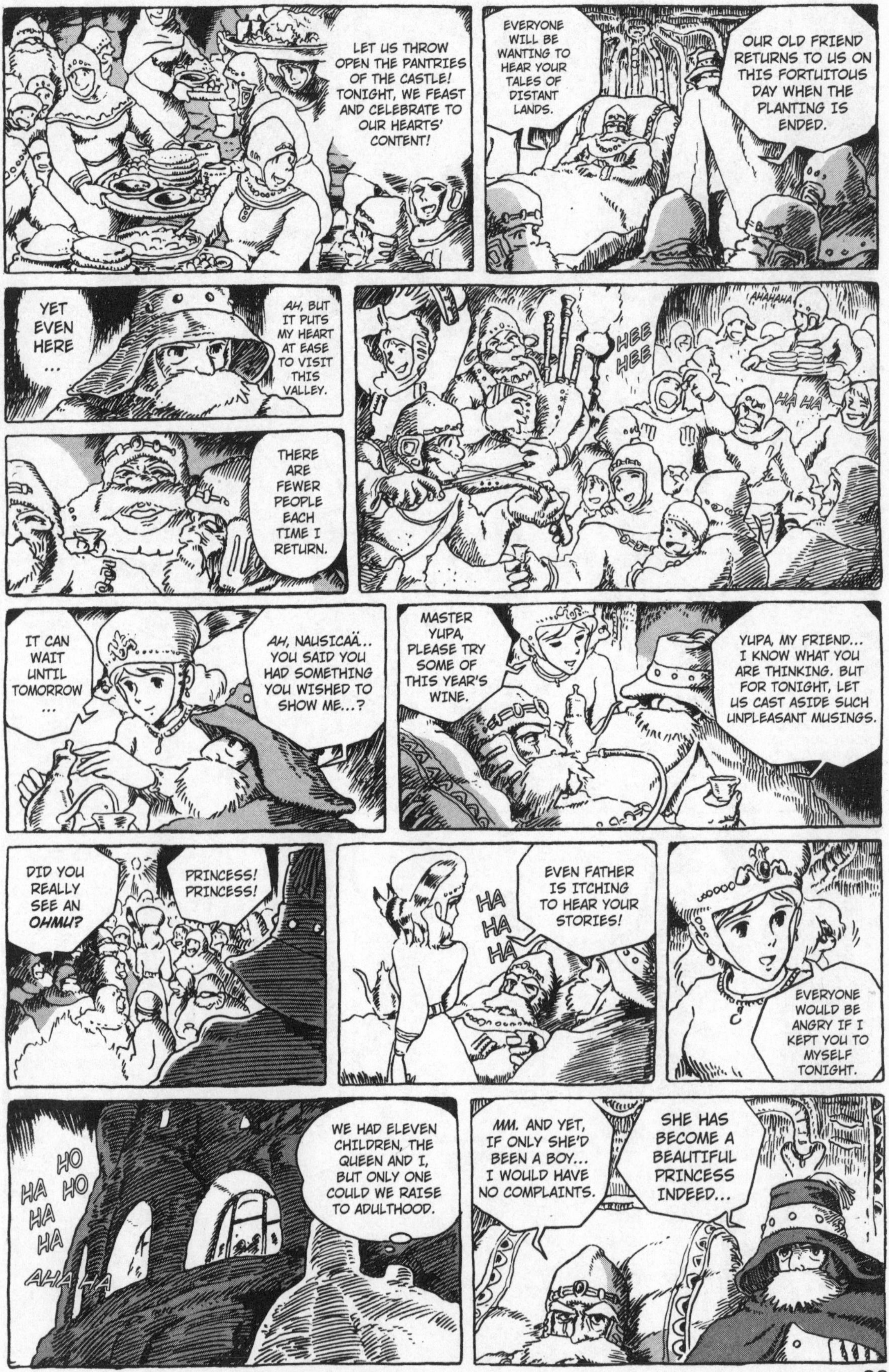
OUR OLD FRIEND RETURNS TO US ON THIS FORTUITOUS DAY WHEN THE PLANTING IS ENDED.
EVERYONE WILL BE WANTING TO HEAR YOUR TALES OF DISTANT LANDS.
LET US THROW OPEN THE PANTRIES OF THE CASTLE! TONIGHT, WE FEAST AND CELEBRATE TO OUR HEARTS' CONTENT!
AHAHAHA
HEE HEE
HA HA
*AH*, BUT IT PUTS MY HEART AT EASE TO VISIT THIS VALLEY.
YET EVEN HERE ...
THERE ARE FEWER PEOPLE EACH TIME I RETURN.
YUPA, MY FRIEND... I KNOW WHAT YOU ARE THINKING. BUT FOR TONIGHT, LET US CAST ASIDE SUCH UNPLEASANT MUSINGS.
MASTER YUPA, PLEASE TRY SOME OF THIS YEAR'S WINE.
*AH*, NAUSICAÄ... YOU SAID YOU HAD SOMETHING YOU WISHED TO SHOW ME...?
IT CAN WAIT UNTIL TOMORROW ...
EVERYONE WOULD BE ANGRY IF I KEPT YOU TO MYSELF TONIGHT.
EVEN FATHER IS ITCHING TO HEAR YOUR STORIES!
HA HA HA
PRINCESS! PRINCESS!
DID YOU REALLY SEE AN ***OHMU?***
SHE HAS BECOME A BEAUTIFUL PRINCESS INDEED...
*MM.* AND YET, IF ONLY SHE'D BEEN A BOY... I WOULD HAVE NO COMPLAINTS.
WE HAD ELEVEN CHILDREN, THE QUEEN AND I, BUT ONLY ONE COULD WE RAISE TO ADULTHOOD.
HO HO
HA HA HA
AHAHA

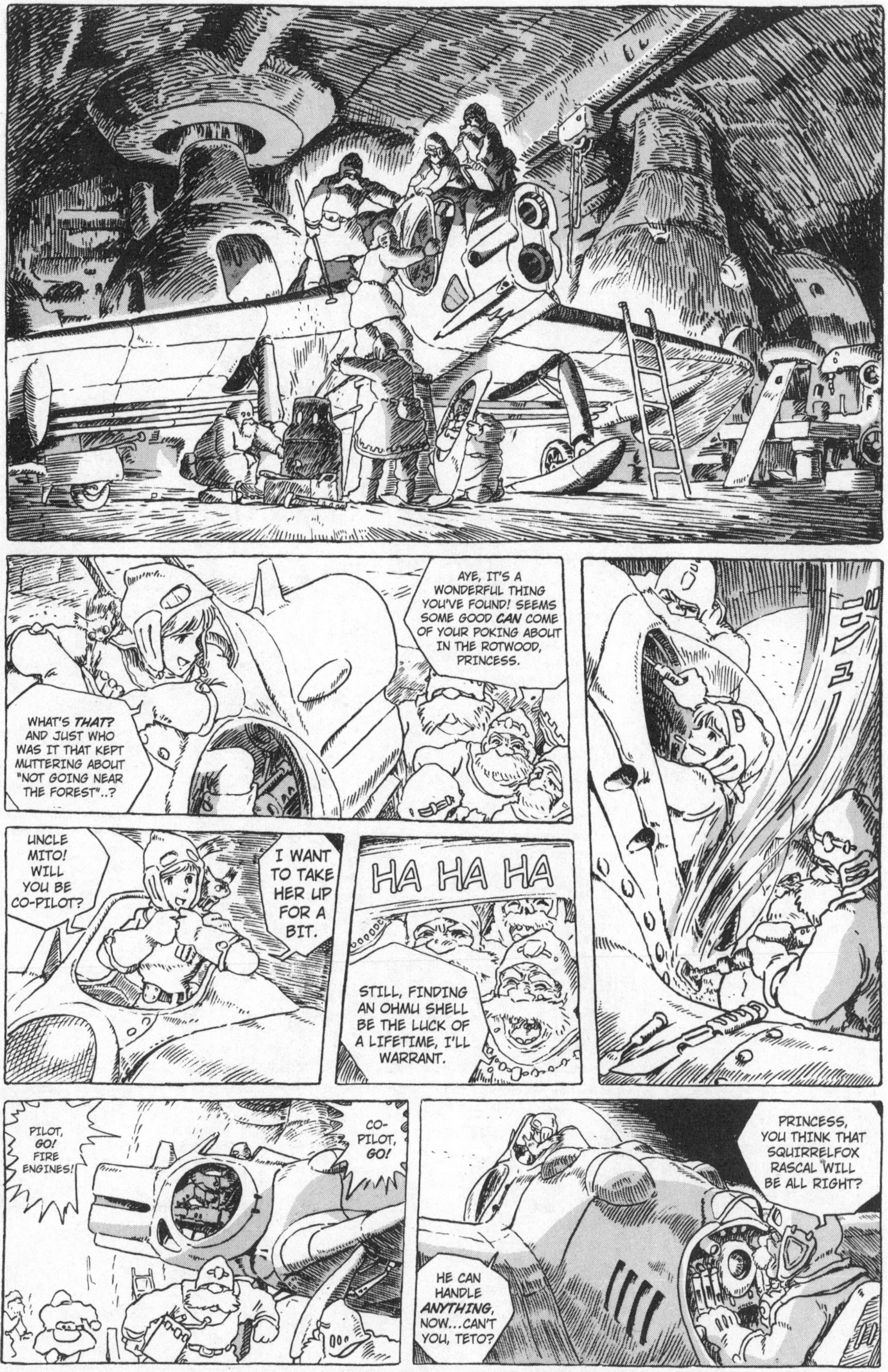

AYE, IT'S A WONDERFUL THING YOU'VE FOUND! SEEMS SOME GOOD **CAN** COME OF YOUR POKING ABOUT IN THE ROTWOOD, PRINCESS.
WHAT'S **THAT?** AND JUST WHO WAS IT THAT KEPT MUTTERING ABOUT "NOT GOING NEAR THE FOREST"..?
HA HA HA
STILL, FINDING AN OHMU SHELL BE THE LUCK OF A LIFETIME, I'LL WARRANT.
I WANT TO TAKE HER UP FOR A BIT.
UNCLE MITO! WILL YOU BE CO-PILOT?
PRINCESS, YOU THINK THAT SQUIRRELFOX RASCAL WILL BE ALL RIGHT?
HE CAN HANDLE **ANYTHING**, NOW...CAN'T YOU, TETO?
CO-PILOT, **GO!**
PILOT, **GO!** FIRE ENGINES!

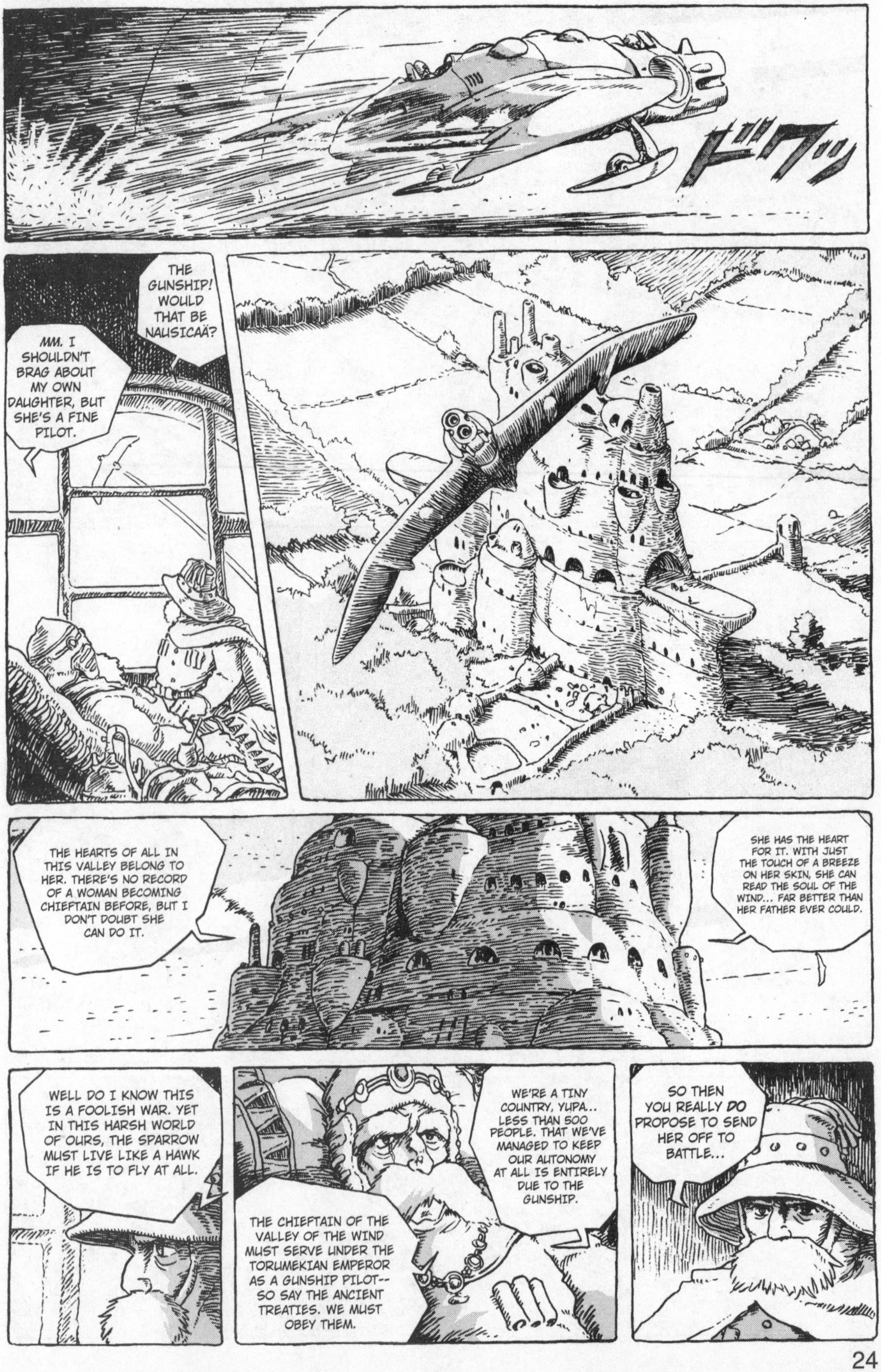
ドワッ
THE GUNSHIP! WOULD THAT BE NAUSICAÄ?
MM. I SHOULDN'T BRAG ABOUT MY OWN DAUGHTER, BUT SHE'S A FINE PILOT.
SHE HAS THE HEART FOR IT. WITH JUST THE TOUCH OF A BREEZE ON HER SKIN, SHE CAN READ THE SOUL OF THE WIND... FAR BETTER THAN HER FATHER EVER COULD.
THE HEARTS OF ALL IN THIS VALLEY BELONG TO HER. THERE'S NO RECORD OF A WOMAN BECOMING CHIEFTAIN BEFORE, BUT I DON'T DOUBT SHE CAN DO IT.
SO THEN YOU REALLY **DO** PROPOSE TO SEND HER OFF TO BATTLE...
WE'RE A TINY COUNTRY, YUPA... LESS THAN 500 PEOPLE. THAT WE'VE MANAGED TO KEEP OUR AUTONOMY AT ALL IS ENTIRELY DUE TO THE GUNSHIP.
THE CHIEFTAIN OF THE VALLEY OF THE WIND MUST SERVE UNDER THE TORUMEKIAN EMPEROR AS A GUNSHIP PILOT-- SO SAY THE ANCIENT TREATIES. WE MUST OBEY THEM.
WELL DO I KNOW THIS IS A FOOLISH WAR. YET IN THIS HARSH WORLD OF OURS, THE SPARROW MUST LIVE LIKE A HAWK IF HE IS TO FLY AT ALL.

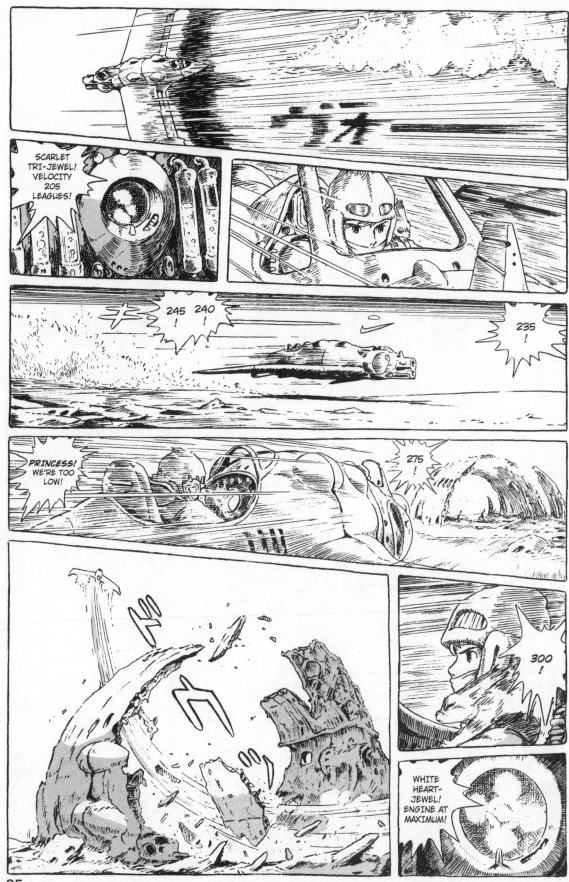

SCARLET TRI-JEWEL! VELOCITY 205 LEAGUES!

245
!

240
!

235
!

PRINCESS! WE'RE TOO LOW!

275
!

300
!

WHITE HEART-JEWEL! ENGINE AT MAXIMUM!

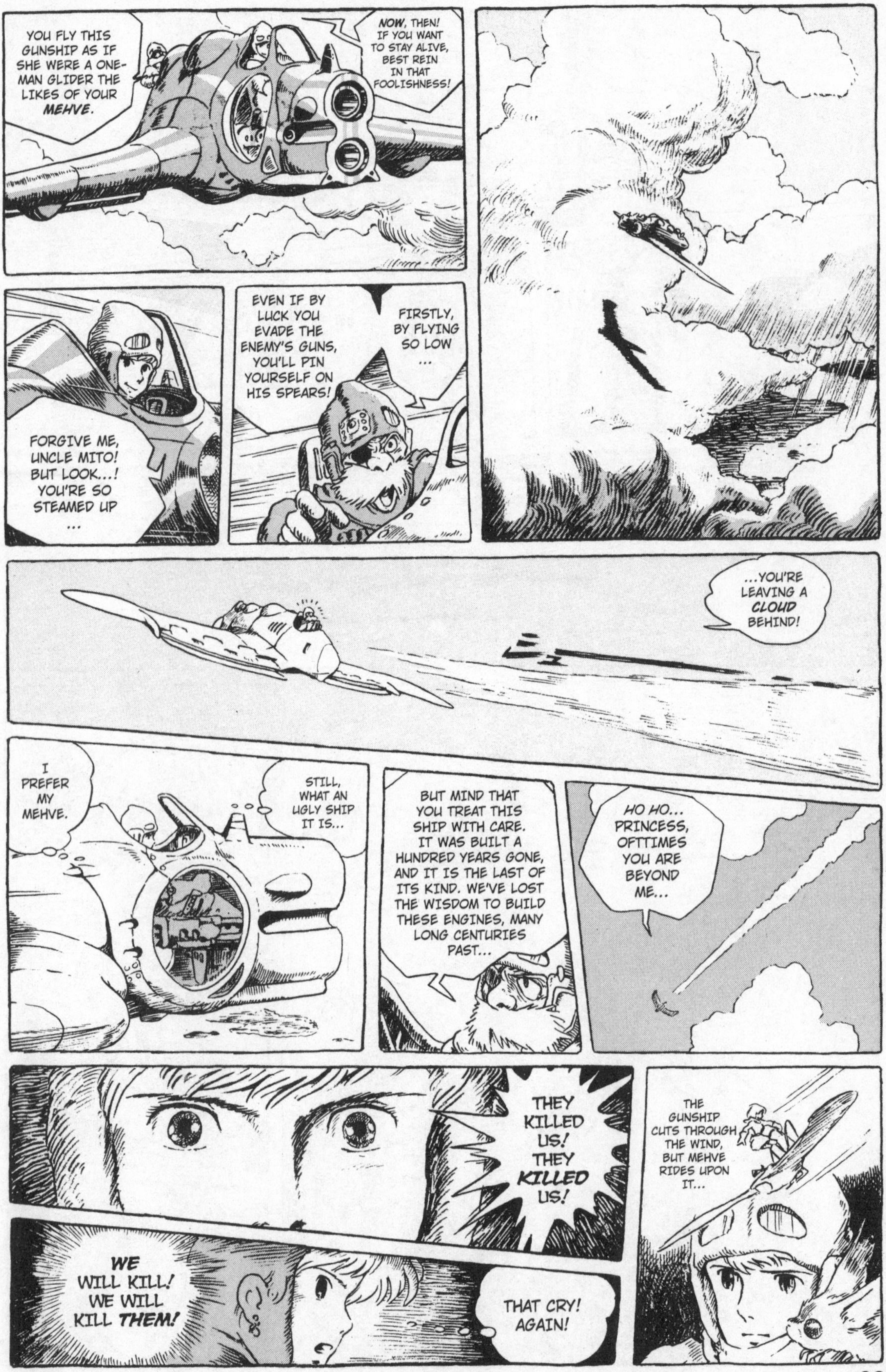
NOW, THEN! IF YOU WANT TO STAY ALIVE, BEST REIN IN THAT FOOLISHNESS!
YOU FLY THIS GUNSHIP AS IF SHE WERE A ONE-MAN GLIDER THE LIKES OF YOUR MEHVE.
FIRSTLY, BY FLYING SO LOW ...
EVEN IF BY LUCK YOU EVADE THE ENEMY'S GUNS, YOU'LL PIN YOURSELF ON HIS SPEARS!
FORGIVE ME, UNCLE MITO! BUT LOOK...! YOU'RE SO STEAMED UP ...
...YOU'RE LEAVING A CLOUD BEHIND!
HO HO... PRINCESS, OFTTIMES YOU ARE BEYOND ME...
BUT MIND THAT YOU TREAT THIS SHIP WITH CARE. IT WAS BUILT A HUNDRED YEARS GONE, AND IT IS THE LAST OF ITS KIND. WE'VE LOST THE WISDOM TO BUILD THESE ENGINES, MANY LONG CENTURIES PAST...
STILL, WHAT AN UGLY SHIP IT IS...
I PREFER MY MEHVE.
THE GUNSHIP CUTS THROUGH THE WIND, BUT MEHVE RIDES UPON IT...
THEY KILLED US! THEY KILLED US!
THAT CRY! AGAIN!
WE WILL KILL! WE WILL KILL THEM!

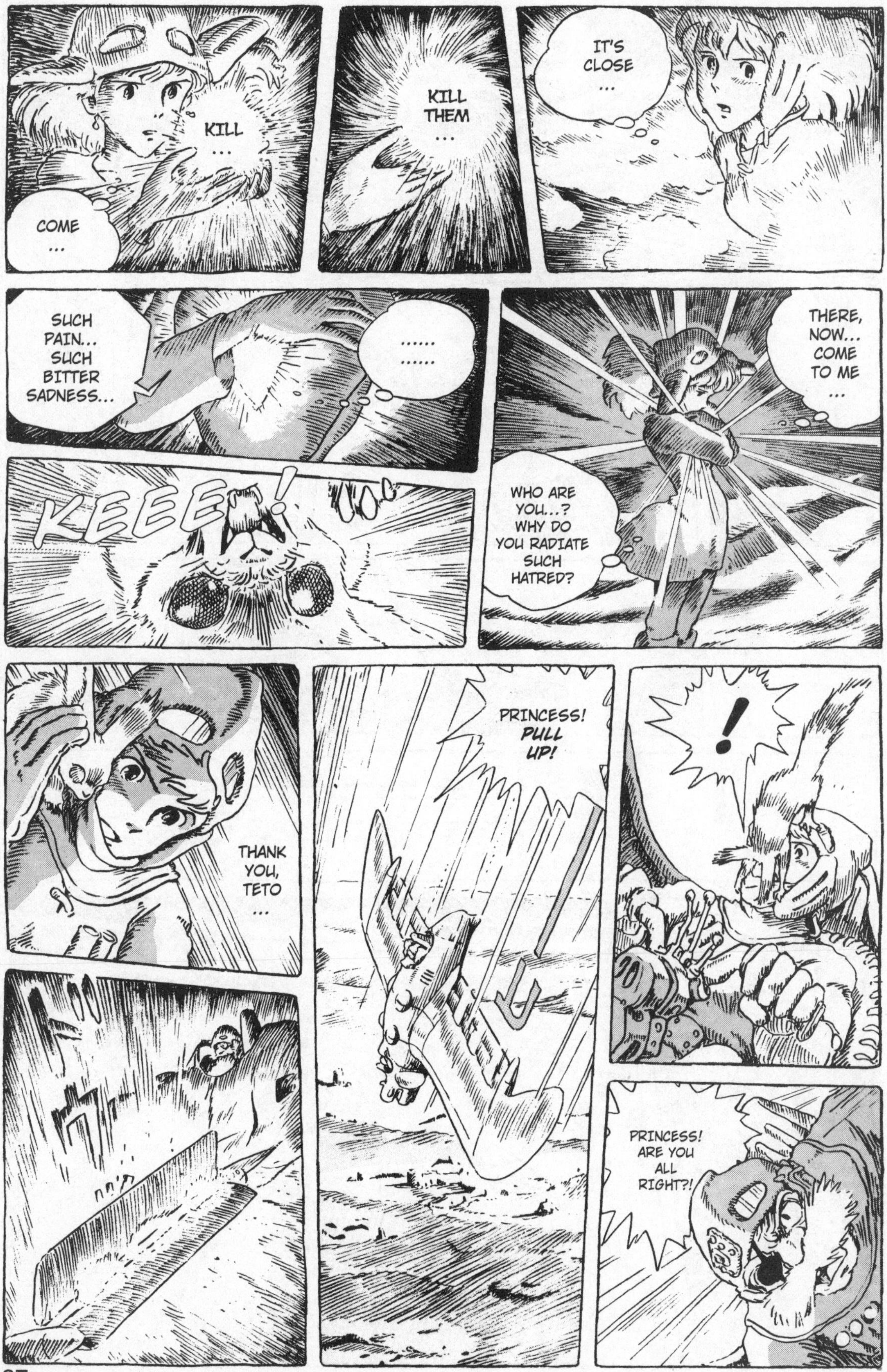
COME ...
KILL ...
KILL THEM ...
IT'S CLOSE ...
SUCH PAIN... SUCH BITTER SADNESS...
...... ......
KEEEE!
WHO ARE YOU...? WHY DO YOU RADIATE SUCH HATRED?
THERE, NOW... COME TO ME ...
THANK YOU, TETO ...
PRINCESS! PULL UP!
!
PRINCESS! ARE YOU ALL RIGHT?!

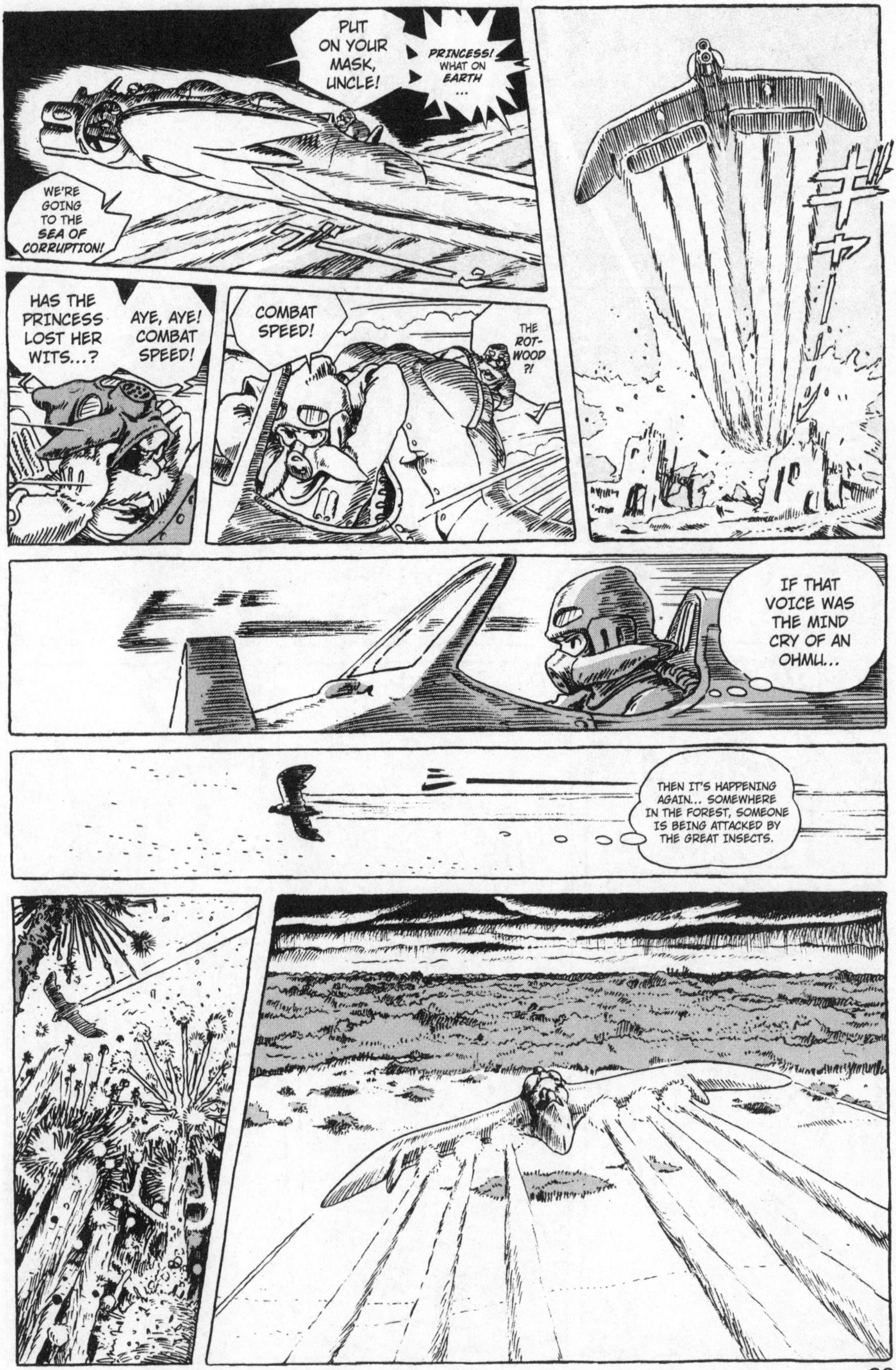
ギャー
PUT ON YOUR MASK, UNCLE!
PRINCESS! WHAT ON EARTH...
WE'RE GOING TO THE SEA OF CORRUPTION!
COMBAT SPEED!
THE ROT-WOOD?!
AYE, AYE! COMBAT SPEED!
HAS THE PRINCESS LOST HER WITS...?
IF THAT VOICE WAS THE MIND CRY OF AN OHMU...
THEN IT'S HAPPENING AGAIN... SOMEWHERE IN THE FOREST, SOMEONE IS BEING ATTACKED BY THE GREAT INSECTS.

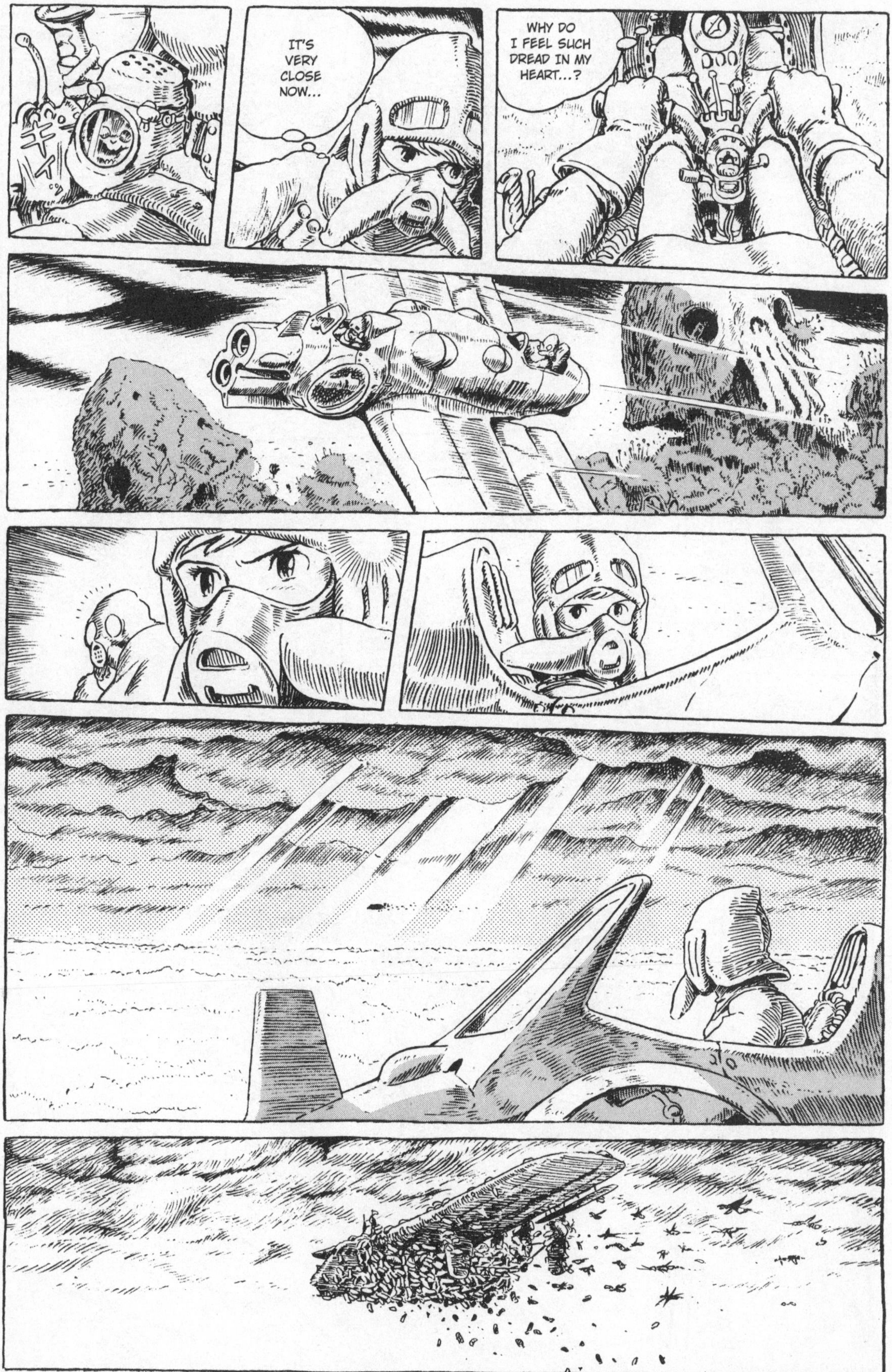
WHY DO I FEEL SUCH DREAD IN MY HEART...?
IT'S VERY CLOSE NOW...
ギイ

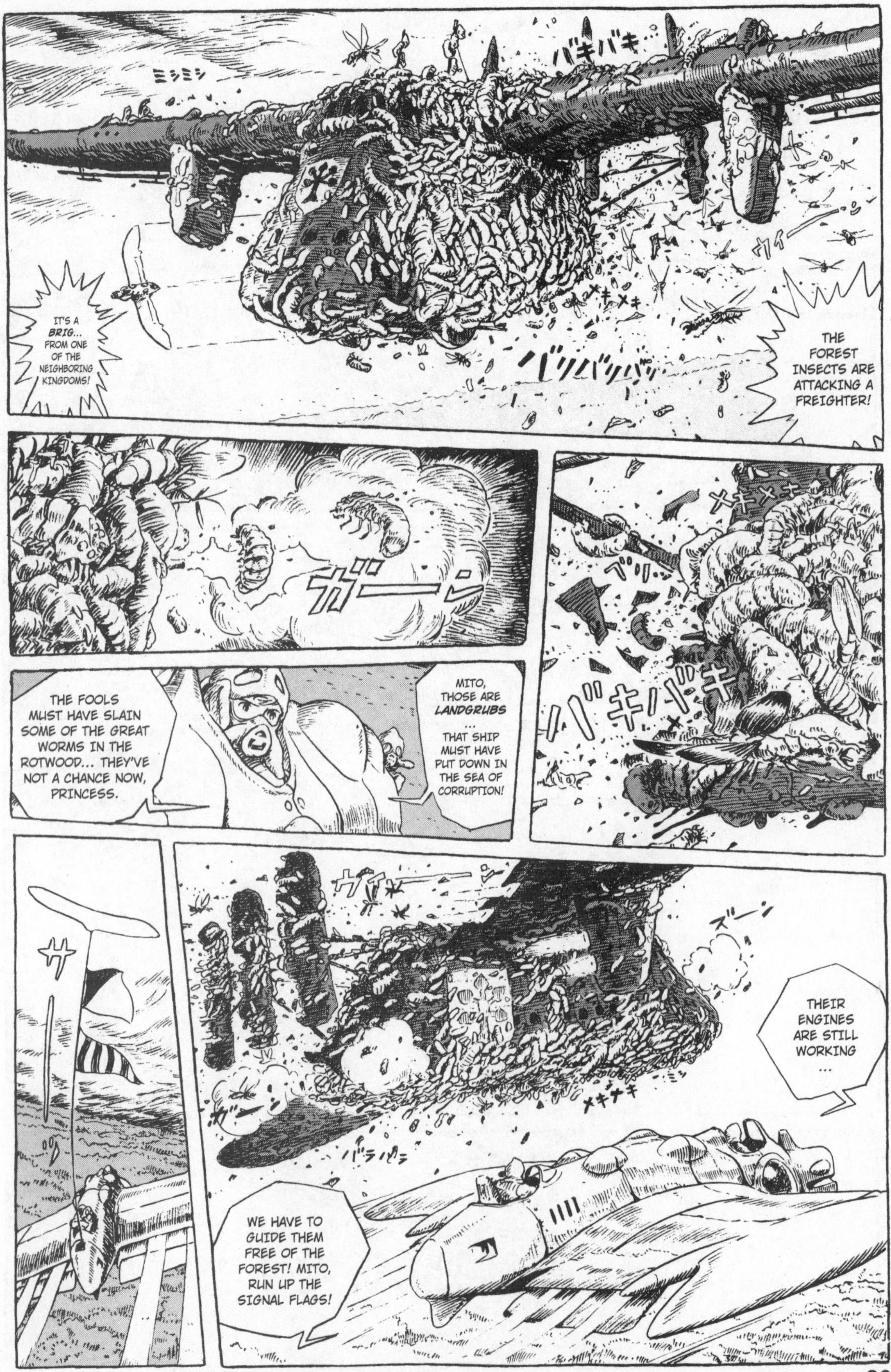
バキバキ
ミシミシ
THE FOREST INSECTS ARE ATTACKING A FREIGHTER!
IT'S A BRIG... FROM ONE OF THE NEIGHBORING KINGDOMS!
メキメキ
バキバキ
ガーン
MITO, THOSE ARE LANDGRUBS ... THAT SHIP MUST HAVE PUT DOWN IN THE SEA OF CORRUPTION!
THE FOOLS MUST HAVE SLAIN SOME OF THE GREAT WORMS IN THE ROTWOOD... THEY'VE NOT A CHANCE NOW, PRINCESS.
ズーン
THEIR ENGINES ARE STILL WORKING ...
WE HAVE TO GUIDE THEM FREE OF THE FOREST! MITO, RUN UP THE SIGNAL FLAGS!
サー

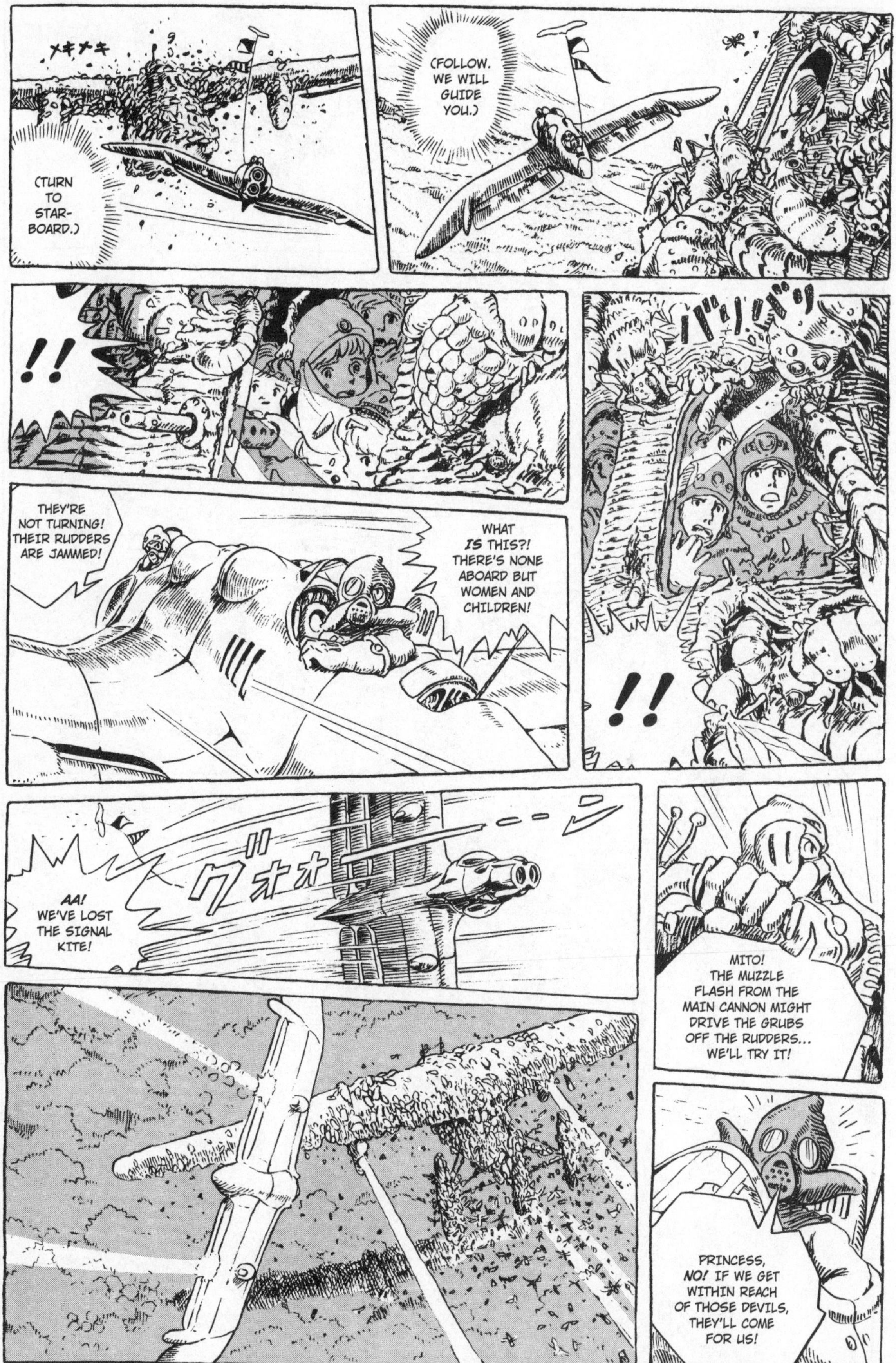
(FOLLOW. WE WILL GUIDE YOU.)
メキメキ
(TURN TO STARBOARD.)
バリバリ
!!
!!
WHAT *IS* THIS?! THERE'S NONE ABOARD BUT WOMEN AND CHILDREN!
THEY'RE NOT TURNING! THEIR RUDDERS ARE JAMMED!
MITO! THE MUZZLE FLASH FROM THE MAIN CANNON MIGHT DRIVE THE GRUBS OFF THE RUDDERS... WE'LL TRY IT!
グオオ
*AA!* WE'VE LOST THE SIGNAL KITE!
PRINCESS, *NO!* IF WE GET WITHIN REACH OF THOSE DEVILS, THEY'LL COME FOR US!

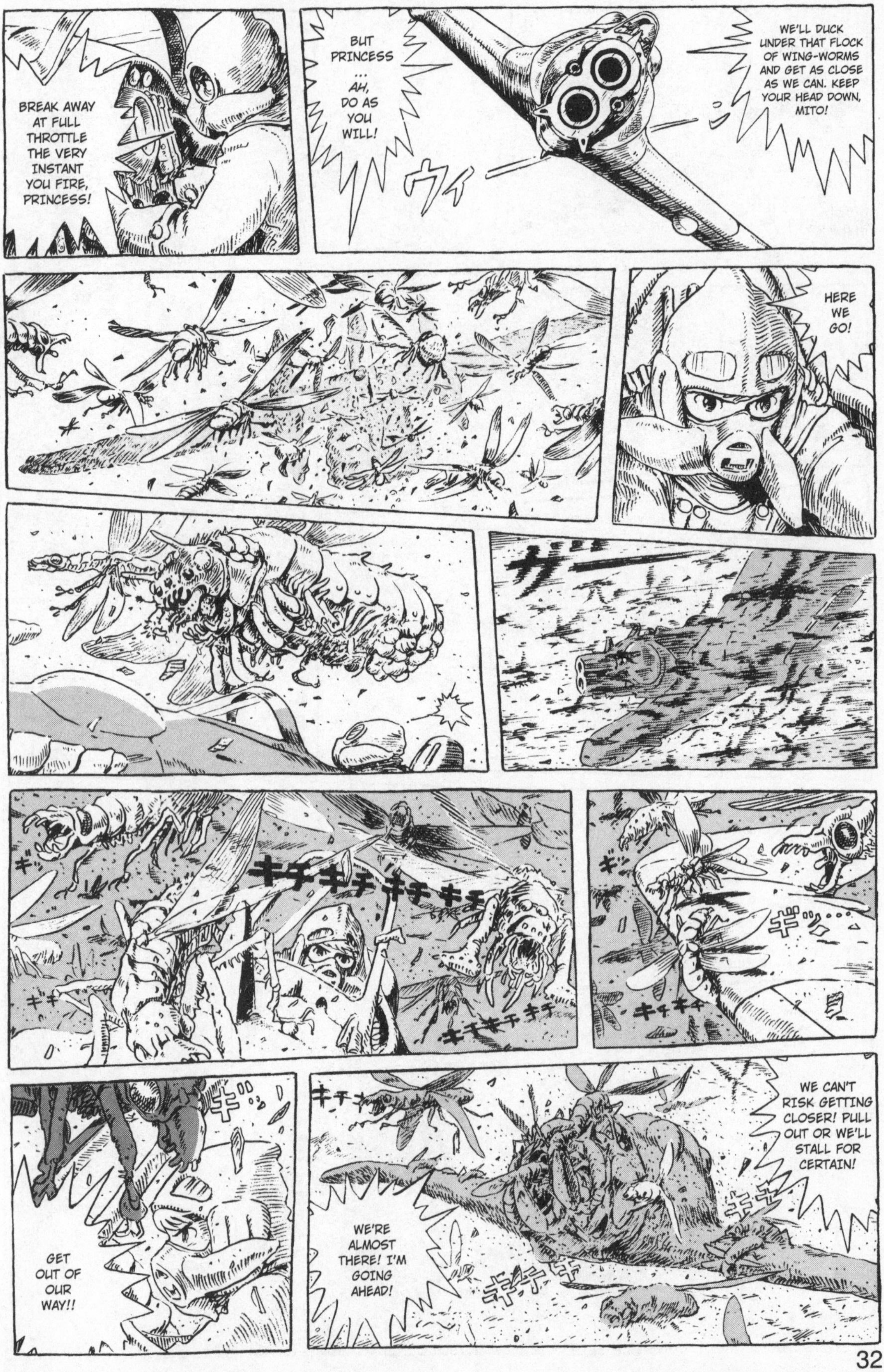
WE'LL DUCK UNDER THAT FLOCK OF WING-WORMS AND GET AS CLOSE AS WE CAN. KEEP YOUR HEAD DOWN, MITO!
BUT PRINCESS ... AH, DO AS YOU WILL!
ウィー
BREAK AWAY AT FULL THROTTLE THE VERY INSTANT YOU FIRE, PRINCESS!
HERE WE GO!
WE CAN'T RISK GETTING CLOSER! PULL OUT OR WE'LL STALL FOR CERTAIN!
WE'RE ALMOST THERE! I'M GOING AHEAD!
GET OUT OF OUR WAY!!

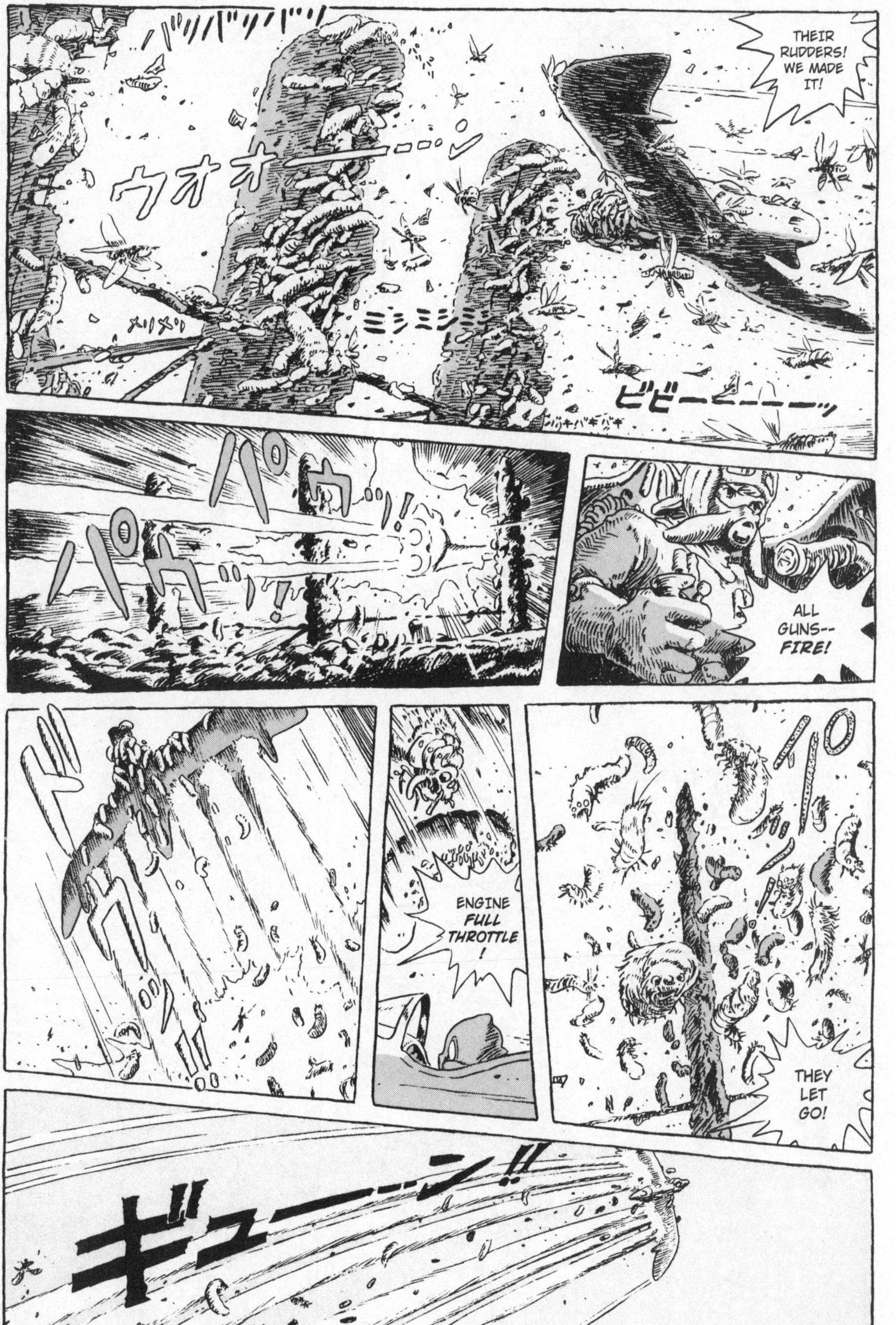
THEIR RUDDERS! WE MADE IT!
ウオオーーーン
ミシミシミシ
ALL GUNS-- FIRE!
パウッ!
パウッ!
THEY LET GO!
ENGINE FULL THROTTLE!
ギューーーン!!

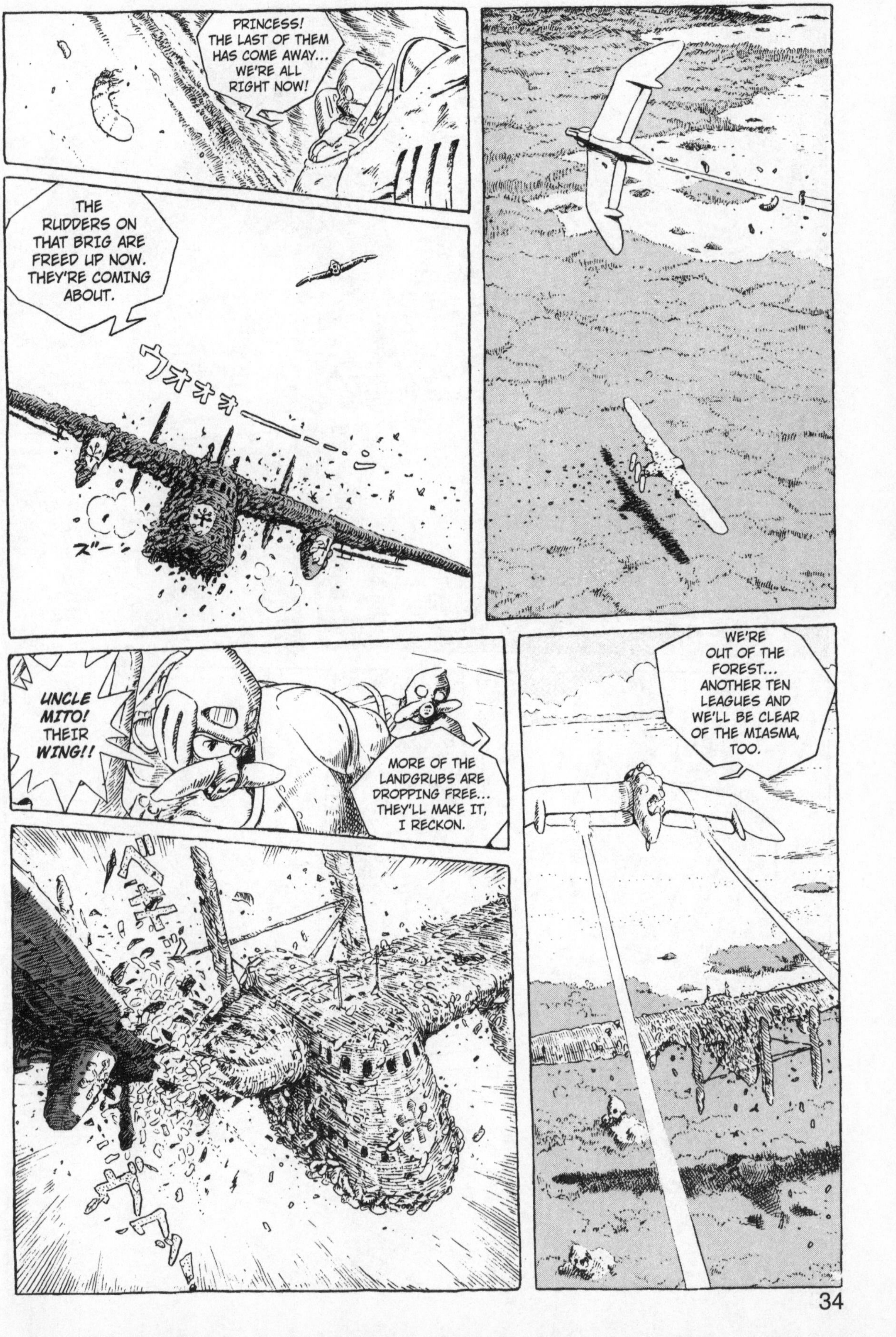
PRINCESS! THE LAST OF THEM HAS COME AWAY... WE'RE ALL RIGHT NOW!
THE RUDDERS ON THAT BRIG ARE FREED UP NOW. THEY'RE COMING ABOUT.
ウオオオー
ズー
WE'RE OUT OF THE FOREST... ANOTHER TEN LEAGUES AND WE'LL BE CLEAR OF THE MIASMA, TOO.
MORE OF THE LANDGRUBS ARE DROPPING FREE... THEY'LL MAKE IT, I RECKON.
***UNCLE MITO!*** THEIR ***WING!!***

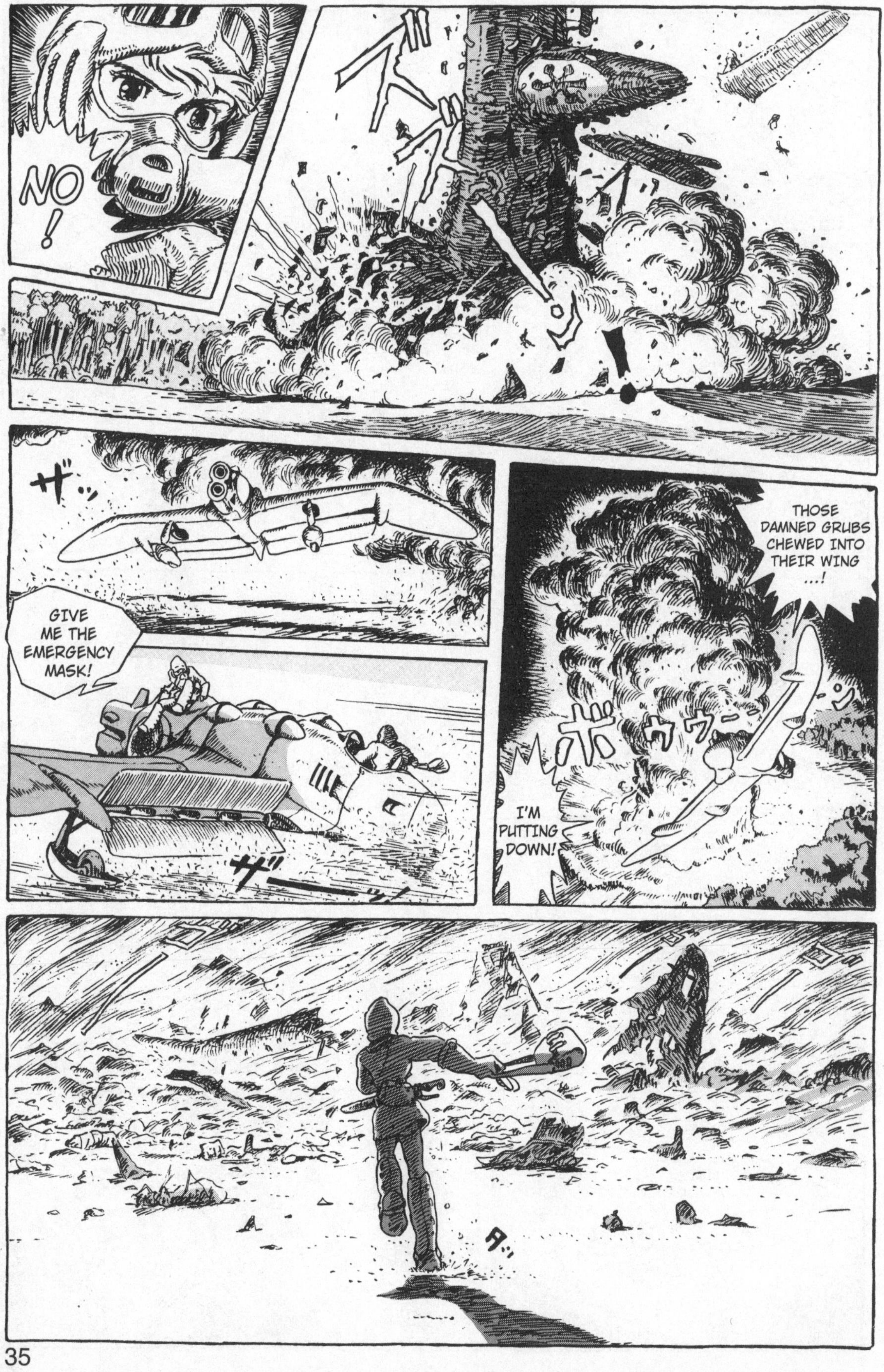
NO!
THOSE DAMNED GRUBS CHEWED INTO THEIR WING ...!
I'M PUTTING DOWN!
GIVE ME THE EMERGENCY MASK!

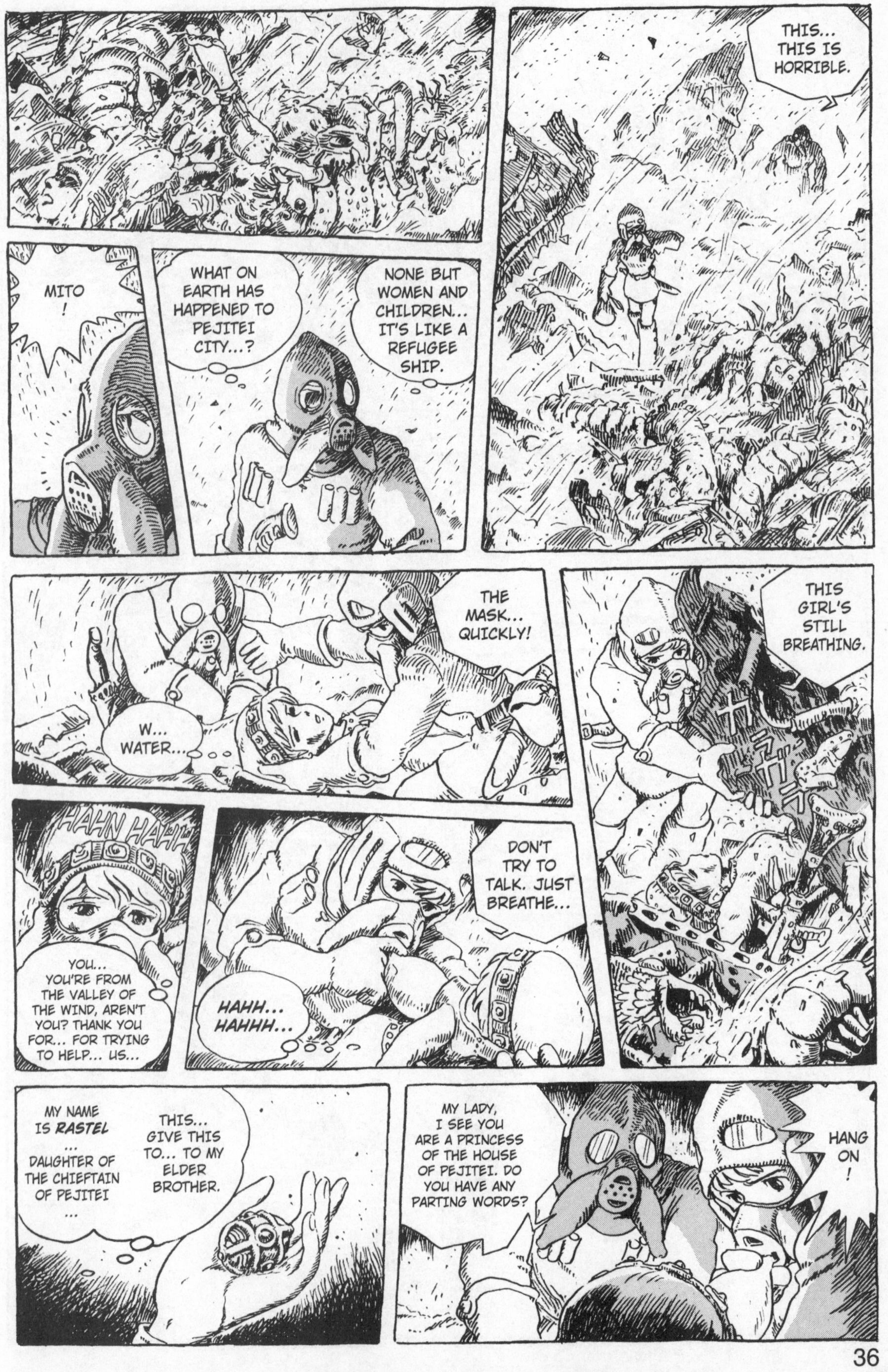
THIS... THIS IS HORRIBLE.
NONE BUT WOMEN AND CHILDREN... IT'S LIKE A REFUGEE SHIP.
WHAT ON EARTH HAS HAPPENED TO PEJITEI CITY...?
MITO!
THIS GIRL'S STILL BREATHING.
THE MASK... QUICKLY!
W... WATER...
DON'T TRY TO TALK. JUST BREATHE...
HAHH... HAHHH...
HAHN HAHH
YOU... YOU'RE FROM THE VALLEY OF THE WIND, AREN'T YOU? THANK YOU FOR... FOR TRYING TO HELP... US...
HANG ON!
MY LADY, I SEE YOU ARE A PRINCESS OF THE HOUSE OF PEJITEI. DO YOU HAVE ANY PARTING WORDS?
THIS... GIVE THIS TO... TO MY ELDER BROTHER.
MY NAME IS RASTEL ... DAUGHTER OF THE CHIEFTAIN OF PEJITEI ...

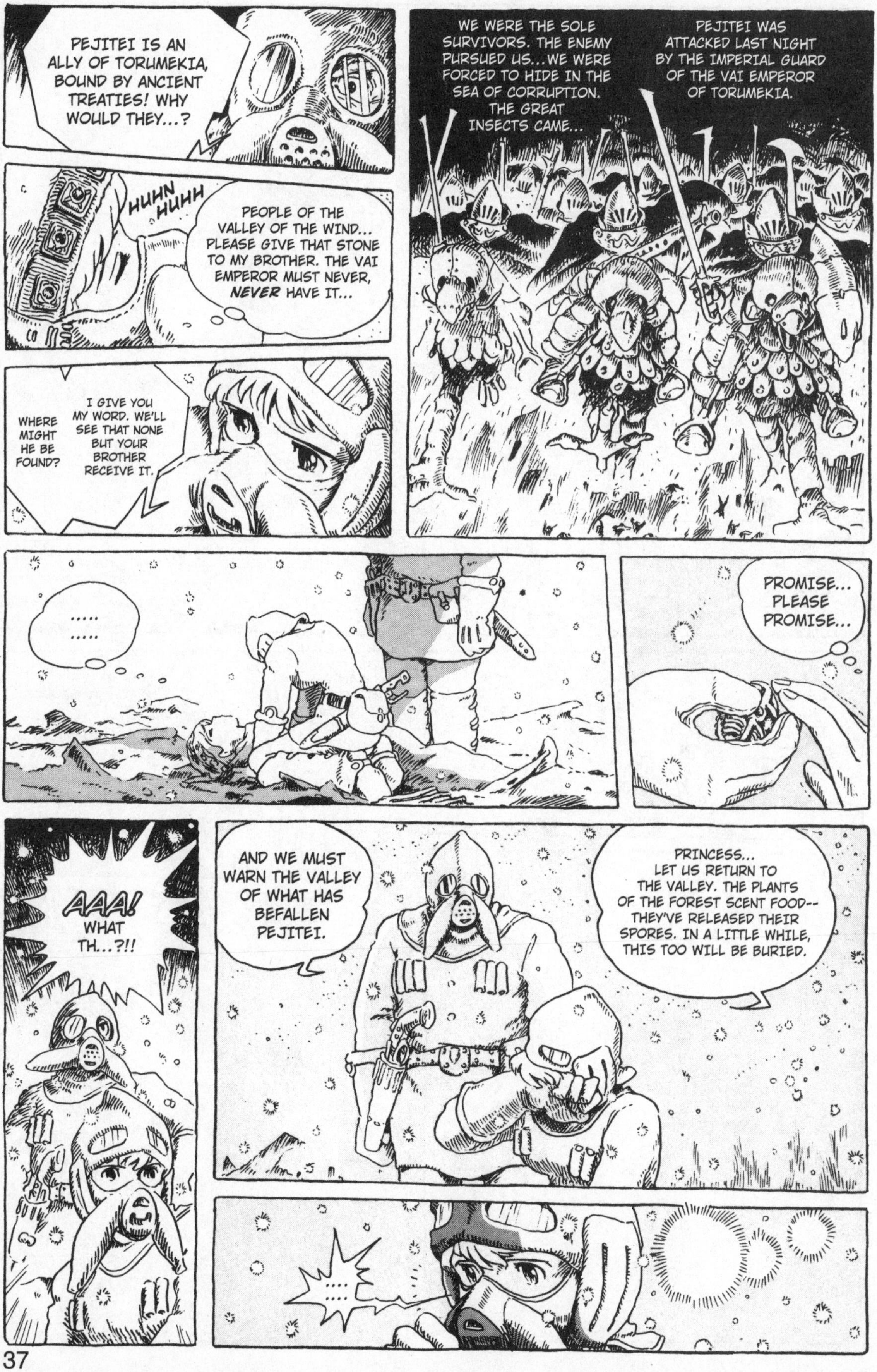
PEJITEI WAS ATTACKED LAST NIGHT BY THE IMPERIAL GUARD OF THE VAI EMPEROR OF TORUMEKIA.
WE WERE THE SOLE SURVIVORS. THE ENEMY PURSUED US... WE WERE FORCED TO HIDE IN THE SEA OF CORRUPTION. THE GREAT INSECTS CAME...
PEJITEI IS AN ALLY OF TORUMEKIA, BOUND BY ANCIENT TREATIES! WHY WOULD THEY...?
HUHN HUHH
PEOPLE OF THE VALLEY OF THE WIND... PLEASE GIVE THAT STONE TO MY BROTHER. THE VAI EMPEROR MUST NEVER, ***NEVER*** HAVE IT...
I GIVE YOU MY WORD. WE'LL SEE THAT NONE BUT YOUR BROTHER RECEIVE IT.
WHERE MIGHT HE BE FOUND?
PROMISE... PLEASE PROMISE...
..... .....
PRINCESS... LET US RETURN TO THE VALLEY. THE PLANTS OF THE FOREST SCENT FOOD-- THEY'VE RELEASED THEIR SPORES. IN A LITTLE WHILE, THIS TOO WILL BE BURIED.
AND WE MUST WARN THE VALLEY OF WHAT HAS BEFALLEN PEJITEI.
..... .....
AAA! WHAT TH...?!!

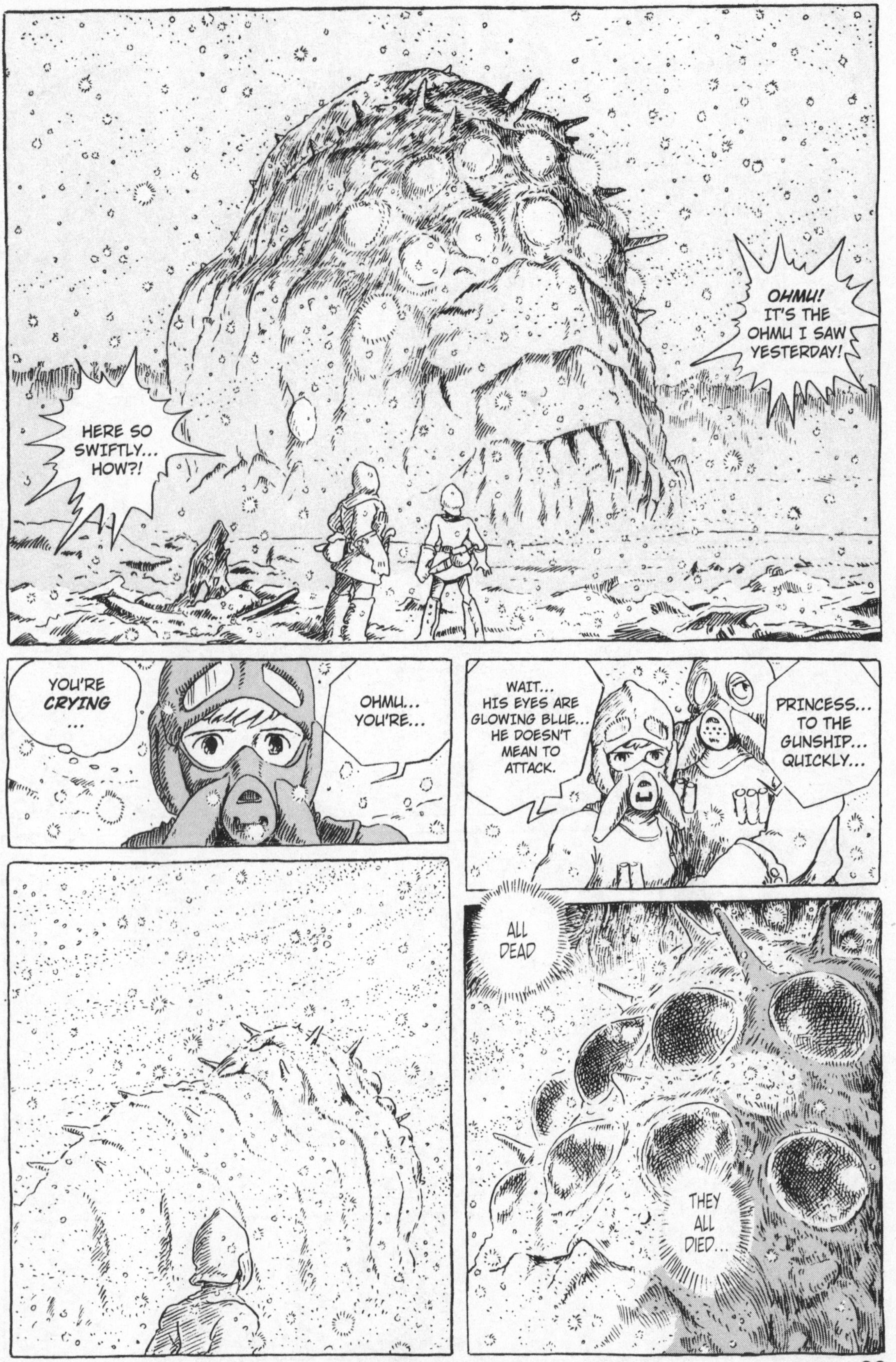
**OHMU!** IT'S THE OHMU I SAW YESTERDAY!
HERE SO SWIFTLY... HOW?!
PRINCESS... TO THE GUNSHIP... QUICKLY...
WAIT... HIS EYES ARE GLOWING BLUE... HE DOESN'T MEAN TO ATTACK.
OHMU... YOU'RE...
YOU'RE **CRYING** ...
ALL DEAD
THEY ALL DIED...

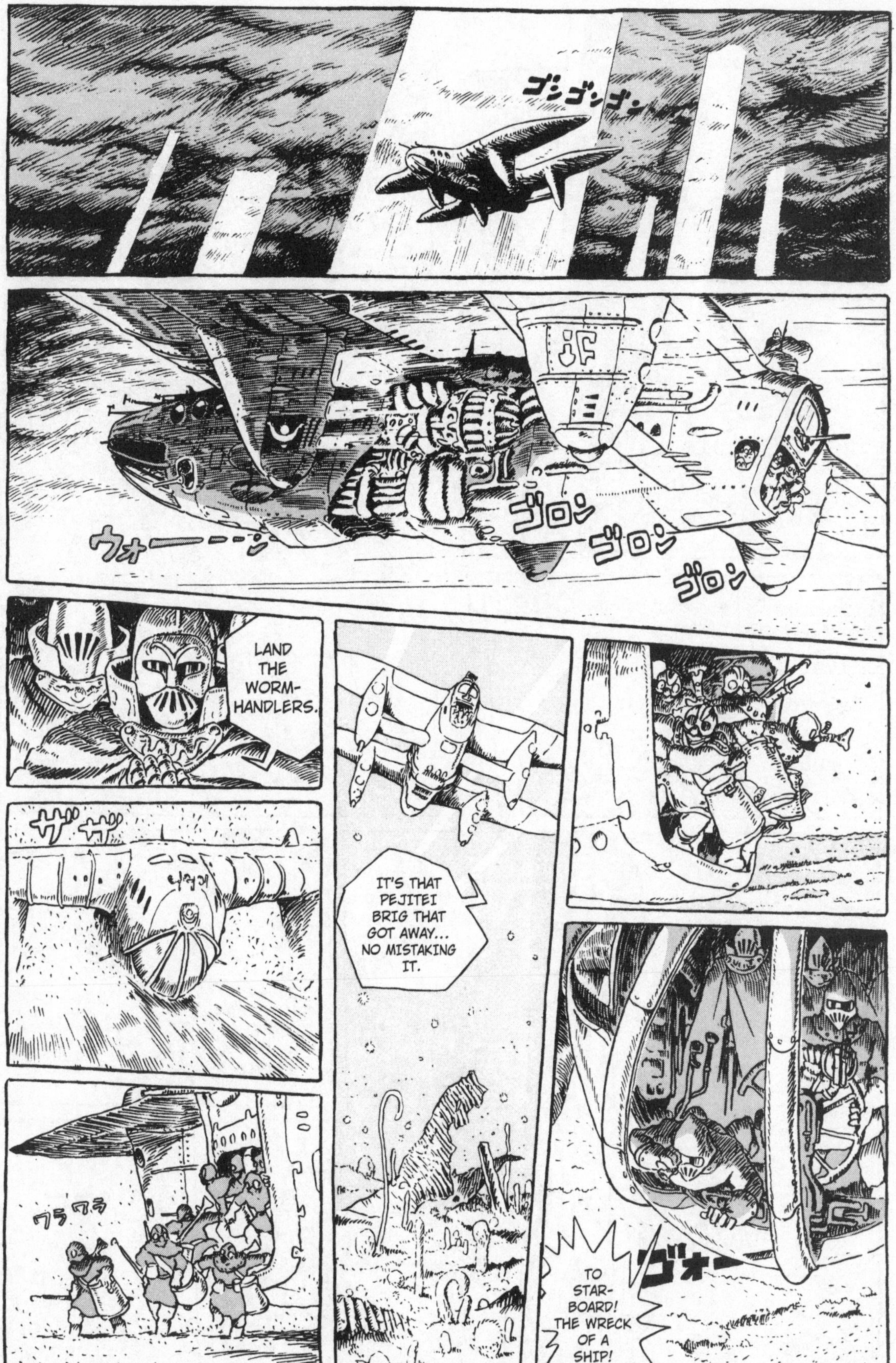

ゴンゴンゴン
ウォーーーン
ゴロン
ゴロン
ゴロン
ゴォー
TO STAR-BOARD! THE WRECK OF A SHIP!
IT'S THAT PEJITEI BRIG THAT GOT AWAY... NO MISTAKING IT.
LAND THE WORM-HANDLERS.
ザザ
ワラワラ

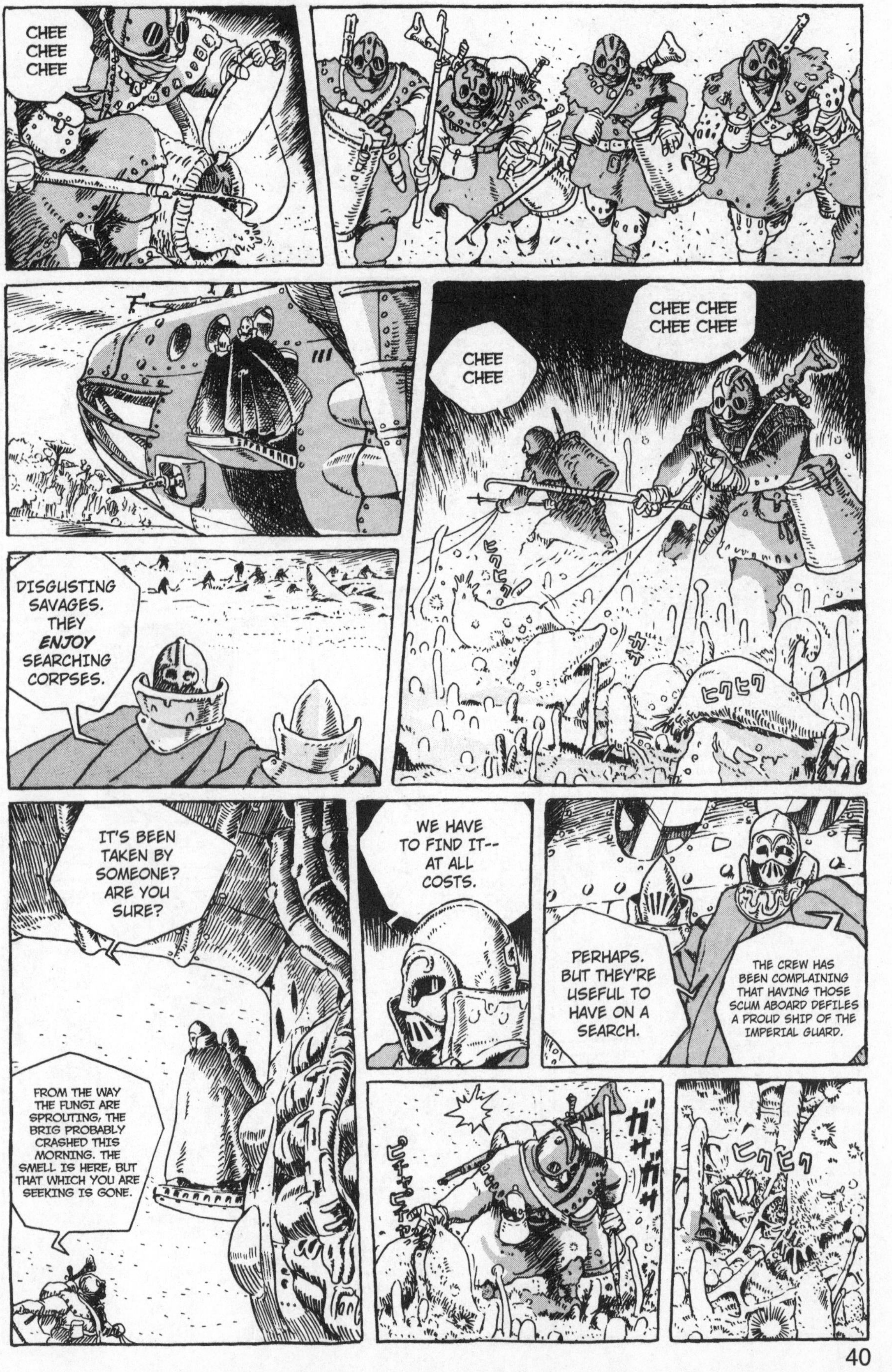
CHEE CHEE CHEE
CHEE CHEE CHEE CHEE
CHEE CHEE
ヒクヒク
ヒクヒク
DISGUSTING SAVAGES. THEY *ENJOY* SEARCHING CORPSES.
PERHAPS. BUT THEY'RE USEFUL TO HAVE ON A SEARCH.
THE CREW HAS BEEN COMPLAINING THAT HAVING THOSE SCUM ABOARD DEFILES A PROUD SHIP OF THE IMPERIAL GUARD.
WE HAVE TO FIND IT-- AT ALL COSTS.
ヒクヒク
IT'S BEEN TAKEN BY SOMEONE? ARE YOU SURE?
FROM THE WAY THE FUNGI ARE SPROUTING, THE BRIG PROBABLY CRASHED THIS MORNING. THE SMELL IS HERE, BUT THAT WHICH YOU ARE SEEKING IS GONE.

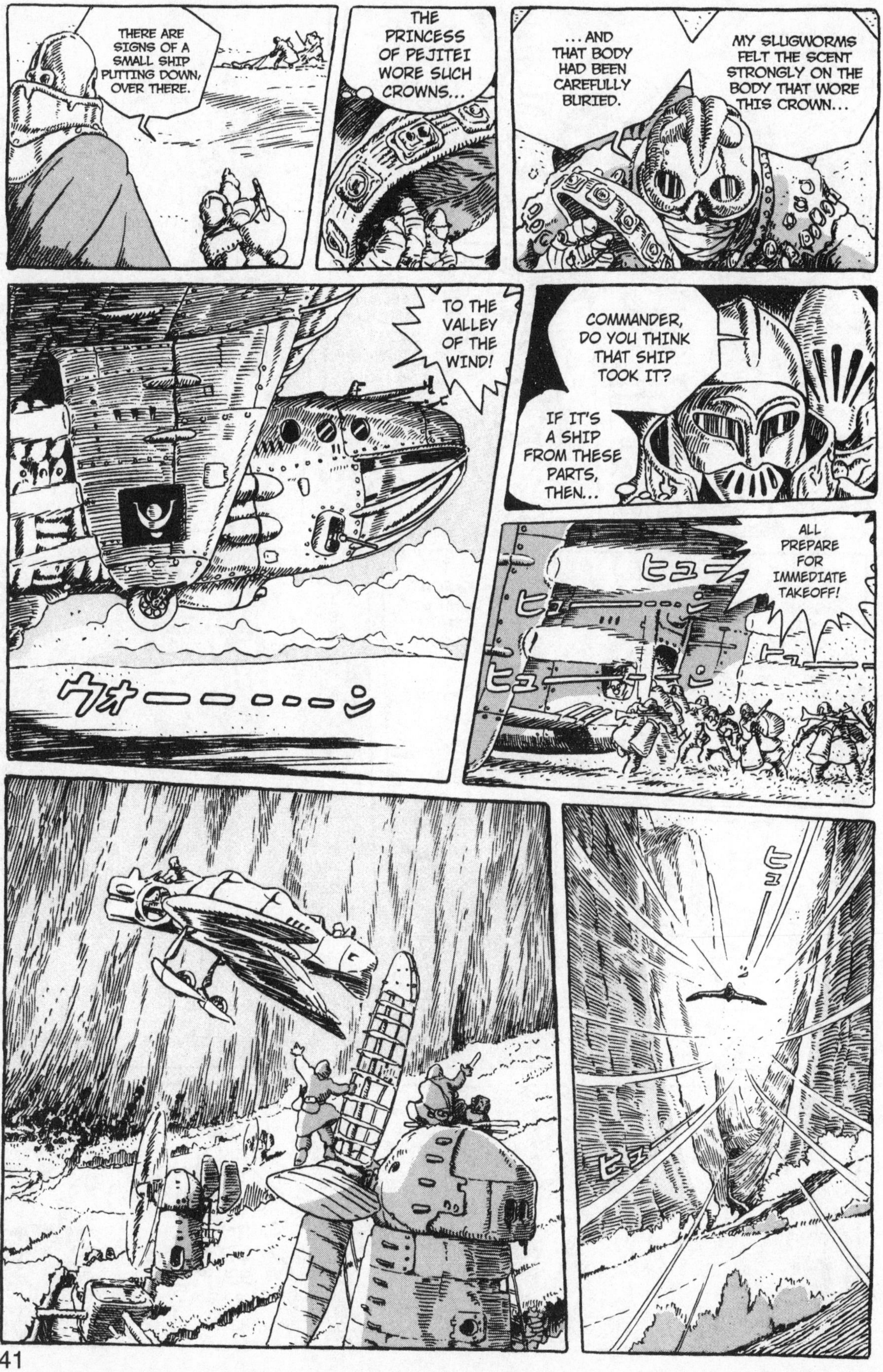
MY SLUGWORMS FELT THE SCENT STRONGLY ON THE BODY THAT WORE THIS CROWN...
...AND THAT BODY HAD BEEN CAREFULLY BURIED.
THE PRINCESS OF PEJITEI WORE SUCH CROWNS...
THERE ARE SIGNS OF A SMALL SHIP PUTTING DOWN, OVER THERE.
COMMANDER, DO YOU THINK THAT SHIP TOOK IT?
IF IT'S A SHIP FROM THESE PARTS, THEN...
ALL PREPARE FOR IMMEDIATE TAKEOFF!
ヒュー
ヒューーン
ヒューーン
ヒューー
TO THE VALLEY OF THE WIND!
ウォーーーーーン
ヒュー
ヒュ

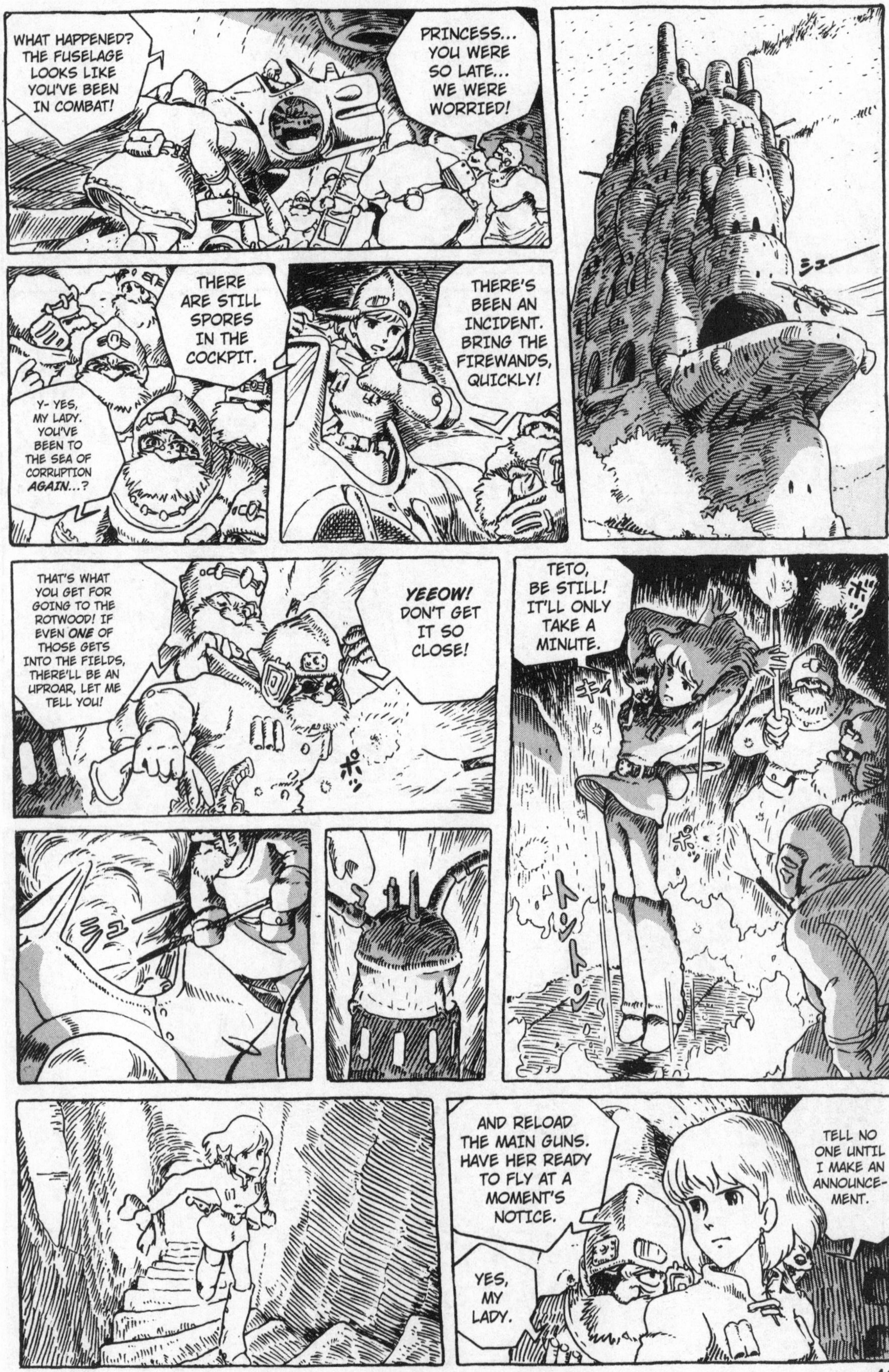
シュー
PRINCESS... YOU WERE SO LATE... WE WERE WORRIED!
WHAT HAPPENED? THE FUSELAGE LOOKS LIKE YOU'VE BEEN IN COMBAT!
THERE'S BEEN AN INCIDENT. BRING THE FIREWANDS, QUICKLY!
THERE ARE STILL SPORES IN THE COCKPIT.
Y- YES, MY LADY. YOU'VE BEEN TO THE SEA OF CORRUPTION ***AGAIN***...?
TETO, BE STILL! IT'LL ONLY TAKE A MINUTE.
ボッ
キイ
トントン
***YEEOW!*** DON'T GET IT SO CLOSE!
THAT'S WHAT YOU GET FOR GOING TO THE ROTWOOD! IF EVEN ***ONE*** OF THOSE GETS INTO THE FIELDS, THERE'LL BE AN UPROAR, LET ME TELL YOU!
ポッ
TELL NO ONE UNTIL I MAKE AN ANNOUNCEMENT.
AND RELOAD THE MAIN GUNS. HAVE HER READY TO FLY AT A MOMENT'S NOTICE.
YES, MY LADY.

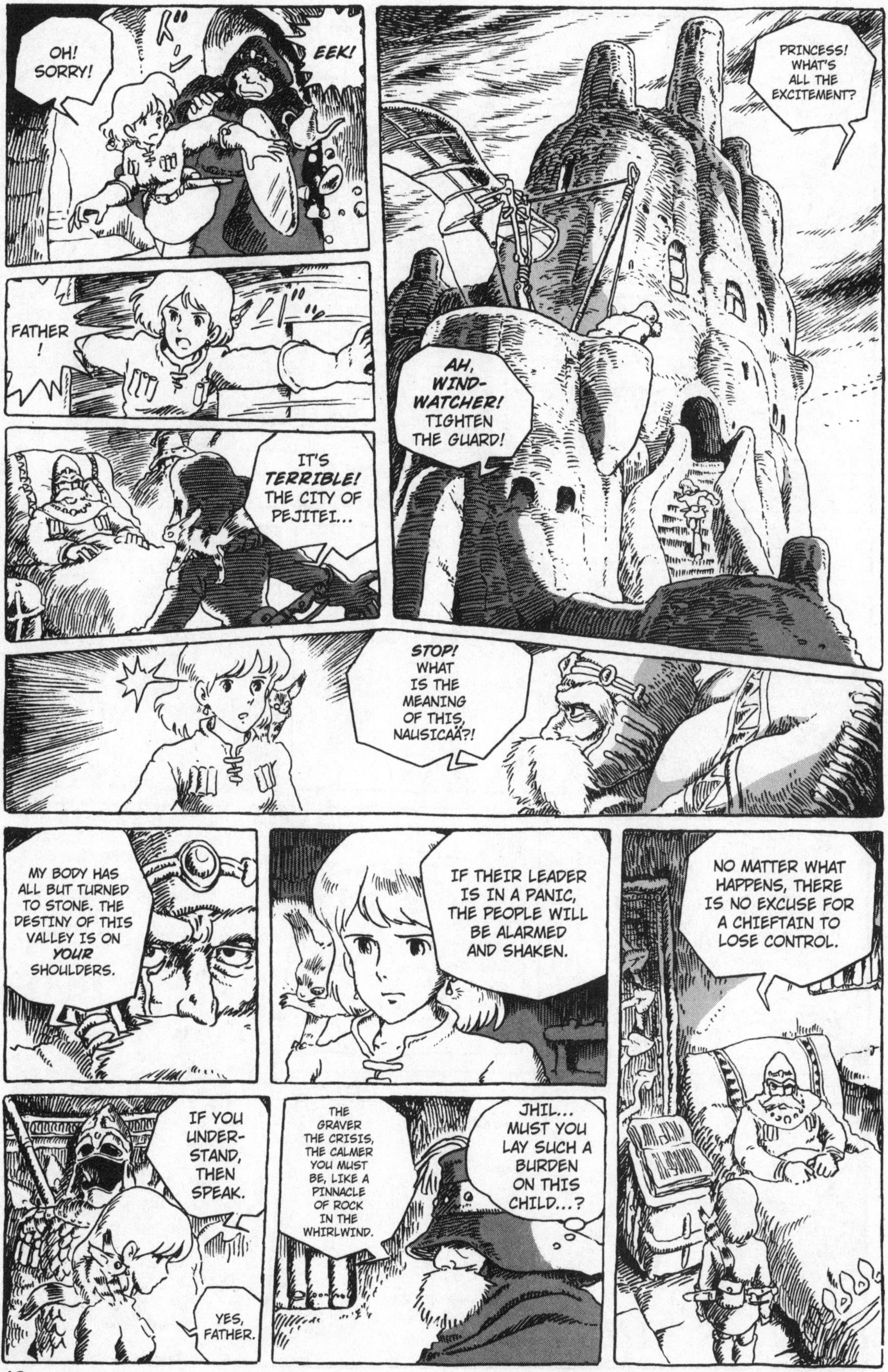
PRINCESS! WHAT'S ALL THE EXCITEMENT?
AH, WIND-WATCHER! TIGHTEN THE GUARD!
EEK!
OH! SORRY!
FATHER!
IT'S TERRIBLE! THE CITY OF PEJITEI...
STOP! WHAT IS THE MEANING OF THIS, NAUSICAÄ?!
NO MATTER WHAT HAPPENS, THERE IS NO EXCUSE FOR A CHIEFTAIN TO LOSE CONTROL.
IF THEIR LEADER IS IN A PANIC, THE PEOPLE WILL BE ALARMED AND SHAKEN.
MY BODY HAS ALL BUT TURNED TO STONE. THE DESTINY OF THIS VALLEY IS ON YOUR SHOULDERS.
JHIL... MUST YOU LAY SUCH A BURDEN ON THIS CHILD...?
THE GRAVER THE CRISIS, THE CALMER YOU MUST BE, LIKE A PINNACLE OF ROCK IN THE WHIRLWIND.
IF YOU UNDER-STAND, THEN SPEAK.
YES, FATHER.

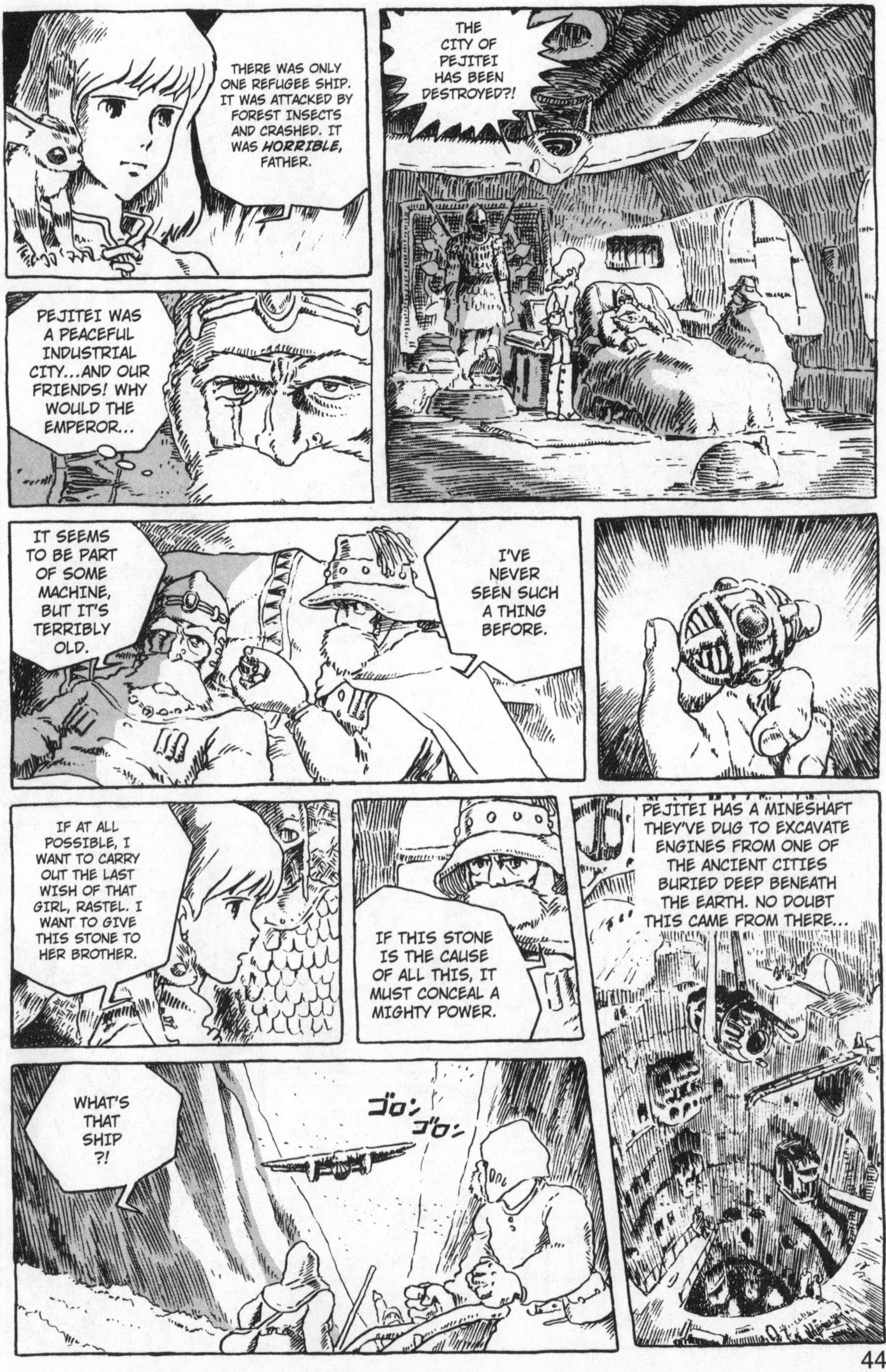
THE CITY OF PEJITEI HAS BEEN DESTROYED?!
THERE WAS ONLY ONE REFUGEE SHIP. IT WAS ATTACKED BY FOREST INSECTS AND CRASHED. IT WAS *HORRIBLE*, FATHER.
PEJITEI WAS A PEACEFUL INDUSTRIAL CITY...AND OUR FRIENDS! WHY WOULD THE EMPEROR...
I'VE NEVER SEEN SUCH A THING BEFORE.
IT SEEMS TO BE PART OF SOME MACHINE, BUT IT'S TERRIBLY OLD.
PEJITEI HAS A MINESHAFT THEY'VE DUG TO EXCAVATE ENGINES FROM ONE OF THE ANCIENT CITIES BURIED DEEP BENEATH THE EARTH. NO DOUBT THIS CAME FROM THERE...
IF THIS STONE IS THE CAUSE OF ALL THIS, IT MUST CONCEAL A MIGHTY POWER.
IF AT ALL POSSIBLE, I WANT TO CARRY OUT THE LAST WISH OF THAT GIRL, RASTEL. I WANT TO GIVE THIS STONE TO HER BROTHER.
ゴロン
ゴロン
WHAT'S THAT SHIP ?!

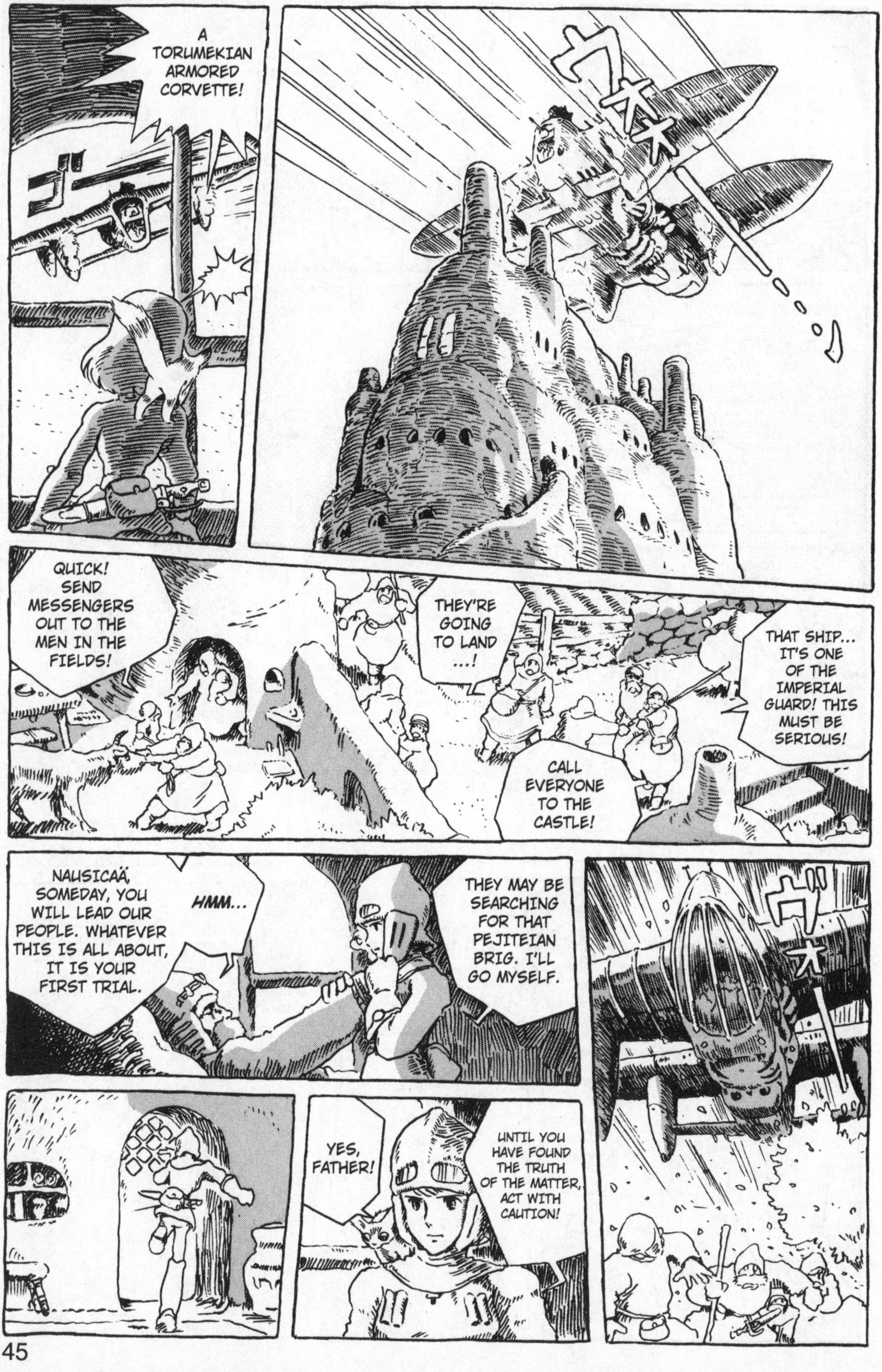
A TORUMEKIAN ARMORED CORVETTE!
THAT SHIP... IT'S ONE OF THE IMPERIAL GUARD! THIS MUST BE SERIOUS!
THEY'RE GOING TO LAND ...!
CALL EVERYONE TO THE CASTLE!
QUICK! SEND MESSENGERS OUT TO THE MEN IN THE FIELDS!
THEY MAY BE SEARCHING FOR THAT PEJITEIAN BRIG. I'LL GO MYSELF.
HMM...
NAUSICAÄ, SOMEDAY, YOU WILL LEAD OUR PEOPLE. WHATEVER THIS IS ALL ABOUT, IT IS YOUR FIRST TRIAL.
UNTIL YOU HAVE FOUND THE TRUTH OF THE MATTER, ACT WITH CAUTION!
YES, FATHER!

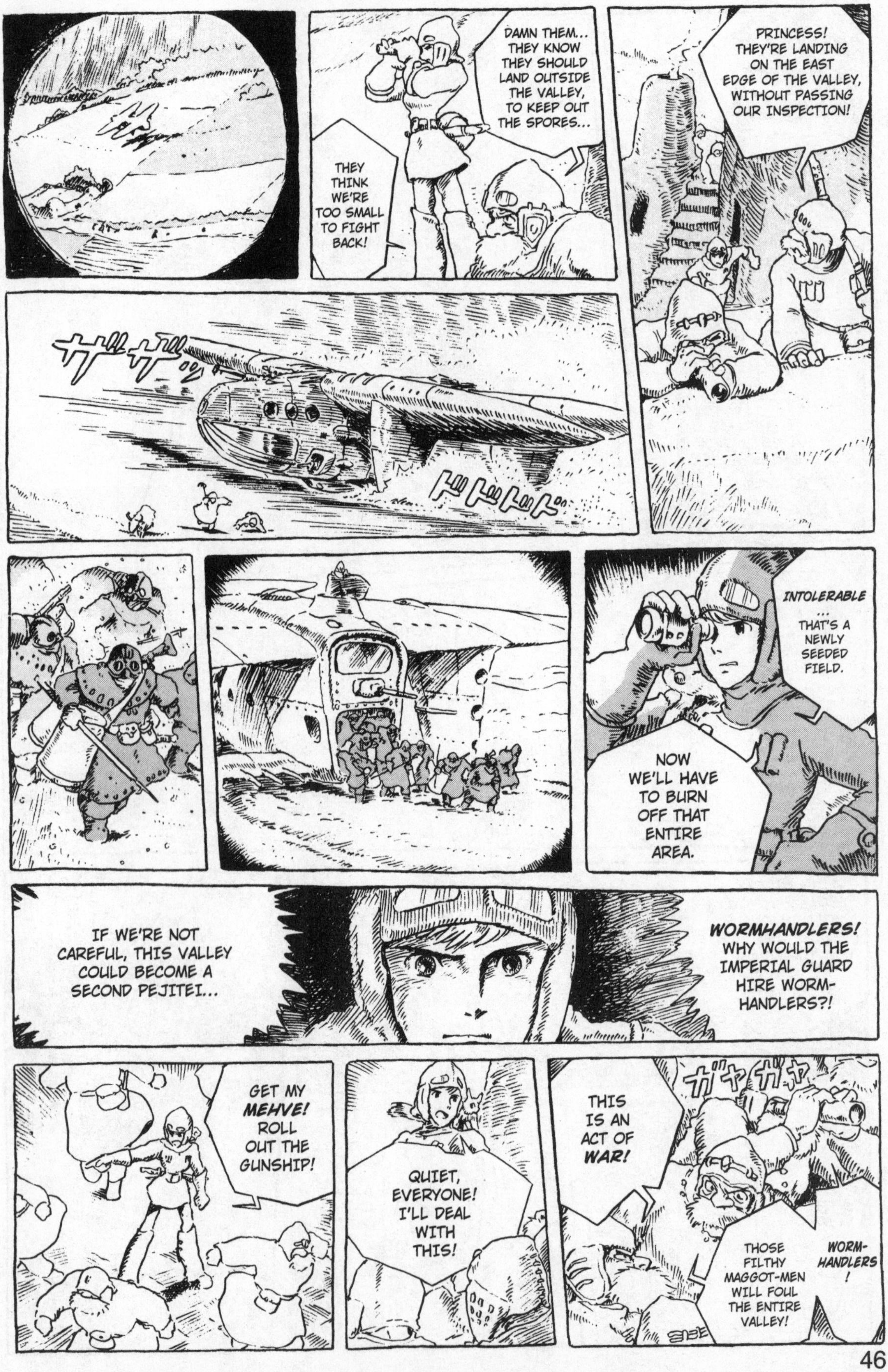
PRINCESS! THEY'RE LANDING ON THE EAST EDGE OF THE VALLEY, WITHOUT PASSING OUR INSPECTION!
DAMN THEM... THEY KNOW THEY SHOULD LAND OUTSIDE THE VALLEY, TO KEEP OUT THE SPORES...
THEY THINK WE'RE TOO SMALL TO FIGHT BACK!
*INTOLERABLE* ... THAT'S A NEWLY SEEDED FIELD.
NOW WE'LL HAVE TO BURN OFF THAT ENTIRE AREA.
*WORMHANDLERS!* WHY WOULD THE IMPERIAL GUARD HIRE WORM-HANDLERS?!
IF WE'RE NOT CAREFUL, THIS VALLEY COULD BECOME A SECOND PEJITEI...
THIS IS AN ACT OF *WAR!*
*WORM-HANDLERS!*
THOSE FILTHY MAGGOT-MEN WILL FOUL THE ENTIRE VALLEY!
QUIET, EVERYONE! I'LL DEAL WITH THIS!
GET MY *MEHVE!* ROLL OUT THE GUNSHIP!

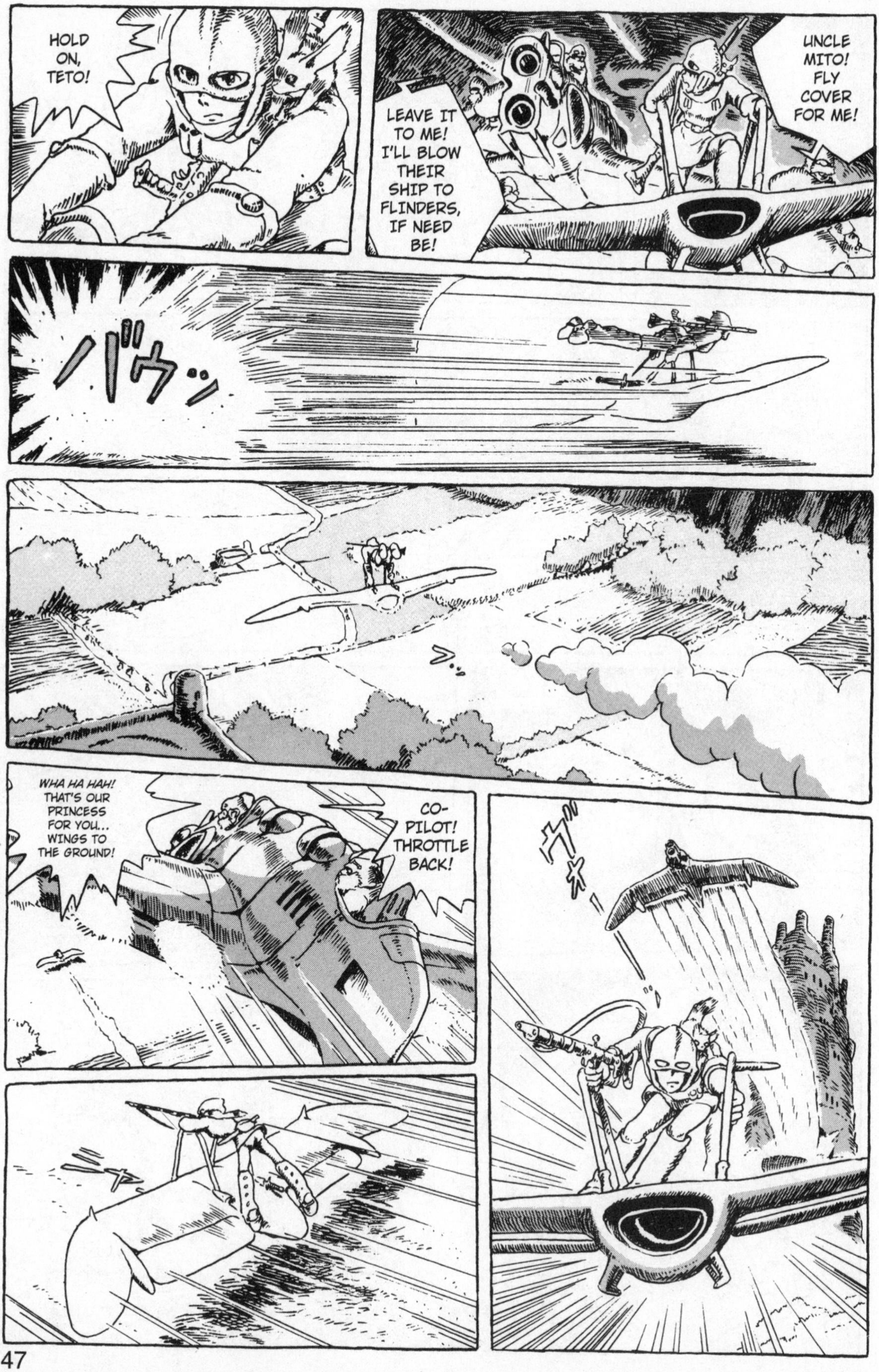
UNCLE MITO! FLY COVER FOR ME!
LEAVE IT TO ME! I'LL BLOW THEIR SHIP TO FLINDERS, IF NEED BE!
HOLD ON, TETO!
バウッ
CO-PILOT! THROTTLE BACK!
WHA HA HAH! THAT'S OUR PRINCESS FOR YOU... WINGS TO THE GROUND!

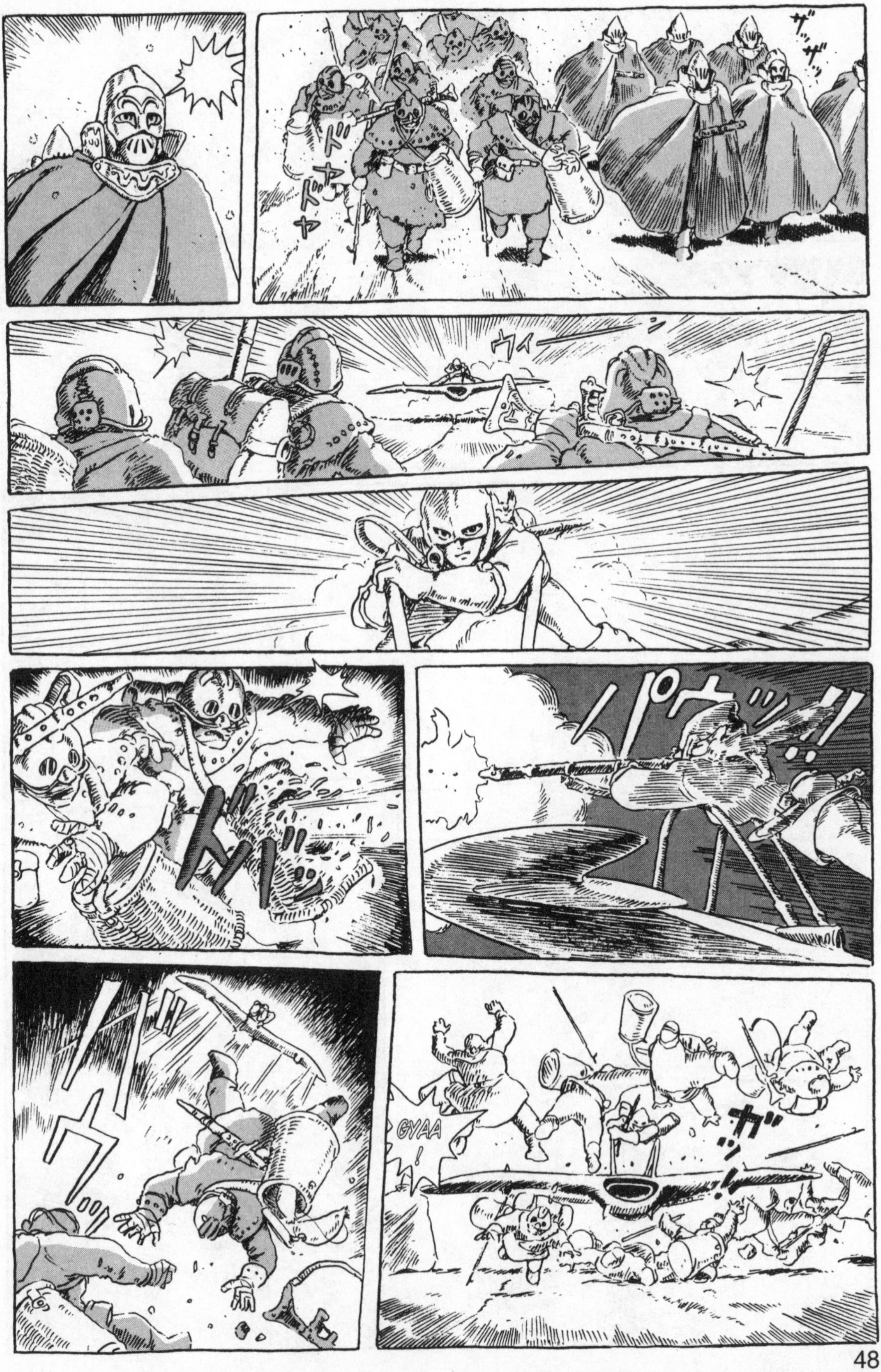
ザッ
ザッ
ドヤ
ドヤ
ウィーーン
パウッ!!
GYAA!
ガッ

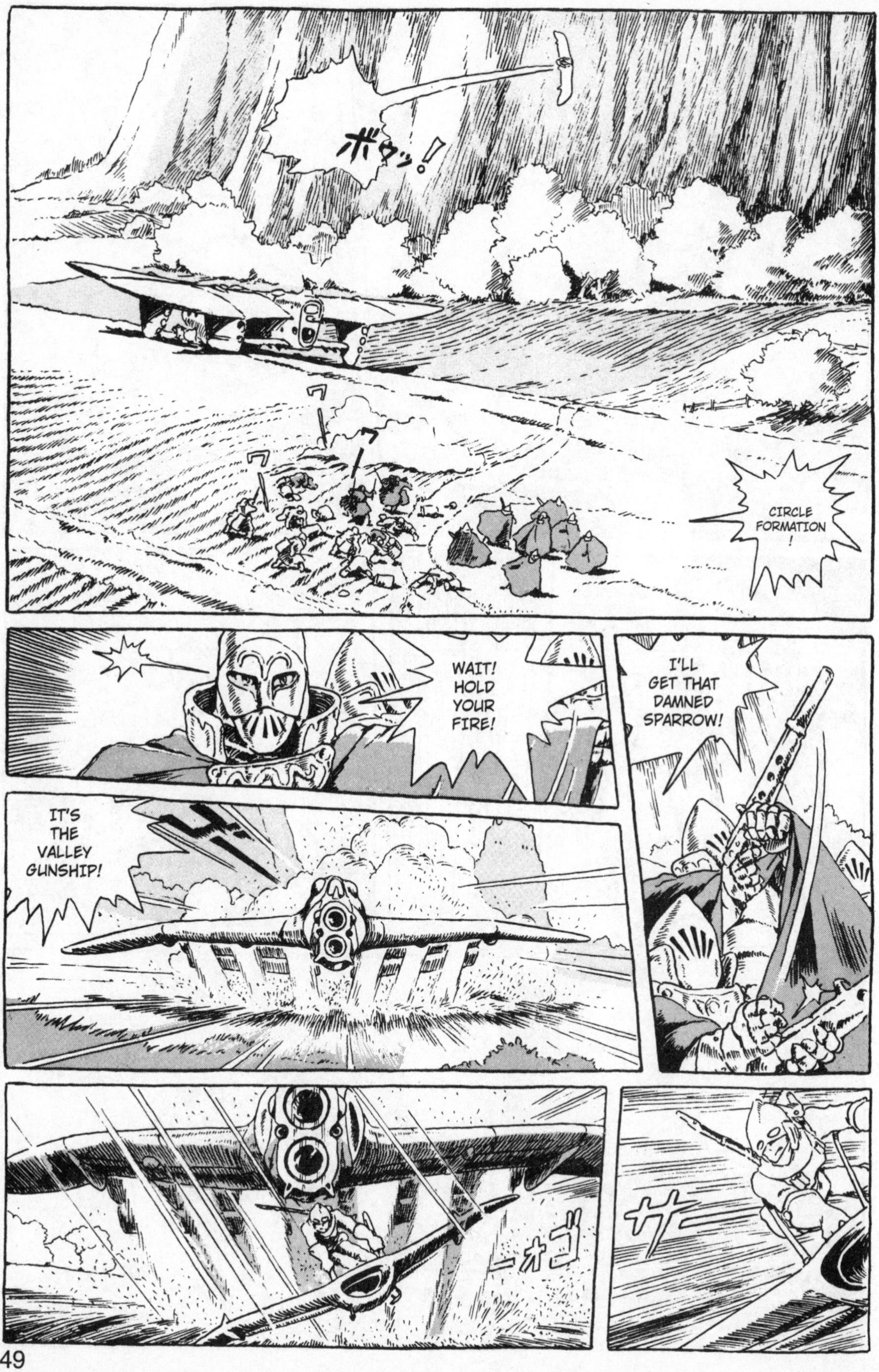
ボタッ!
ワー
ワー
ワー
CIRCLE FORMATION!
I'LL GET THAT DAMNED SPARROW!
WAIT! HOLD YOUR FIRE!
IT'S THE VALLEY GUNSHIP!
サー
ゴォー

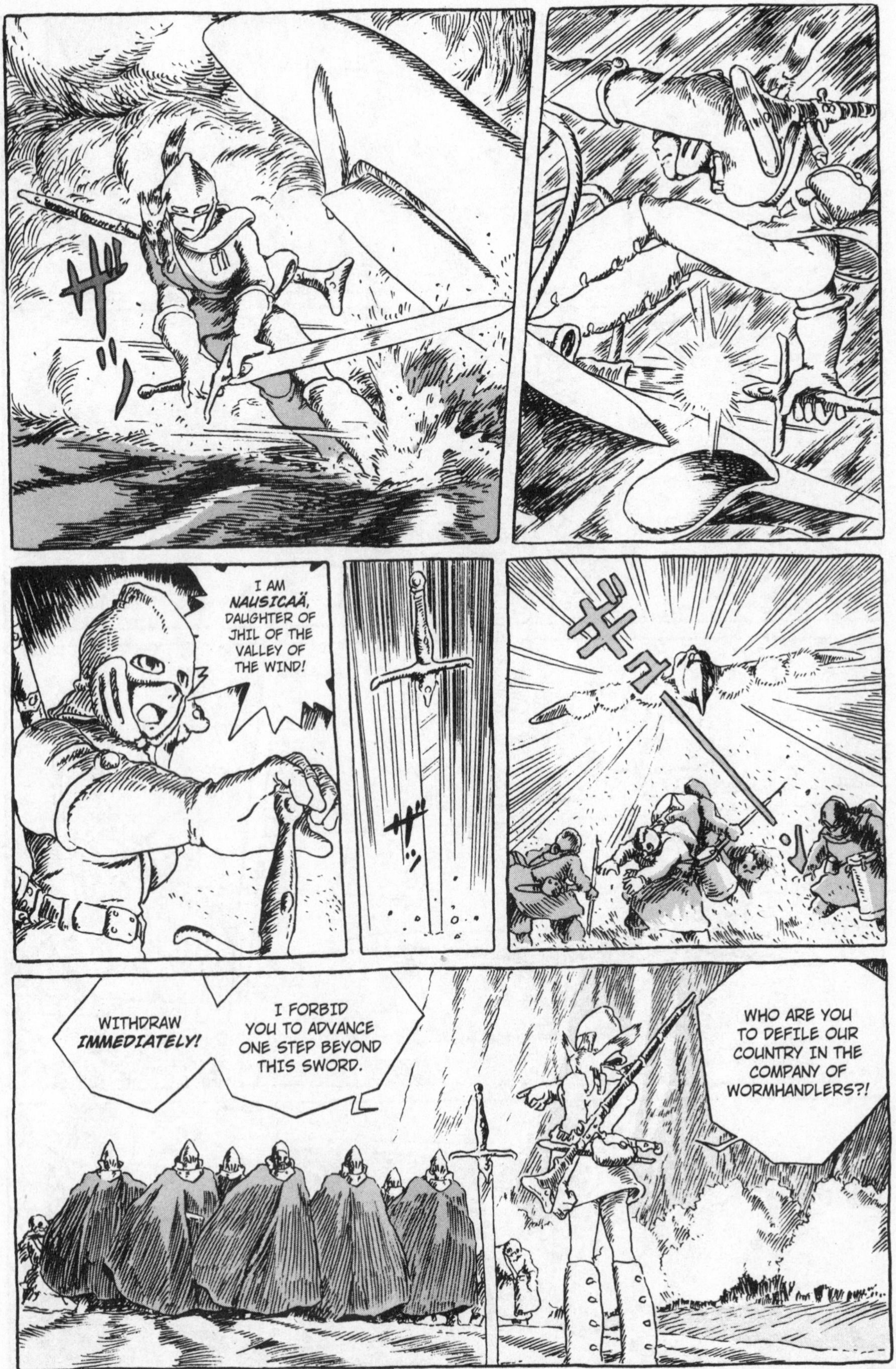
I AM NAUSICAÄ, DAUGHTER OF JHIL OF THE VALLEY OF THE WIND!
WHO ARE YOU TO DEFILE OUR COUNTRY IN THE COMPANY OF WORMHANDLERS?!
I FORBID YOU TO ADVANCE ONE STEP BEYOND THIS SWORD.
WITHDRAW IMMEDIATELY!

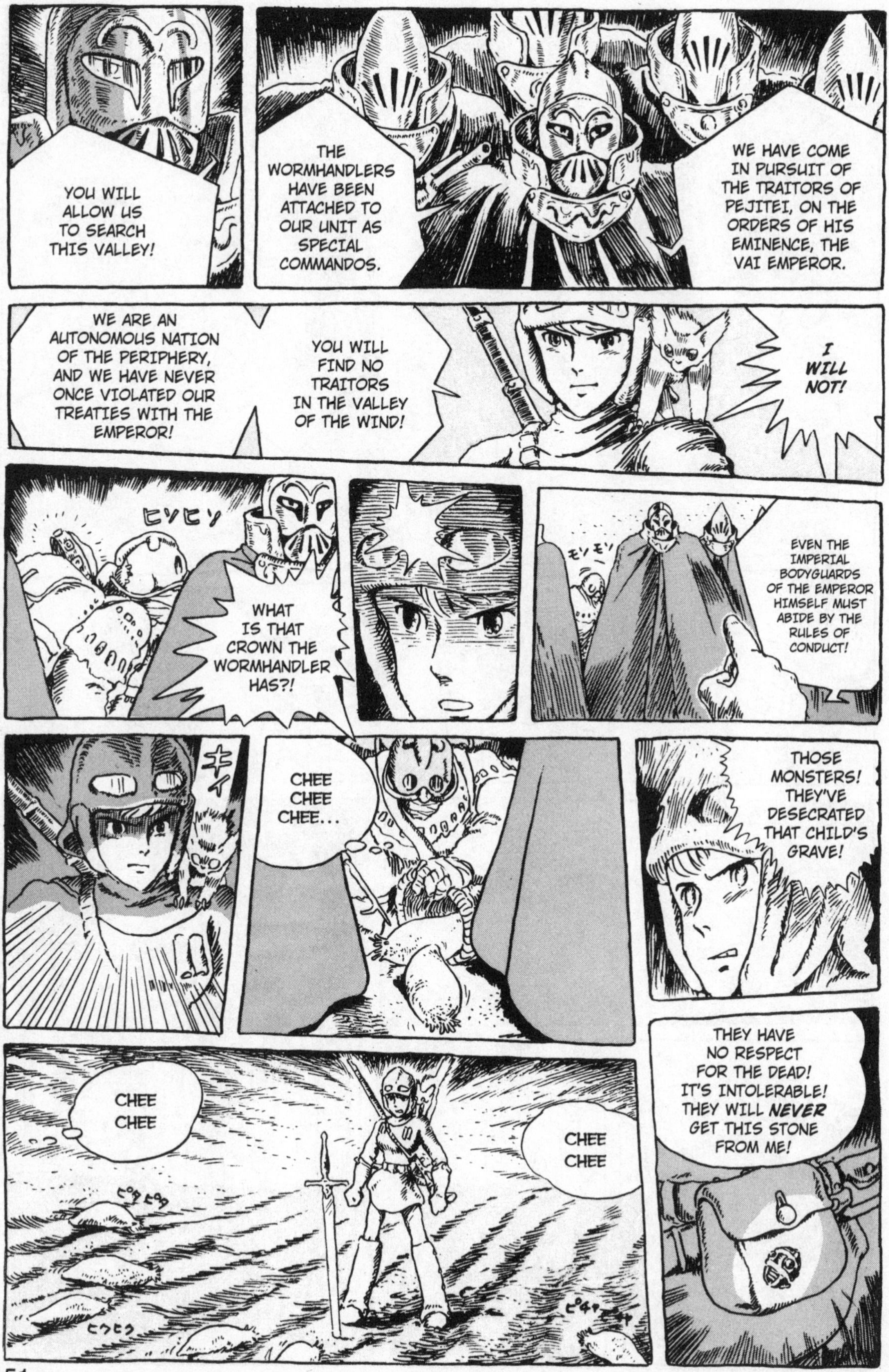
WE HAVE COME IN PURSUIT OF THE TRAITORS OF PEJITEI, ON THE ORDERS OF HIS EMINENCE, THE VAI EMPEROR.
THE WORMHANDLERS HAVE BEEN ATTACHED TO OUR UNIT AS SPECIAL COMMANDOS.
YOU WILL ALLOW US TO SEARCH THIS VALLEY!
I WILL NOT!
YOU WILL FIND NO TRAITORS IN THE VALLEY OF THE WIND!
WE ARE AN AUTONOMOUS NATION OF THE PERIPHERY, AND WE HAVE NEVER ONCE VIOLATED OUR TREATIES WITH THE EMPEROR!
EVEN THE IMPERIAL BODYGUARDS OF THE EMPEROR HIMSELF MUST ABIDE BY THE RULES OF CONDUCT!
モソモソ
ヒソヒソ
WHAT IS THAT CROWN THE WORMHANDLER HAS?!
THOSE MONSTERS! THEY'VE DESECRATED THAT CHILD'S GRAVE!
CHEE CHEE CHEE...
キイ
THEY HAVE NO RESPECT FOR THE DEAD! IT'S INTOLERABLE! THEY WILL *NEVER* GET THIS STONE FROM ME!
CHEE CHEE
CHEE CHEE

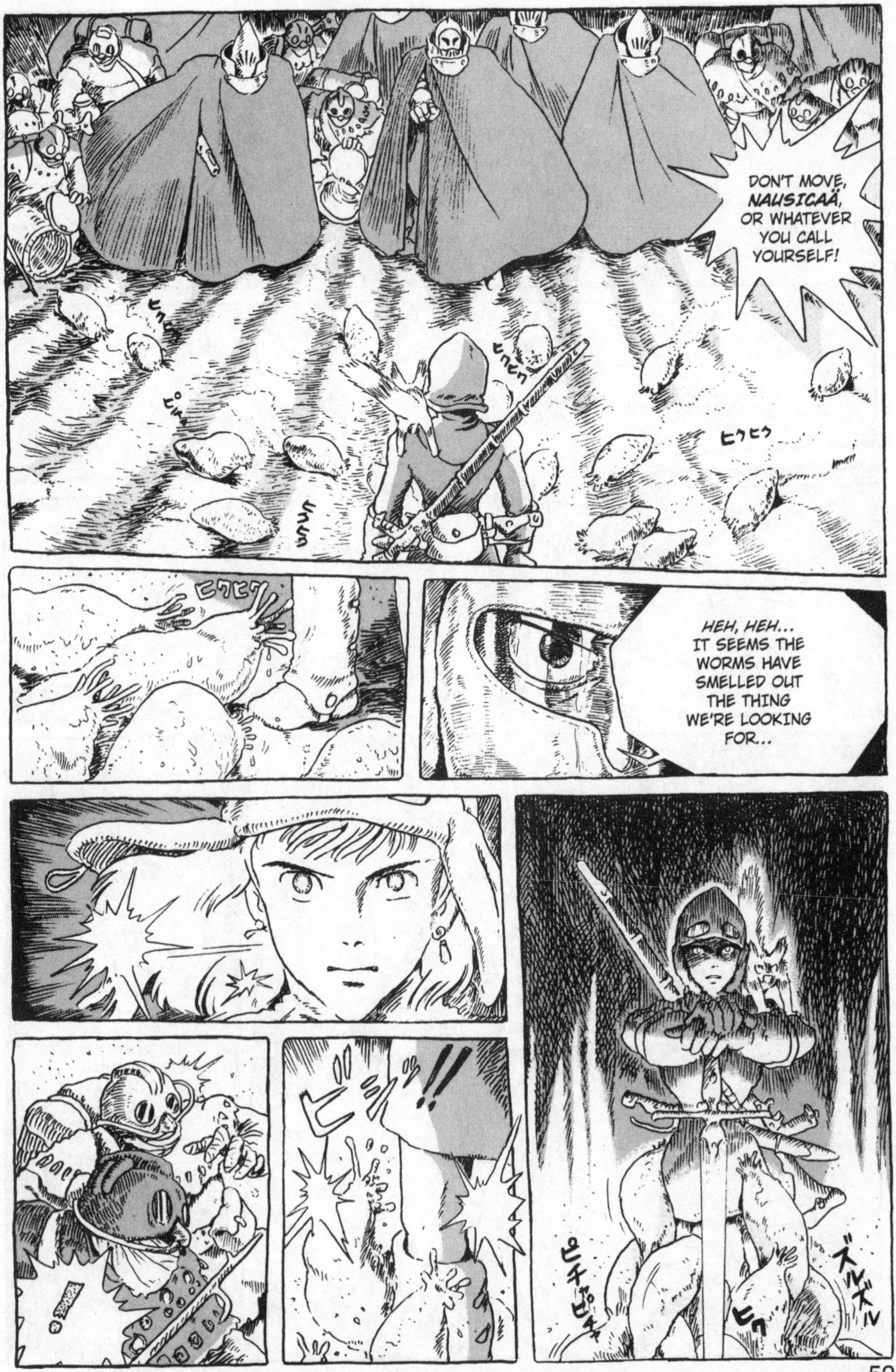
DON'T MOVE, *NAUSICAÄ*, OR WHATEVER YOU CALL YOURSELF!
*HEH, HEH...* IT SEEMS THE WORMS HAVE SMELLED OUT THE THING WE'RE LOOKING FOR...
ヒクヒク
ズルズル
ピチャピチャ
ヒク
ビシッ!!

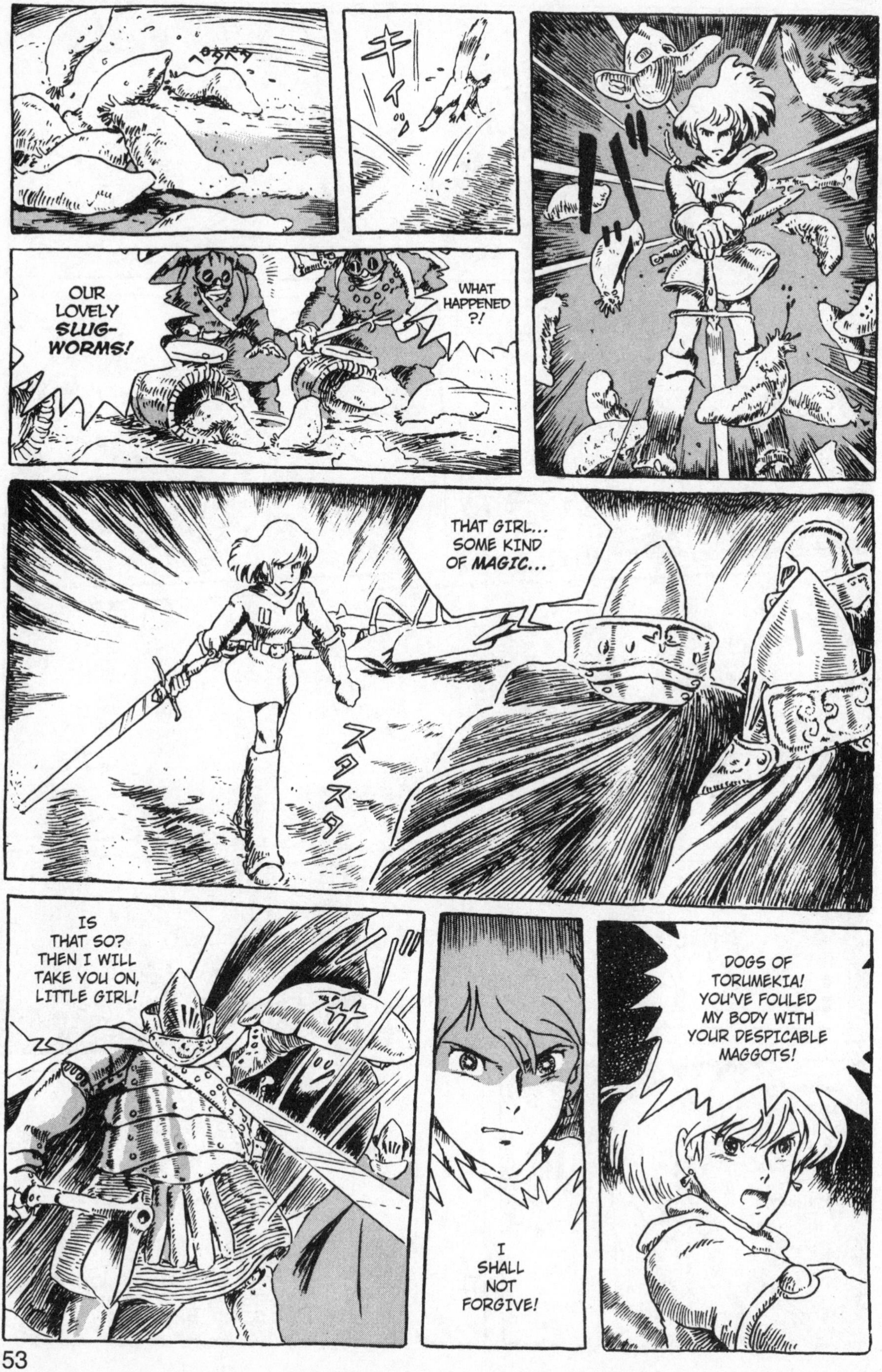
キイ
WHAT HAPPENED ?!
OUR LOVELY SLUG-WORMS!
THAT GIRL... SOME KIND OF MAGIC...
スタスタ
DOGS OF TORUMEKIA! YOU'VE FOULED MY BODY WITH YOUR DESPICABLE MAGGOTS!
I SHALL NOT FORGIVE!
IS THAT SO? THEN I WILL TAKE YOU ON, LITTLE GIRL!

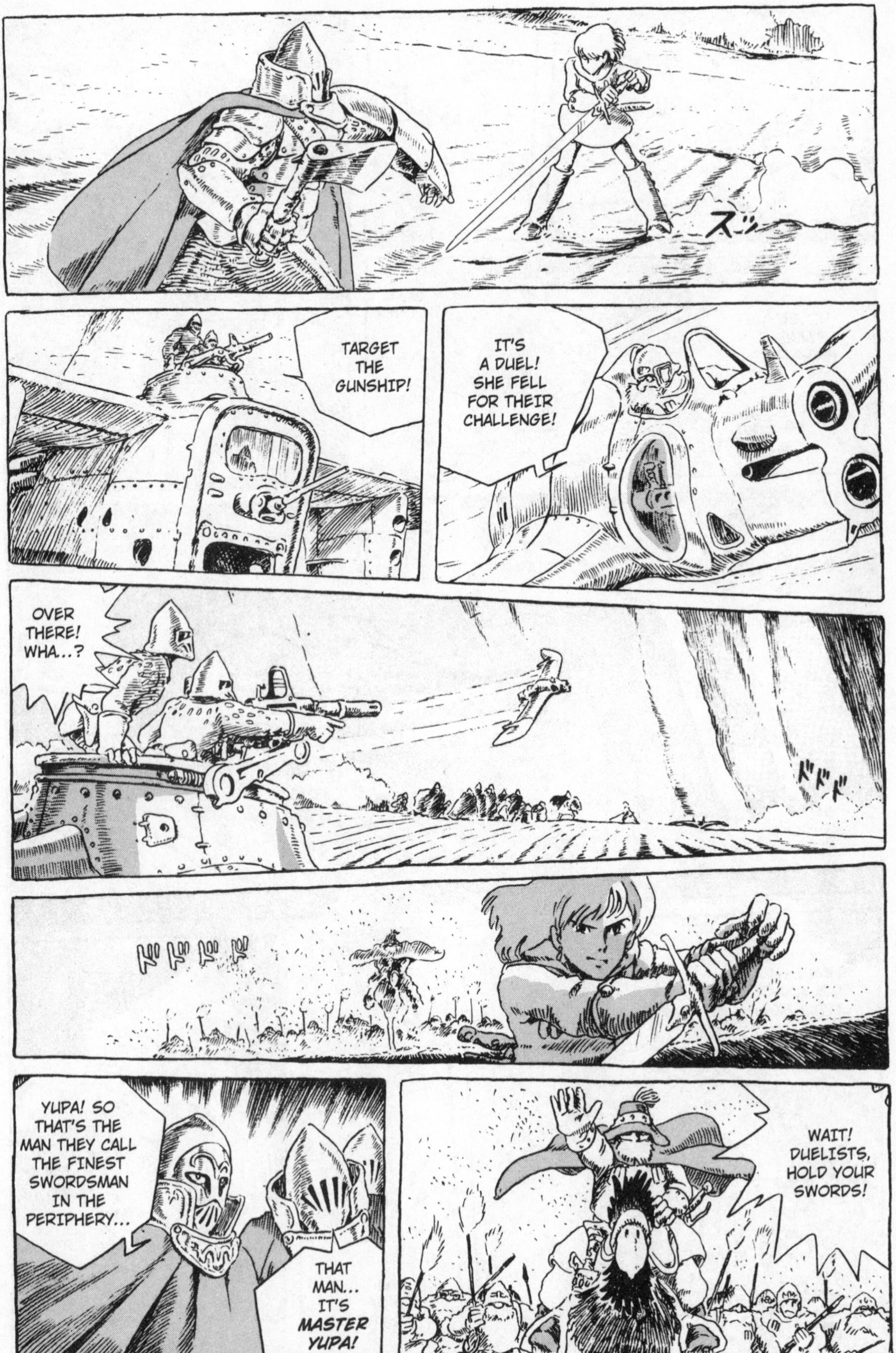
ズッ
IT'S A DUEL! SHE FELL FOR THEIR CHALLENGE!
TARGET THE GUNSHIP!
OVER THERE! WHA...?
ドドド
ドドドド
WAIT! DUELISTS, HOLD YOUR SWORDS!
YUPA! SO THAT'S THE MAN THEY CALL THE FINEST SWORDSMAN IN THE PERIPHERY...
THAT MAN... IT'S *MASTER YUPA!*

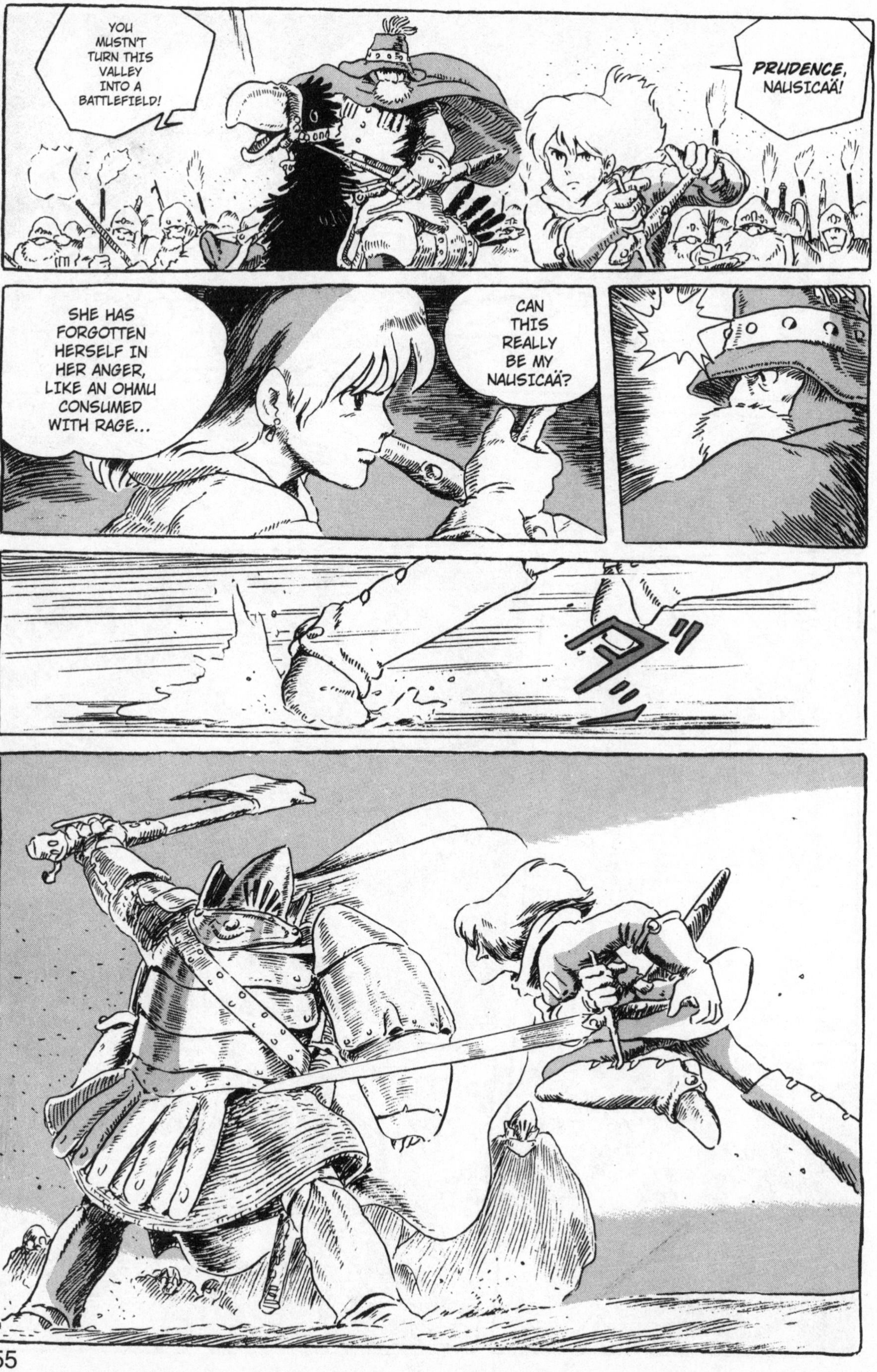
PRUDENCE, NAUSICAÄ!
YOU MUSTN'T TURN THIS VALLEY INTO A BATTLEFIELD!
CAN THIS REALLY BE MY NAUSICAÄ?
SHE HAS FORGOTTEN HERSELF IN HER ANGER, LIKE AN OHMU CONSUMED WITH RAGE...
ダッ

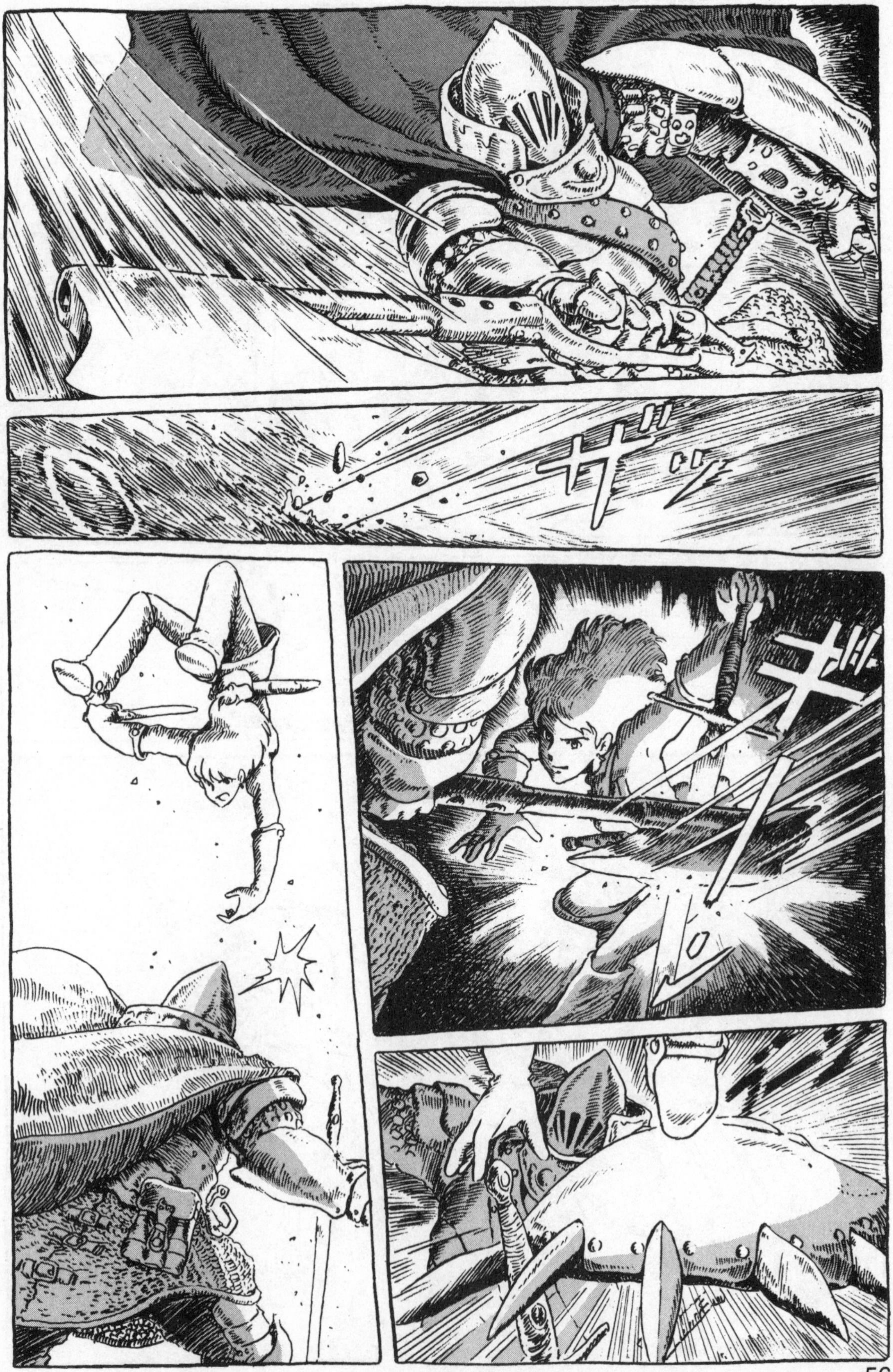
ザッ

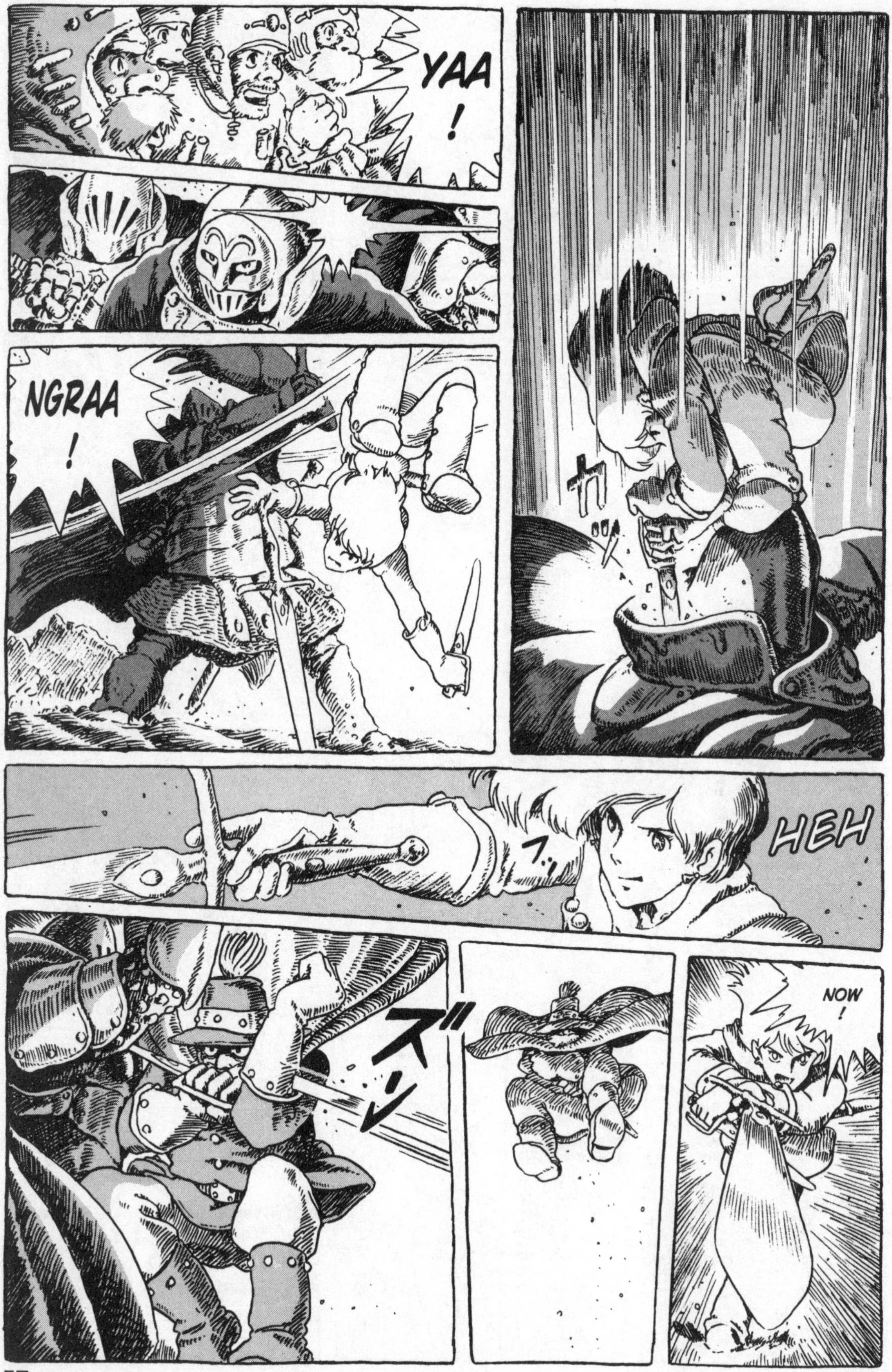
ガッ
YAA!
NGRAA!
HEH
フッ
NOW!
ズン

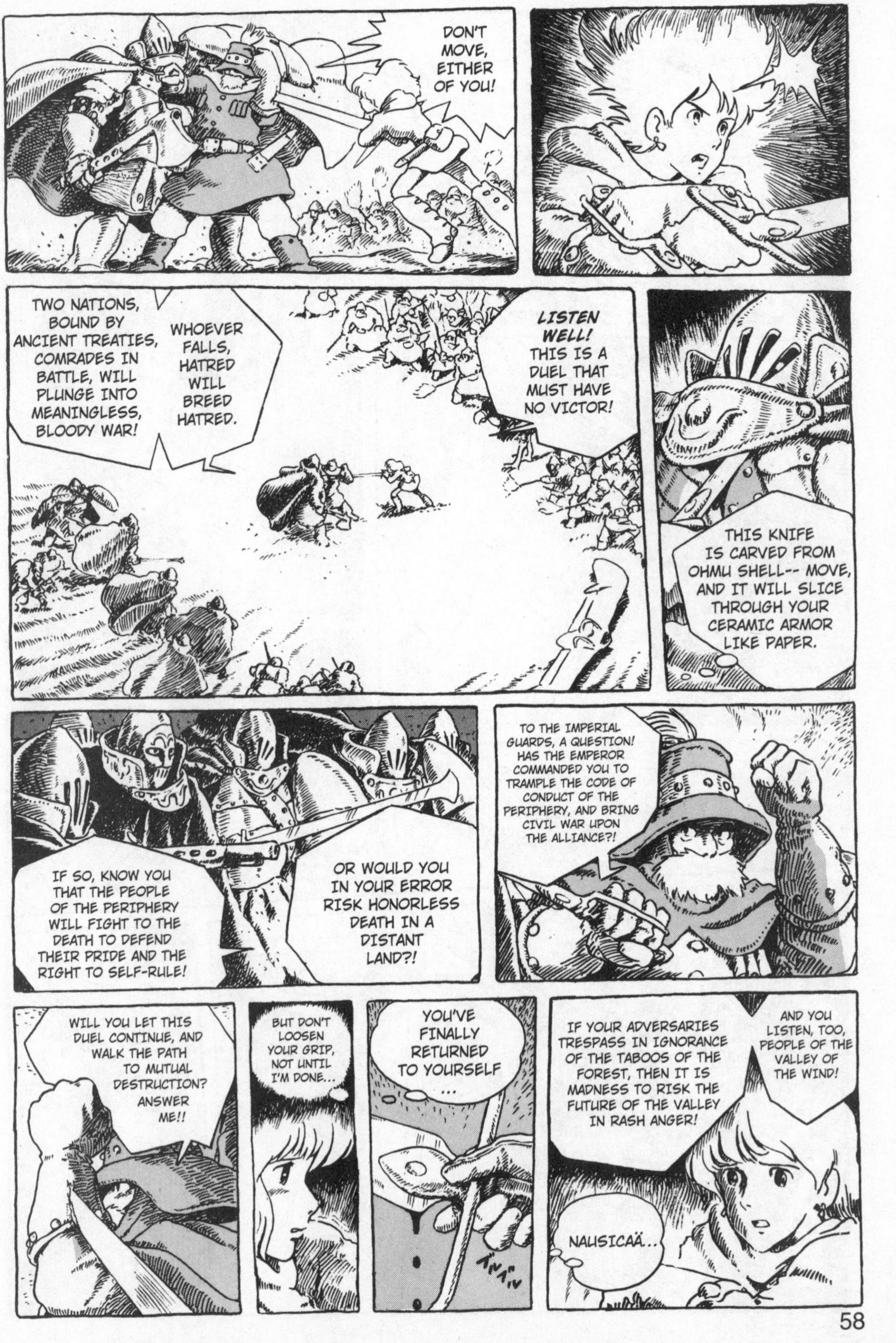
DON'T MOVE, EITHER OF YOU!
THIS KNIFE IS CARVED FROM OHMU SHELL-- MOVE, AND IT WILL SLICE THROUGH YOUR CERAMIC ARMOR LIKE PAPER.
LISTEN WELL! THIS IS A DUEL THAT MUST HAVE NO VICTOR!
WHOEVER FALLS, HATRED WILL BREED HATRED.
TWO NATIONS, BOUND BY ANCIENT TREATIES, COMRADES IN BATTLE, WILL PLUNGE INTO MEANINGLESS, BLOODY WAR!
TO THE IMPERIAL GUARDS, A QUESTION! HAS THE EMPEROR COMMANDED YOU TO TRAMPLE THE CODE OF CONDUCT OF THE PERIPHERY, AND BRING CIVIL WAR UPON THE ALLIANCE?!
OR WOULD YOU IN YOUR ERROR RISK HONORLESS DEATH IN A DISTANT LAND?!
IF SO, KNOW YOU THAT THE PEOPLE OF THE PERIPHERY WILL FIGHT TO THE DEATH TO DEFEND THEIR PRIDE AND THE RIGHT TO SELF-RULE!
AND YOU LISTEN, TOO, PEOPLE OF THE VALLEY OF THE WIND!
IF YOUR ADVERSARIES TRESPASS IN IGNORANCE OF THE TABOOS OF THE FOREST, THEN IT IS MADNESS TO RISK THE FUTURE OF THE VALLEY IN RASH ANGER!
NAUSICAÄ...
YOU'VE FINALLY RETURNED TO YOURSELF ...
BUT DON'T LOOSEN YOUR GRIP, NOT UNTIL I'M DONE...
WILL YOU LET THIS DUEL CONTINUE, AND WALK THE PATH TO MUTUAL DESTRUCTION? ANSWER ME!!

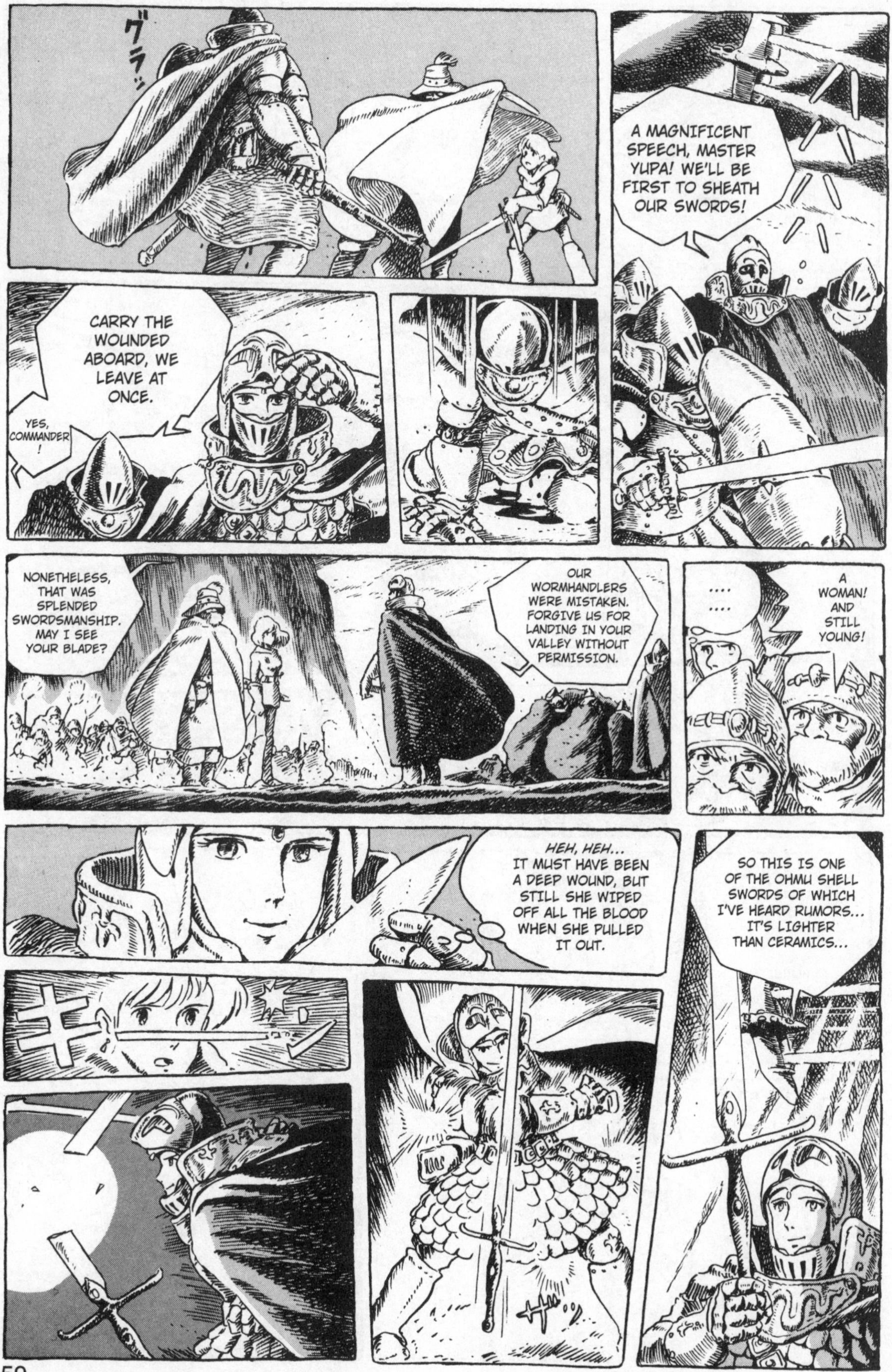
A MAGNIFICENT SPEECH, MASTER YUPA! WE'LL BE FIRST TO SHEATH OUR SWORDS!
グラッ
CARRY THE WOUNDED ABOARD, WE LEAVE AT ONCE.
YES, COMMANDER!
....
....
A WOMAN! AND STILL YOUNG!
OUR WORMHANDLERS WERE MISTAKEN. FORGIVE US FOR LANDING IN YOUR VALLEY WITHOUT PERMISSION.
NONETHELESS, THAT WAS SPLENDID SWORDSMANSHIP. MAY I SEE YOUR BLADE?
SO THIS IS ONE OF THE OHMU SHELL SWORDS OF WHICH I'VE HEARD RUMORS... IT'S LIGHTER THAN CERAMICS...
*HEH, HEH...* IT MUST HAVE BEEN A DEEP WOUND, BUT STILL SHE WIPED OFF ALL THE BLOOD WHEN SHE PULLED IT OUT.

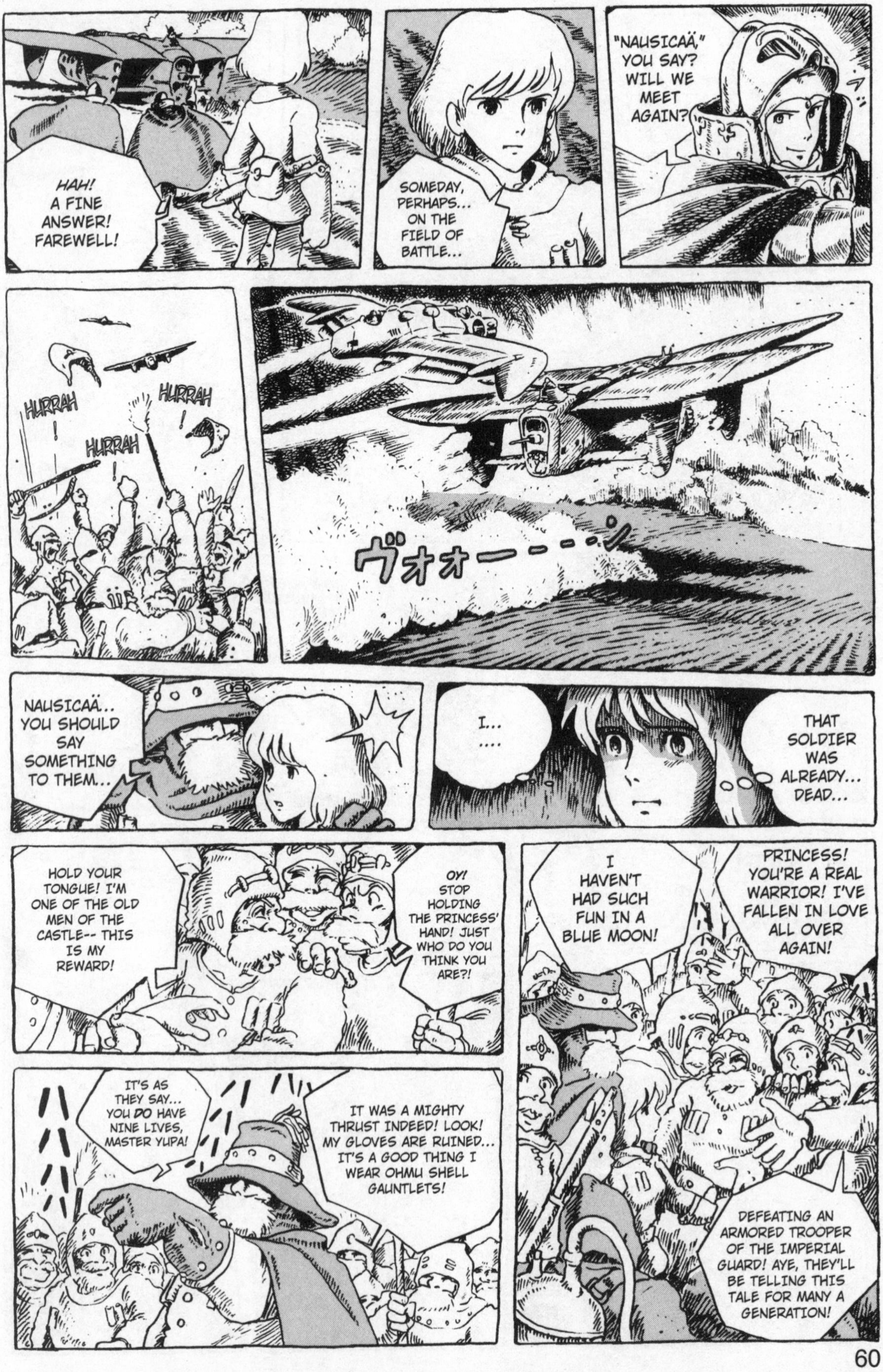
"NAUSICAÄ," YOU SAY? WILL WE MEET AGAIN?
SOMEDAY, PERHAPS... ON THE FIELD OF BATTLE...
HAH! A FINE ANSWER! FAREWELL!
ヴォオーーーーン
HURRAH!
HURRAH!
HURRAH!
I... ....
THAT SOLDIER WAS ALREADY... DEAD...
NAUSICAÄ... YOU SHOULD SAY SOMETHING TO THEM...
PRINCESS! YOU'RE A REAL WARRIOR! I'VE FALLEN IN LOVE ALL OVER AGAIN!
I HAVEN'T HAD SUCH FUN IN A BLUE MOON!
DEFEATING AN ARMORED TROOPER OF THE IMPERIAL GUARD! AYE, THEY'LL BE TELLING THIS TALE FOR MANY A GENERATION!
OY! STOP HOLDING THE PRINCESS' HAND! JUST WHO DO YOU THINK YOU ARE?!
HOLD YOUR TONGUE! I'M ONE OF THE OLD MEN OF THE CASTLE-- THIS IS MY REWARD!
IT WAS A MIGHTY THRUST INDEED! LOOK! MY GLOVES ARE RUINED... IT'S A GOOD THING I WEAR OHMU SHELL GAUNTLETS!
IT'S AS THEY SAY... YOU *DO* HAVE NINE LIVES, MASTER YUPA!

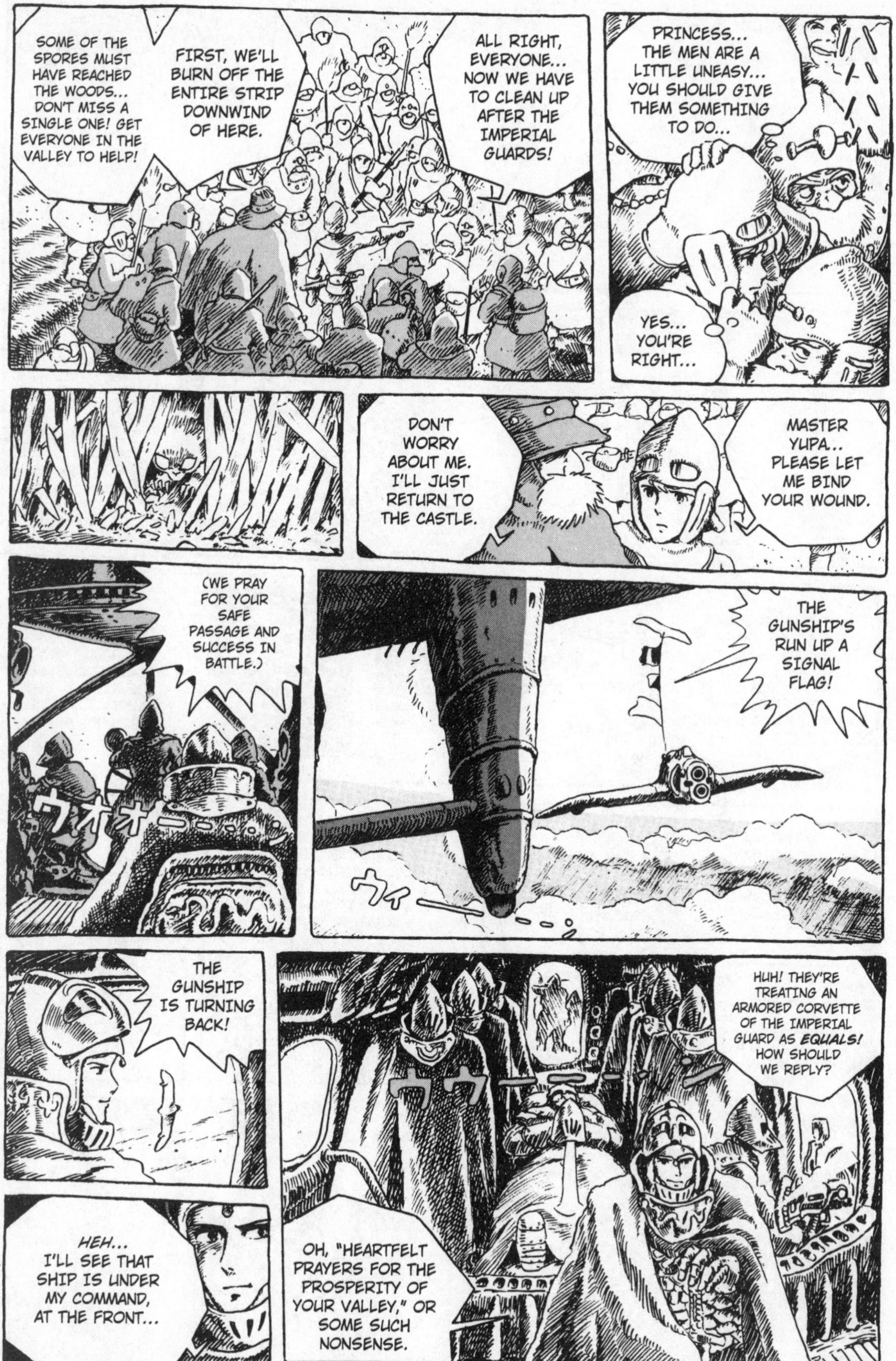
PRINCESS... THE MEN ARE A LITTLE UNEASY... YOU SHOULD GIVE THEM SOMETHING TO DO...
YES... YOU'RE RIGHT...
ALL RIGHT, EVERYONE... NOW WE HAVE TO CLEAN UP AFTER THE IMPERIAL GUARDS!
FIRST, WE'LL BURN OFF THE ENTIRE STRIP DOWNWIND OF HERE.
SOME OF THE SPORES MUST HAVE REACHED THE WOODS... DON'T MISS A SINGLE ONE! GET EVERYONE IN THE VALLEY TO HELP!
MASTER YUPA... PLEASE LET ME BIND YOUR WOUND.
DON'T WORRY ABOUT ME. I'LL JUST RETURN TO THE CASTLE.
THE GUNSHIP'S RUN UP A SIGNAL FLAG!
ウィーー
(WE PRAY FOR YOUR SAFE PASSAGE AND SUCCESS IN BATTLE.)
ウオオーー
HUH! THEY'RE TREATING AN ARMORED CORVETTE OF THE IMPERIAL GUARD AS ***EQUALS!*** HOW SHOULD WE REPLY?
ウウーー
OH, "HEARTFELT PRAYERS FOR THE PROSPERITY OF YOUR VALLEY," OR SOME SUCH NONSENSE.
THE GUNSHIP IS TURNING BACK!
*HEH...* I'LL SEE THAT SHIP IS UNDER MY COMMAND, AT THE FRONT...

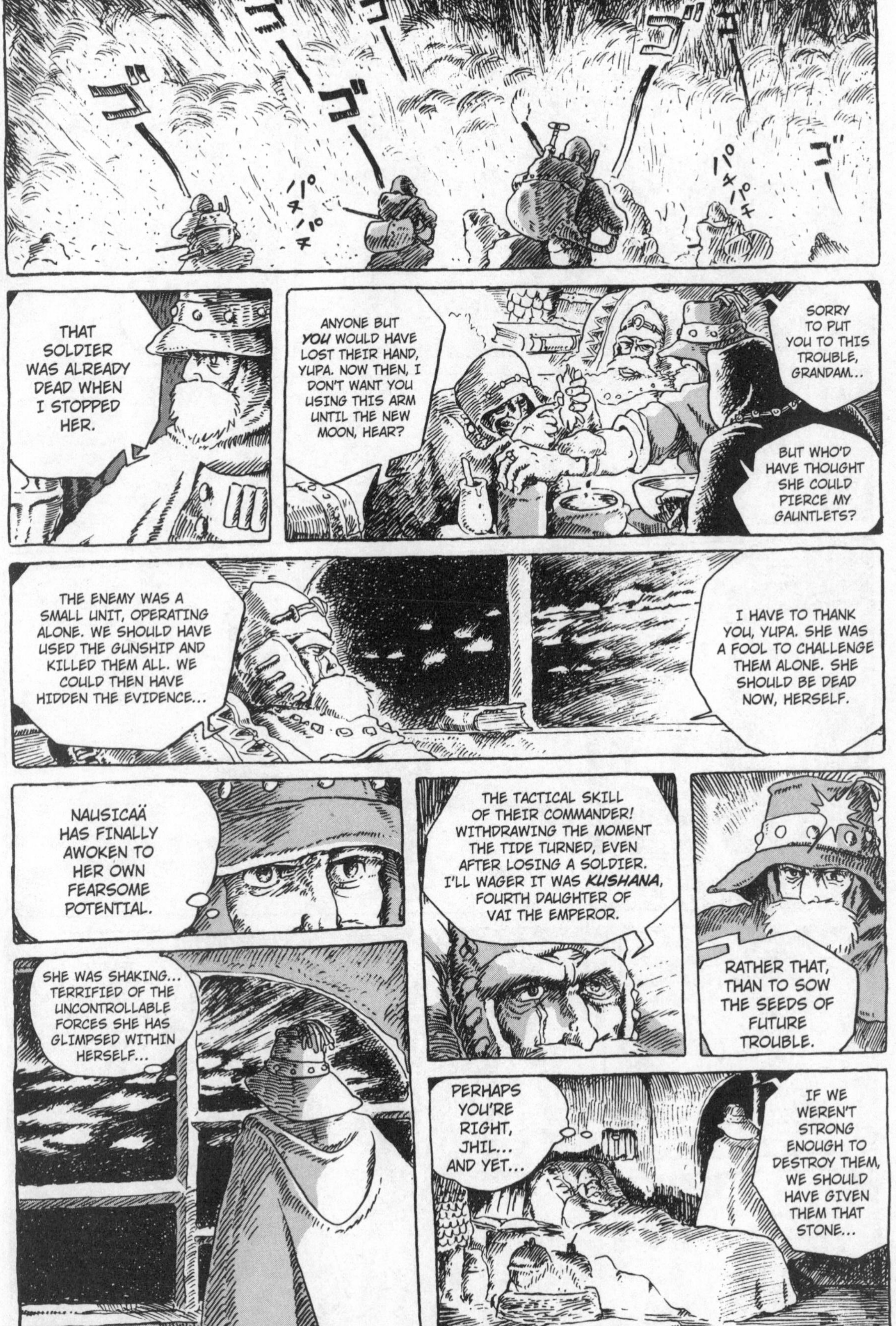
SORRY TO PUT YOU TO THIS TROUBLE, GRANDAM...
BUT WHO'D HAVE THOUGHT SHE COULD PIERCE MY GAUNTLETS?
ANYONE BUT *YOU* WOULD HAVE LOST THEIR HAND, YUPA. NOW THEN, I DON'T WANT YOU USING THIS ARM UNTIL THE NEW MOON, HEAR?
THAT SOLDIER WAS ALREADY DEAD WHEN I STOPPED HER.
I HAVE TO THANK YOU, YUPA. SHE WAS A FOOL TO CHALLENGE THEM ALONE. SHE SHOULD BE DEAD NOW, HERSELF.
THE ENEMY WAS A SMALL UNIT, OPERATING ALONE. WE SHOULD HAVE USED THE GUNSHIP AND KILLED THEM ALL. WE COULD THEN HAVE HIDDEN THE EVIDENCE...
RATHER THAT, THAN TO SOW THE SEEDS OF FUTURE TROUBLE.
THE TACTICAL SKILL OF THEIR COMMANDER! WITHDRAWING THE MOMENT THE TIDE TURNED, EVEN AFTER LOSING A SOLDIER. I'LL WAGER IT WAS *KUSHANA*, FOURTH DAUGHTER OF VAI THE EMPEROR.
IF WE WEREN'T STRONG ENOUGH TO DESTROY THEM, WE SHOULD HAVE GIVEN THEM THAT STONE...
PERHAPS YOU'RE RIGHT, JHIL... AND YET...
NAUSICAÄ HAS FINALLY AWOKEN TO HER OWN FEARSOME POTENTIAL.
SHE WAS SHAKING... TERRIFIED OF THE UNCONTROLLABLE FORCES SHE HAS GLIMPSED WITHIN HERSELF...

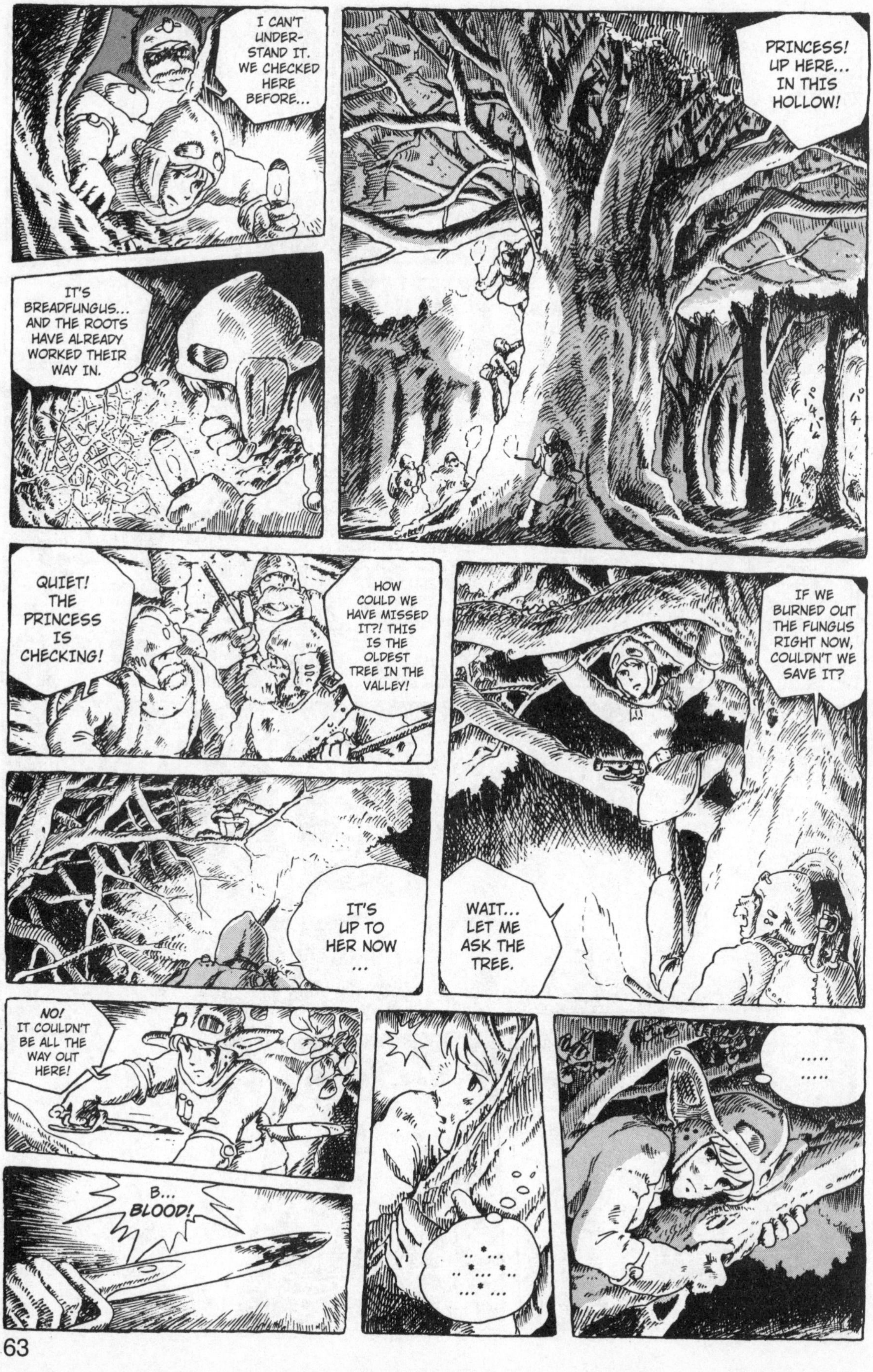
PRINCESS! UP HERE... IN THIS HOLLOW!
I CAN'T UNDER-STAND IT. WE CHECKED HERE BEFORE...
IT'S BREADFUNGUS... AND THE ROOTS HAVE ALREADY WORKED THEIR WAY IN.
IF WE BURNED OUT THE FUNGUS RIGHT NOW, COULDN'T WE SAVE IT?
WAIT... LET ME ASK THE TREE.
HOW COULD WE HAVE MISSED IT?! THIS IS THE OLDEST TREE IN THE VALLEY!
QUIET! THE PRINCESS IS CHECKING!
IT'S UP TO HER NOW ...
.....
.....
NO! IT COULDN'T BE ALL THE WAY OUT HERE!
B... BLOOD!

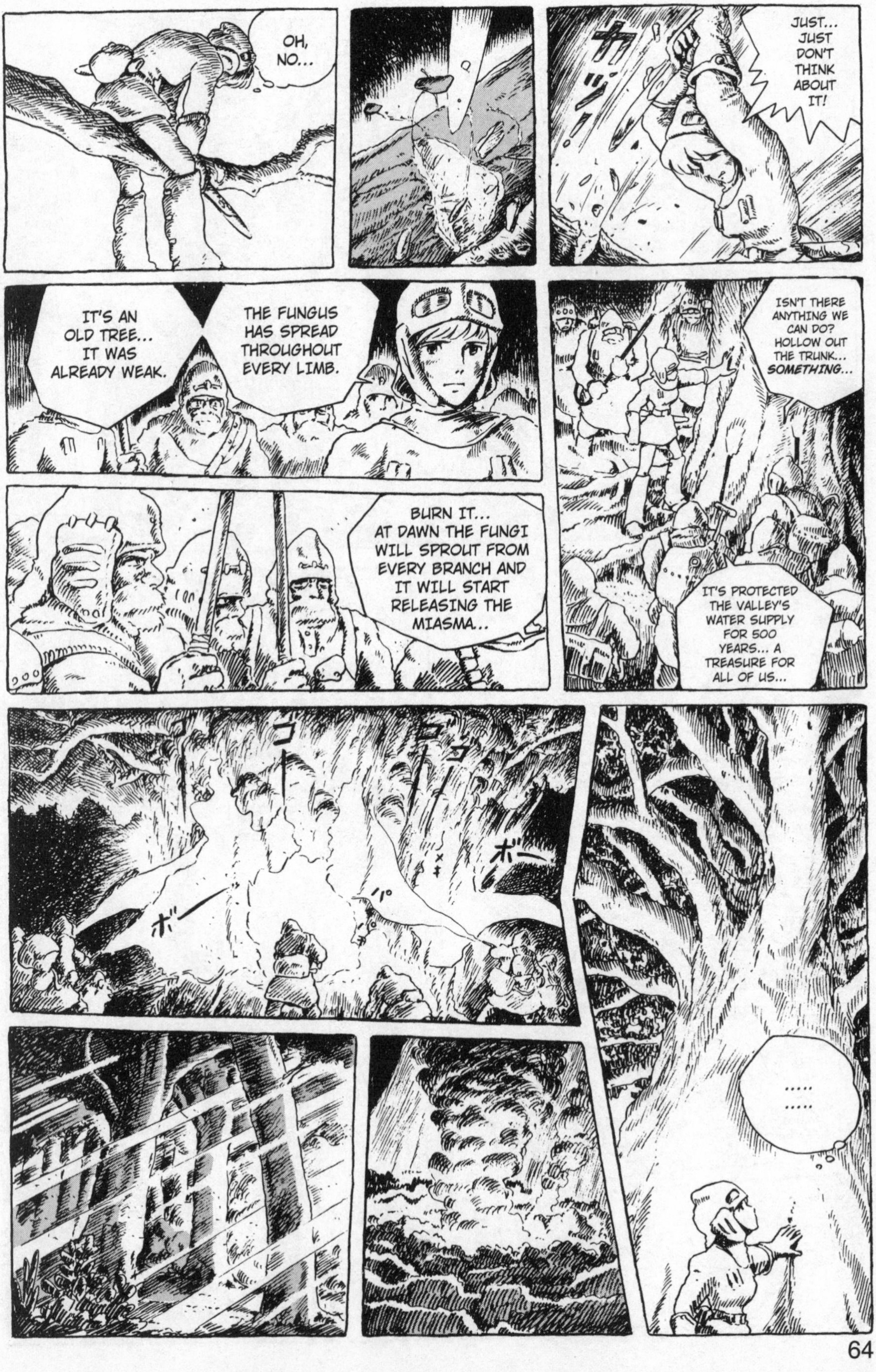
JUST... JUST DON'T THINK ABOUT IT!
OH, NO...
ISN'T THERE ANYTHING WE CAN DO? HOLLOW OUT THE TRUNK... *SOMETHING*...
IT'S PROTECTED THE VALLEY'S WATER SUPPLY FOR 500 YEARS... A TREASURE FOR ALL OF US...
THE FUNGUS HAS SPREAD THROUGHOUT EVERY LIMB.
IT'S AN OLD TREE... IT WAS ALREADY WEAK.
BURN IT... AT DAWN THE FUNGI WILL SPROUT FROM EVERY BRANCH AND IT WILL START RELEASING THE MIASMA...
.....
.....

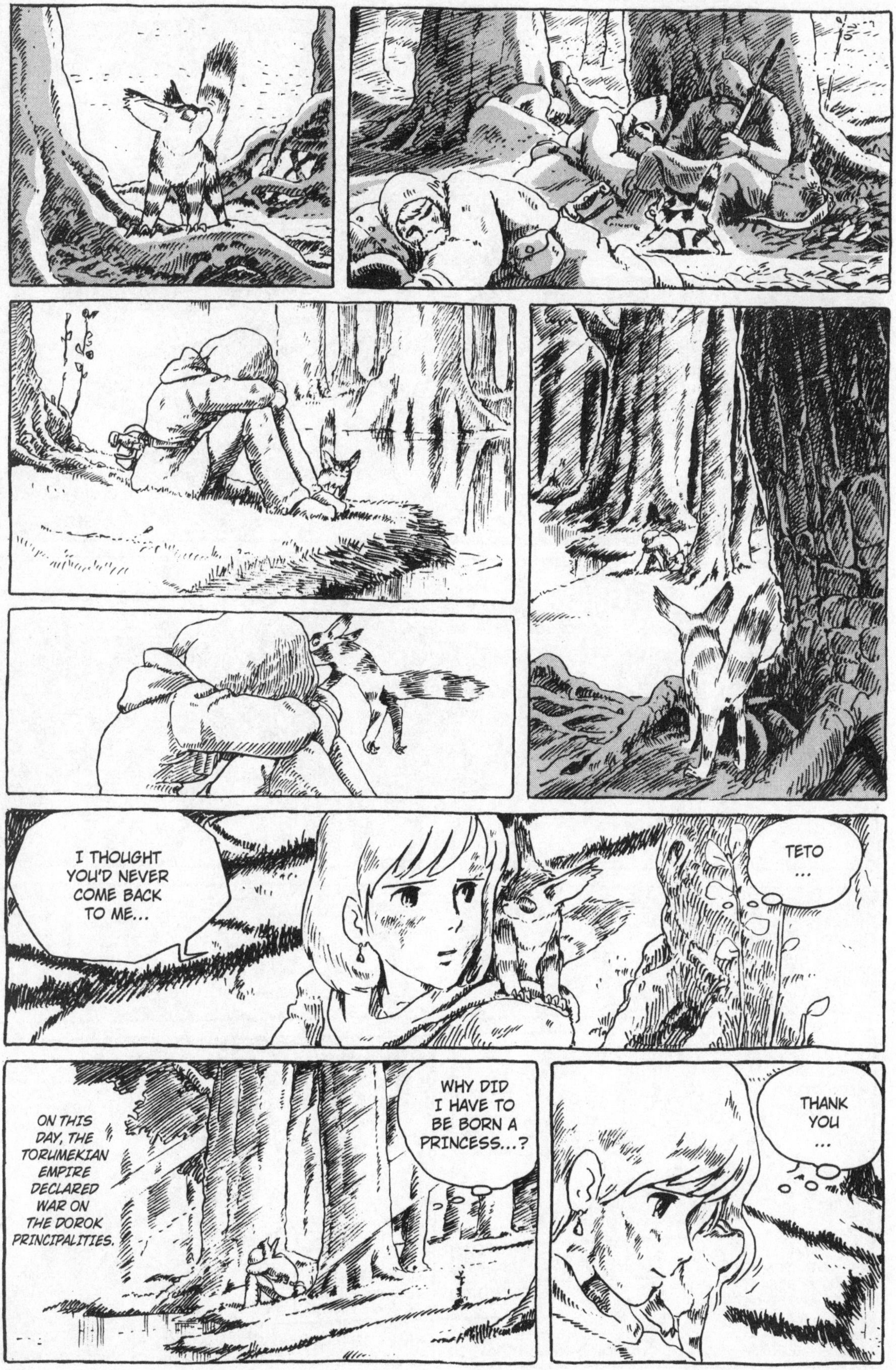
TETO ...
I THOUGHT YOU'D NEVER COME BACK TO ME...
THANK YOU ...
WHY DID I HAVE TO BE BORN A PRINCESS...?
ON THIS DAY, THE TORUMEKIAN EMPIRE DECLARED WAR ON THE DOROK PRINCIPALITIES.

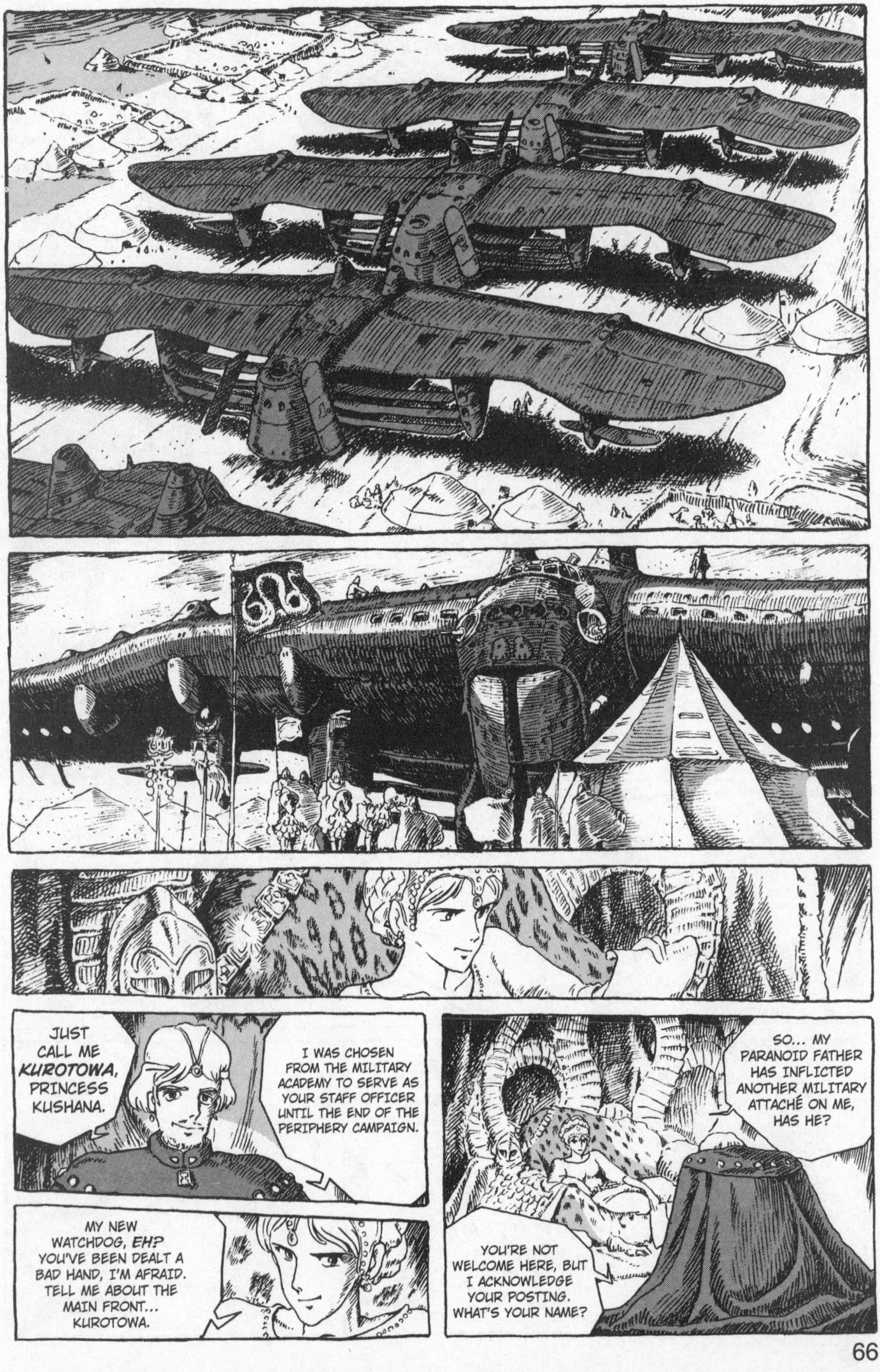

SO... MY PARANOID FATHER HAS INFLICTED ANOTHER MILITARY ATTACHÉ ON ME, HAS HE?
YOU'RE NOT WELCOME HERE, BUT I ACKNOWLEDGE YOUR POSTING. WHAT'S YOUR NAME?
JUST CALL ME **KUROTOWA**, PRINCESS KUSHANA.
I WAS CHOSEN FROM THE MILITARY ACADEMY TO SERVE AS YOUR STAFF OFFICER UNTIL THE END OF THE PERIPHERY CAMPAIGN.
MY NEW WATCHDOG, **EH?** YOU'VE BEEN DEALT A BAD HAND, I'M AFRAID. TELL ME ABOUT THE MAIN FRONT... KUROTOWA.

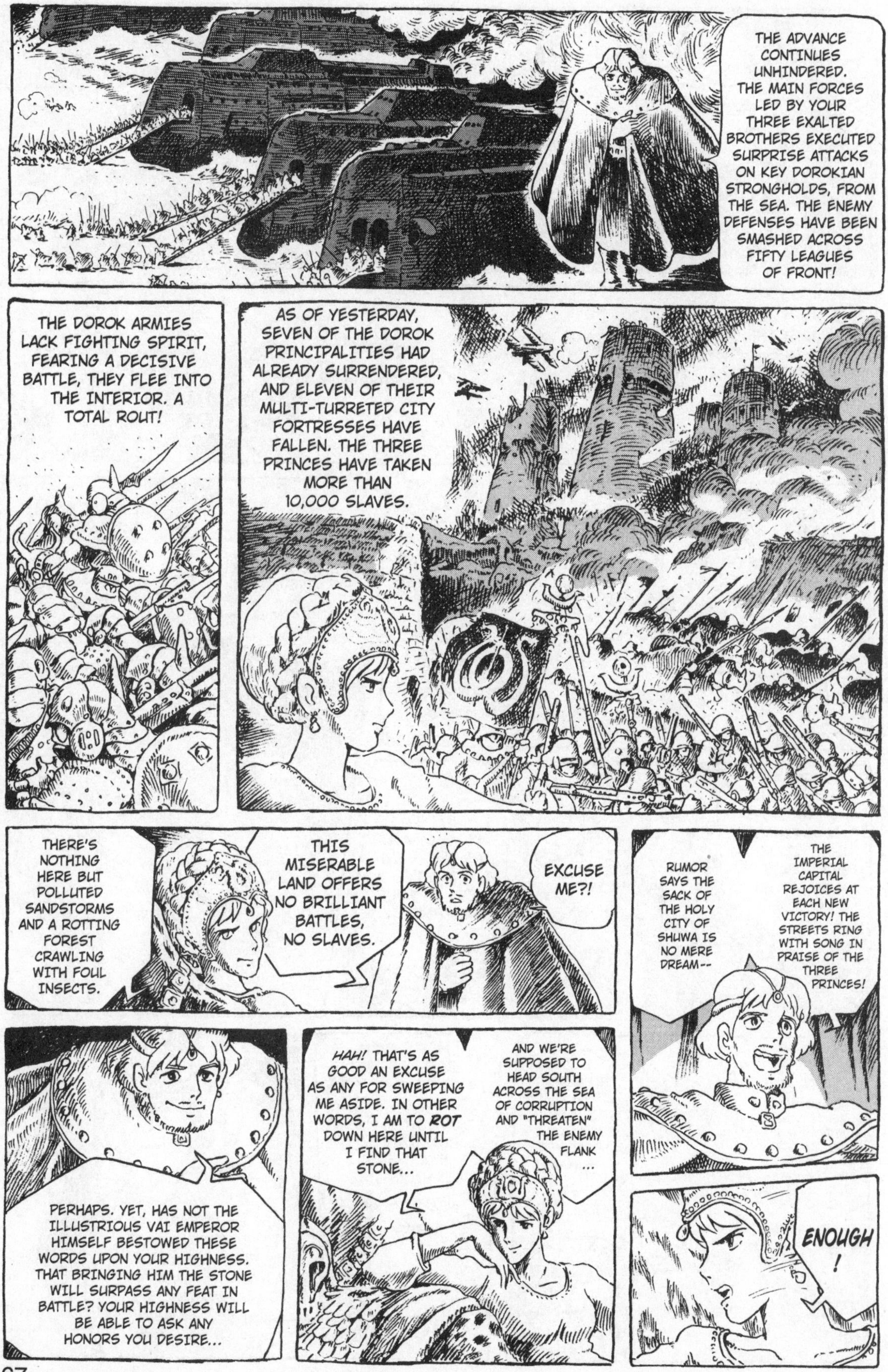
THE ADVANCE CONTINUES UNHINDERED. THE MAIN FORCES LED BY YOUR THREE EXALTED BROTHERS EXECUTED SURPRISE ATTACKS ON KEY DOROKIAN STRONGHOLDS, FROM THE SEA. THE ENEMY DEFENSES HAVE BEEN SMASHED ACROSS FIFTY LEAGUES OF FRONT!
THE DOROK ARMIES LACK FIGHTING SPIRIT, FEARING A DECISIVE BATTLE, THEY FLEE INTO THE INTERIOR. A TOTAL ROUT!
AS OF YESTERDAY, SEVEN OF THE DOROK PRINCIPALITIES HAD ALREADY SURRENDERED, AND ELEVEN OF THEIR MULTI-TURRETED CITY FORTRESSES HAVE FALLEN. THE THREE PRINCES HAVE TAKEN MORE THAN 10,000 SLAVES.
THERE'S NOTHING HERE BUT POLLUTED SANDSTORMS AND A ROTTING FOREST CRAWLING WITH FOUL INSECTS.
THIS MISERABLE LAND OFFERS NO BRILLIANT BATTLES, NO SLAVES.
EXCUSE ME?!
RUMOR SAYS THE SACK OF THE HOLY CITY OF SHUWA IS NO MERE DREAM--
THE IMPERIAL CAPITAL REJOICES AT EACH NEW VICTORY! THE STREETS RING WITH SONG IN PRAISE OF THE THREE PRINCES!
PERHAPS. YET, HAS NOT THE ILLUSTRIOUS VAI EMPEROR HIMSELF BESTOWED THESE WORDS UPON YOUR HIGHNESS. THAT BRINGING HIM THE STONE WILL SURPASS ANY FEAT IN BATTLE? YOUR HIGHNESS WILL BE ABLE TO ASK ANY HONORS YOU DESIRE...
*HAH!* THAT'S AS GOOD AN EXCUSE AS ANY FOR SWEEPING ME ASIDE. IN OTHER WORDS, I AM TO ***ROT*** DOWN HERE UNTIL I FIND THAT STONE...
AND WE'RE SUPPOSED TO HEAD SOUTH ACROSS THE SEA OF CORRUPTION AND "THREATEN" THE ENEMY FLANK ...
ENOUGH!

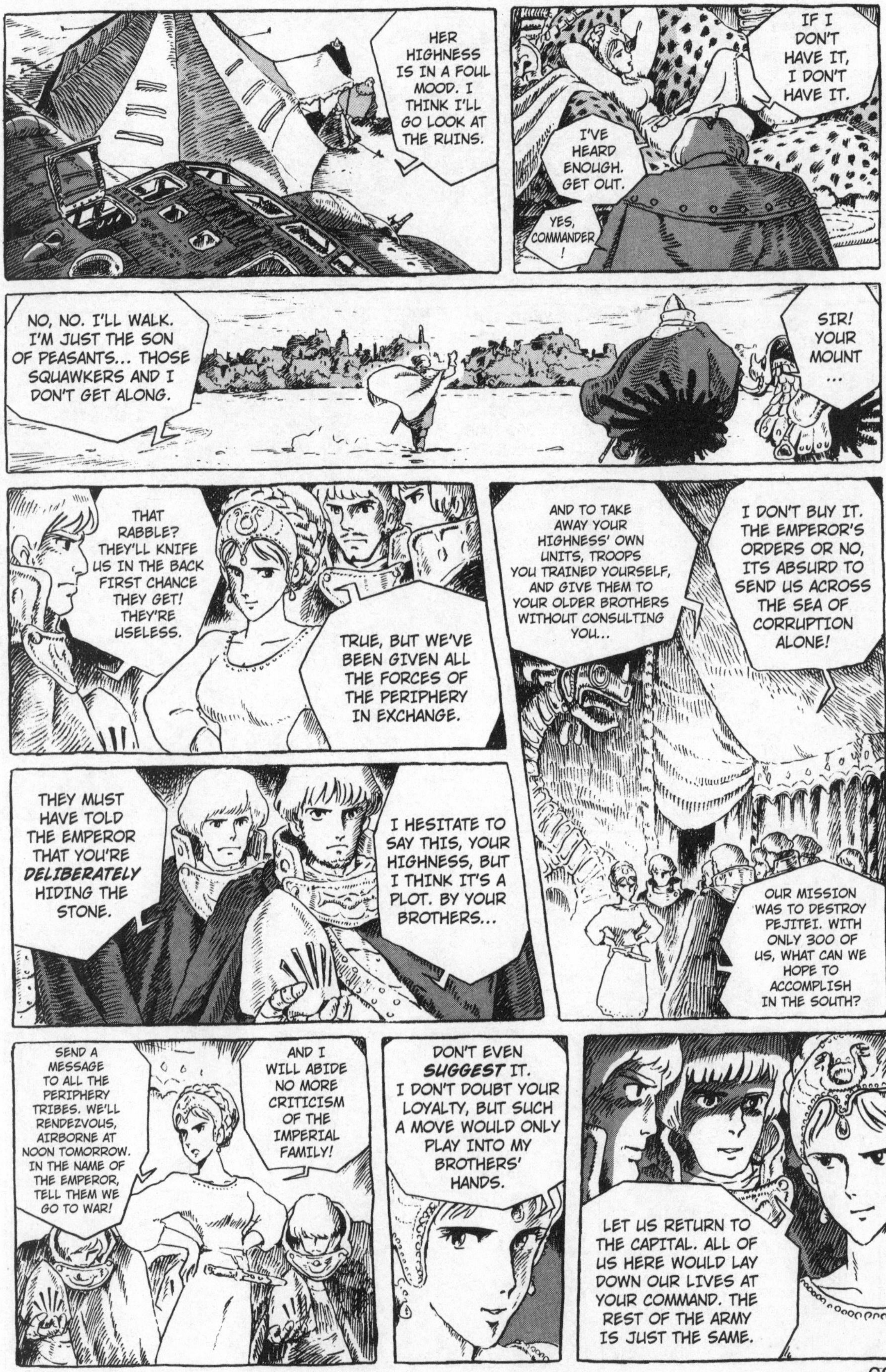
IF I DON'T HAVE IT, I DON'T HAVE IT.
I'VE HEARD ENOUGH. GET OUT.
YES, COMMANDER!
HER HIGHNESS IS IN A FOUL MOOD. I THINK I'LL GO LOOK AT THE RUINS.
SIR! YOUR MOUNT...
NO, NO. I'LL WALK. I'M JUST THE SON OF PEASANTS... THOSE SQUAWKERS AND I DON'T GET ALONG.
I DON'T BUY IT. THE EMPEROR'S ORDERS OR NO, ITS ABSURD TO SEND US ACROSS THE SEA OF CORRUPTION ALONE!
AND TO TAKE AWAY YOUR HIGHNESS' OWN UNITS, TROOPS YOU TRAINED YOURSELF, AND GIVE THEM TO YOUR OLDER BROTHERS WITHOUT CONSULTING YOU...
OUR MISSION WAS TO DESTROY PEJITEI. WITH ONLY 300 OF US, WHAT CAN WE HOPE TO ACCOMPLISH IN THE SOUTH?
TRUE, BUT WE'VE BEEN GIVEN ALL THE FORCES OF THE PERIPHERY IN EXCHANGE.
THAT RABBLE? THEY'LL KNIFE US IN THE BACK FIRST CHANCE THEY GET! THEY'RE USELESS.
I HESITATE TO SAY THIS, YOUR HIGHNESS, BUT I THINK IT'S A PLOT. BY YOUR BROTHERS...
THEY MUST HAVE TOLD THE EMPEROR THAT YOU'RE ***DELIBERATELY*** HIDING THE STONE.
LET US RETURN TO THE CAPITAL. ALL OF US HERE WOULD LAY DOWN OUR LIVES AT YOUR COMMAND. THE REST OF THE ARMY IS JUST THE SAME.
DON'T EVEN ***SUGGEST*** IT. I DON'T DOUBT YOUR LOYALTY, BUT SUCH A MOVE WOULD ONLY PLAY INTO MY BROTHERS' HANDS.
AND I WILL ABIDE NO MORE CRITICISM OF THE IMPERIAL FAMILY!
SEND A MESSAGE TO ALL THE PERIPHERY TRIBES. WE'LL RENDEZVOUS, AIRBORNE AT NOON TOMORROW. IN THE NAME OF THE EMPEROR, TELL THEM WE GO TO WAR!

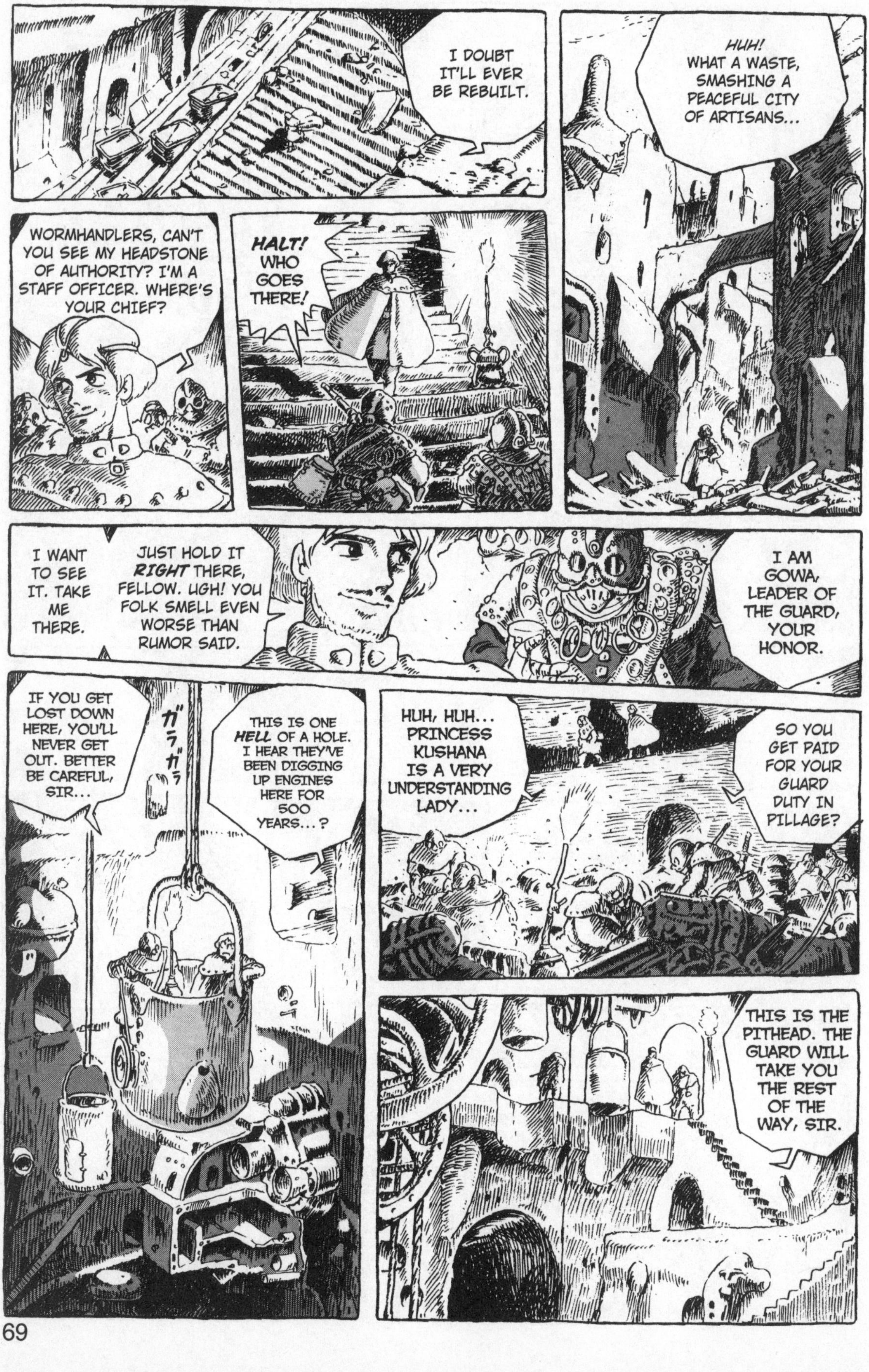

HUH! WHAT A WASTE, SMASHING A PEACEFUL CITY OF ARTISANS...
I DOUBT IT'LL EVER BE REBUILT.
HALT! WHO GOES THERE!
WORMHANDLERS, CAN'T YOU SEE MY HEADSTONE OF AUTHORITY? I'M A STAFF OFFICER. WHERE'S YOUR CHIEF?
I AM GOWA, LEADER OF THE GUARD, YOUR HONOR.
JUST HOLD IT RIGHT THERE, FELLOW. UGH! YOU FOLK SMELL EVEN WORSE THAN RUMOR SAID.
I WANT TO SEE IT. TAKE ME THERE.
SO YOU GET PAID FOR YOUR GUARD DUTY IN PILLAGE?
HUH, HUH... PRINCESS KUSHANA IS A VERY UNDERSTANDING LADY...
THIS IS THE PITHEAD. THE GUARD WILL TAKE YOU THE REST OF THE WAY, SIR.
THIS IS ONE HELL OF A HOLE. I HEAR THEY'VE BEEN DIGGING UP ENGINES HERE FOR 500 YEARS...?
ガラガラ
IF YOU GET LOST DOWN HERE, YOU'LL NEVER GET OUT. BETTER BE CAREFUL, SIR...

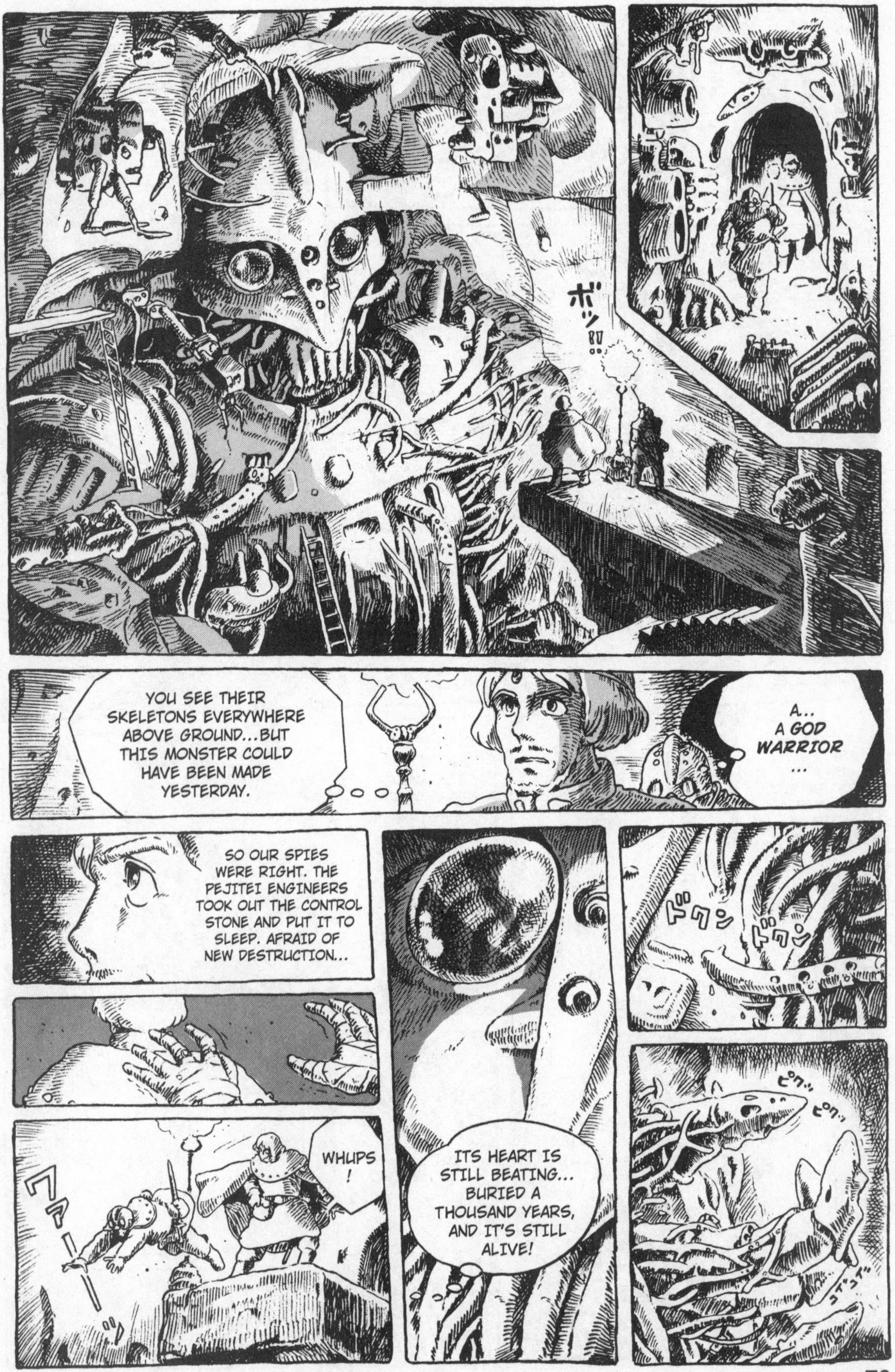
ボッ!!
A... A GOD WARRIOR ...
YOU SEE THEIR SKELETONS EVERYWHERE ABOVE GROUND...BUT THIS MONSTER COULD HAVE BEEN MADE YESTERDAY.
ドクン ドクン
ピクッ ピクッ
ITS HEART IS STILL BEATING... BURIED A THOUSAND YEARS, AND IT'S STILL ALIVE!
SO OUR SPIES WERE RIGHT. THE PEJITEI ENGINEERS TOOK OUT THE CONTROL STONE AND PUT IT TO SLEEP. AFRAID OF NEW DESTRUCTION...
WHUPS !

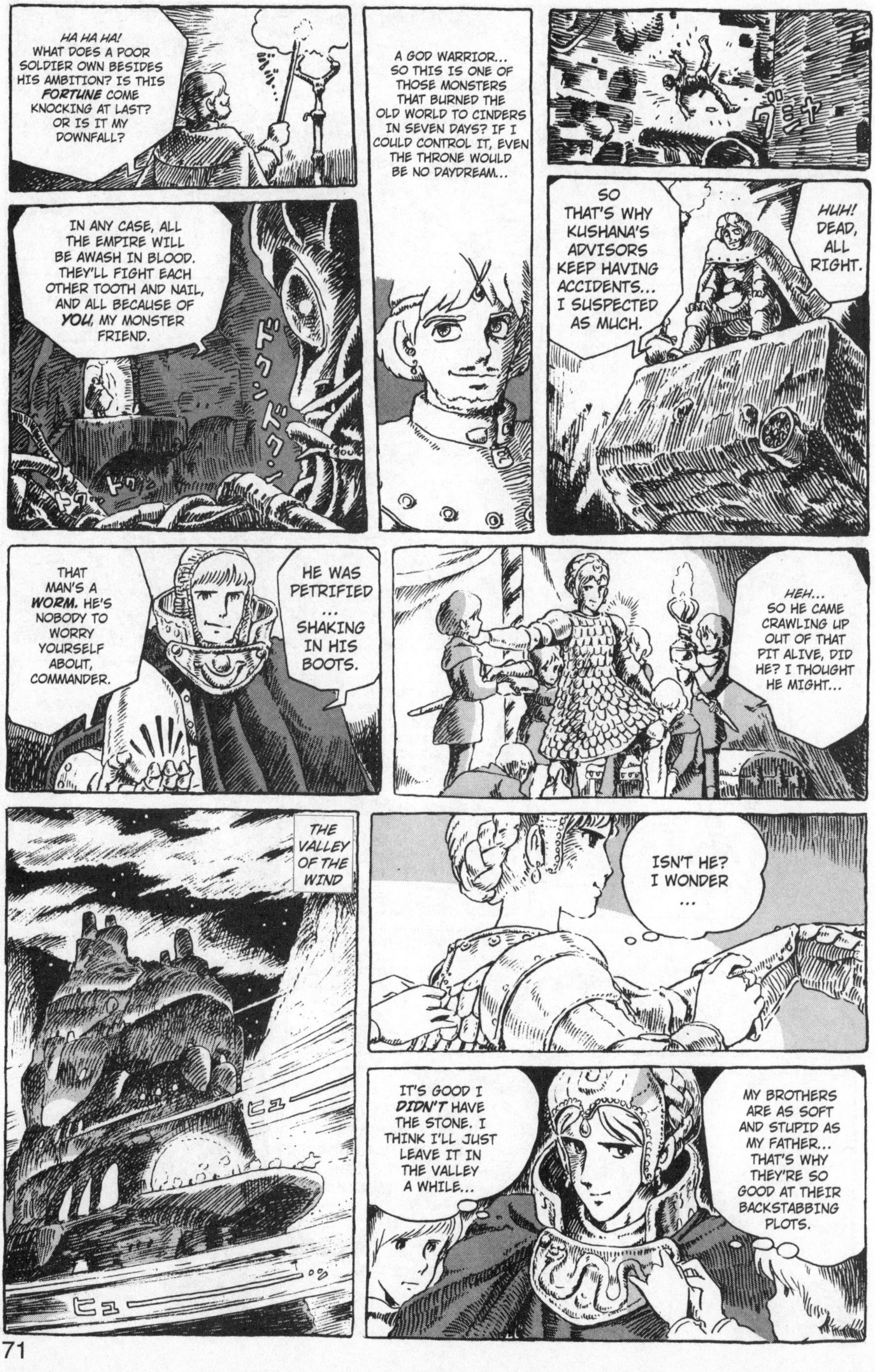
HUH! DEAD, ALL RIGHT.
SO THAT'S WHY KUSHANA'S ADVISORS KEEP HAVING ACCIDENTS... I SUSPECTED AS MUCH.
A GOD WARRIOR... SO THIS IS ONE OF THOSE MONSTERS THAT BURNED THE OLD WORLD TO CINDERS IN SEVEN DAYS? IF I COULD CONTROL IT, EVEN THE THRONE WOULD BE NO DAYDREAM...
HA HA HA! WHAT DOES A POOR SOLDIER OWN BESIDES HIS AMBITION? IS THIS FORTUNE COME KNOCKING AT LAST? OR IS IT MY DOWNFALL?
IN ANY CASE, ALL THE EMPIRE WILL BE AWASH IN BLOOD. THEY'LL FIGHT EACH OTHER TOOTH AND NAIL, AND ALL BECAUSE OF YOU, MY MONSTER FRIEND.
HEH... SO HE CAME CRAWLING UP OUT OF THAT PIT ALIVE, DID HE? I THOUGHT HE MIGHT...
HE WAS PETRIFIED ... SHAKING IN HIS BOOTS.
THAT MAN'S A WORM. HE'S NOBODY TO WORRY YOURSELF ABOUT, COMMANDER.
ISN'T HE? I WONDER ...
MY BROTHERS ARE AS SOFT AND STUPID AS MY FATHER... THAT'S WHY THEY'RE SO GOOD AT THEIR BACKSTABBING PLOTS.
IT'S GOOD I DIDN'T HAVE THE STONE. I THINK I'LL JUST LEAVE IT IN THE VALLEY A WHILE...
THE VALLEY OF THE WIND
ヒュー
ヒュー

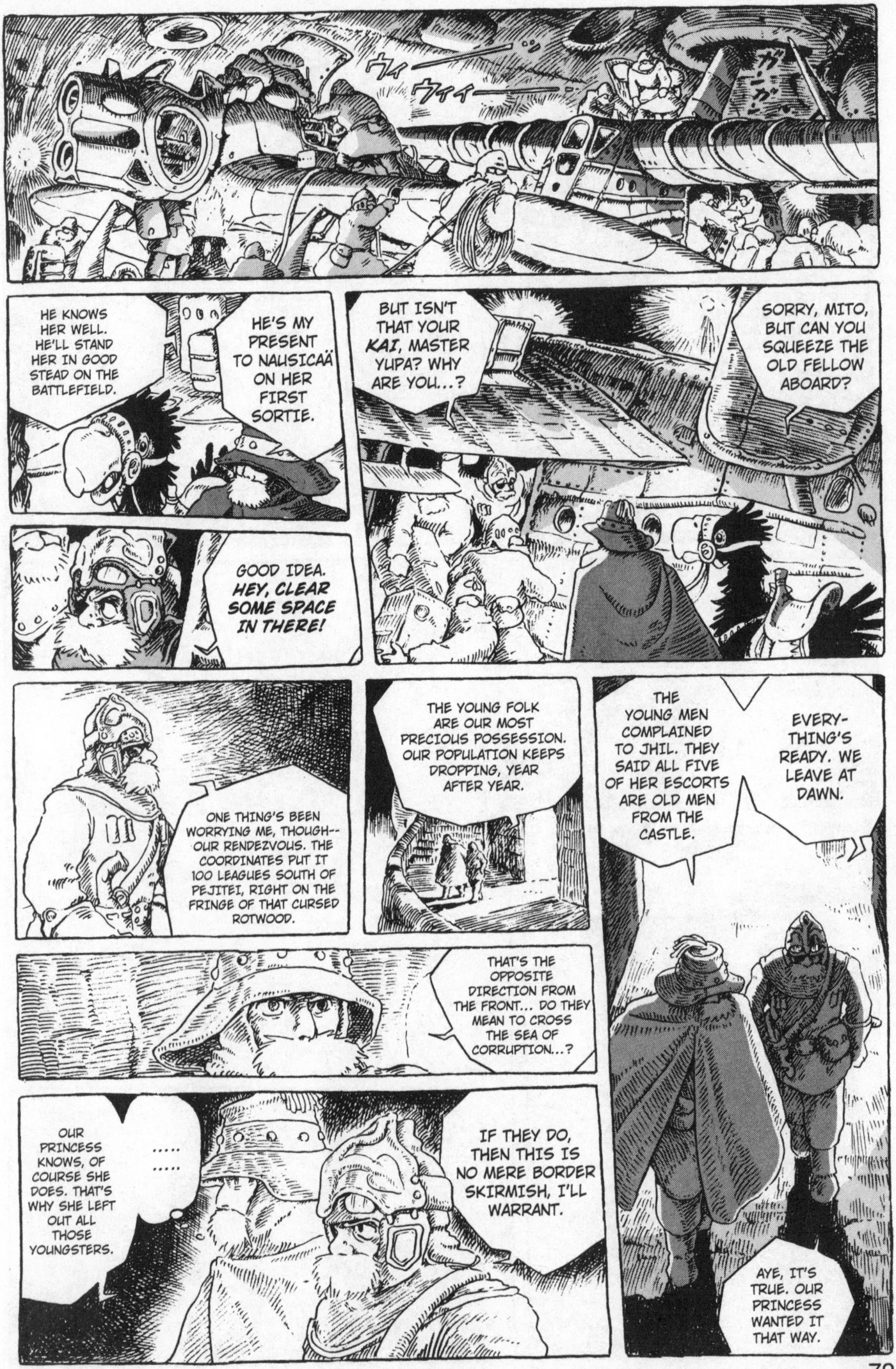
ウィー
ウィィー
SORRY, MITO, BUT CAN YOU SQUEEZE THE OLD FELLOW ABOARD?
BUT ISN'T THAT YOUR *KAI*, MASTER YUPA? WHY ARE YOU...?
HE'S MY PRESENT TO NAUSICAÄ ON HER FIRST SORTIE.
HE KNOWS HER WELL. HE'LL STAND HER IN GOOD STEAD ON THE BATTLEFIELD.
GOOD IDEA. **HEY, CLEAR SOME SPACE IN THERE!**
EVERY-THING'S READY. WE LEAVE AT DAWN.
THE YOUNG MEN COMPLAINED TO JHIL. THEY SAID ALL FIVE OF HER ESCORTS ARE OLD MEN FROM THE CASTLE.
AYE, IT'S TRUE. OUR PRINCESS WANTED IT THAT WAY.
THE YOUNG FOLK ARE OUR MOST PRECIOUS POSSESSION. OUR POPULATION KEEPS DROPPING, YEAR AFTER YEAR.
ONE THING'S BEEN WORRYING ME, THOUGH-- OUR RENDEZVOUS. THE COORDINATES PUT IT 100 LEAGUES SOUTH OF PEJITEI, RIGHT ON THE FRINGE OF THAT CURSED ROTWOOD.
THAT'S THE OPPOSITE DIRECTION FROM THE FRONT... DO THEY MEAN TO CROSS THE SEA OF CORRUPTION...?
IF THEY DO, THEN THIS IS NO MERE BORDER SKIRMISH, I'LL WARRANT.
.....
.....
OUR PRINCESS KNOWS, OF COURSE SHE DOES. THAT'S WHY SHE LEFT OUT ALL THOSE YOUNGSTERS.

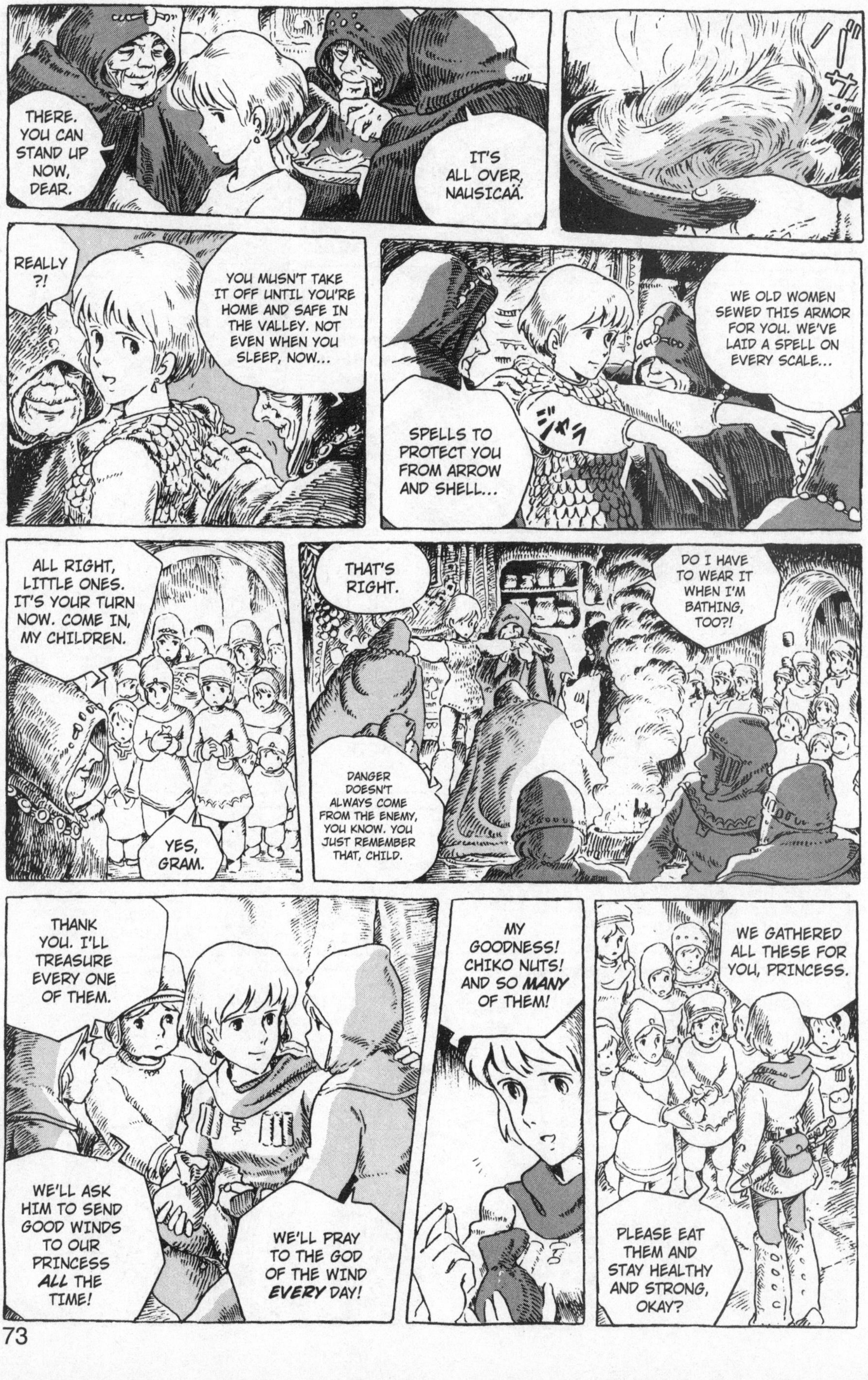
THERE. YOU CAN STAND UP NOW, DEAR.
IT'S ALL OVER, NAUSICAÄ.
WE OLD WOMEN SEWED THIS ARMOR FOR YOU. WE'VE LAID A SPELL ON EVERY SCALE...
SPELLS TO PROTECT YOU FROM ARROW AND SHELL...
YOU MUSN'T TAKE IT OFF UNTIL YOU'RE HOME AND SAFE IN THE VALLEY. NOT EVEN WHEN YOU SLEEP, NOW...
REALLY ?!
DO I HAVE TO WEAR IT WHEN I'M BATHING, TOO?!
THAT'S RIGHT.
DANGER DOESN'T ALWAYS COME FROM THE ENEMY, YOU KNOW. YOU JUST REMEMBER THAT, CHILD.
ALL RIGHT, LITTLE ONES. IT'S YOUR TURN NOW. COME IN, MY CHILDREN.
YES, GRAM.
WE GATHERED ALL THESE FOR YOU, PRINCESS.
PLEASE EAT THEM AND STAY HEALTHY AND STRONG, OKAY?
MY GOODNESS! CHIKO NUTS! AND SO *MANY* OF THEM!
THANK YOU. I'LL TREASURE EVERY ONE OF THEM.
WE'LL PRAY TO THE GOD OF THE WIND *EVERY* DAY!
WE'LL ASK HIM TO SEND GOOD WINDS TO OUR PRINCESS *ALL* THE TIME!

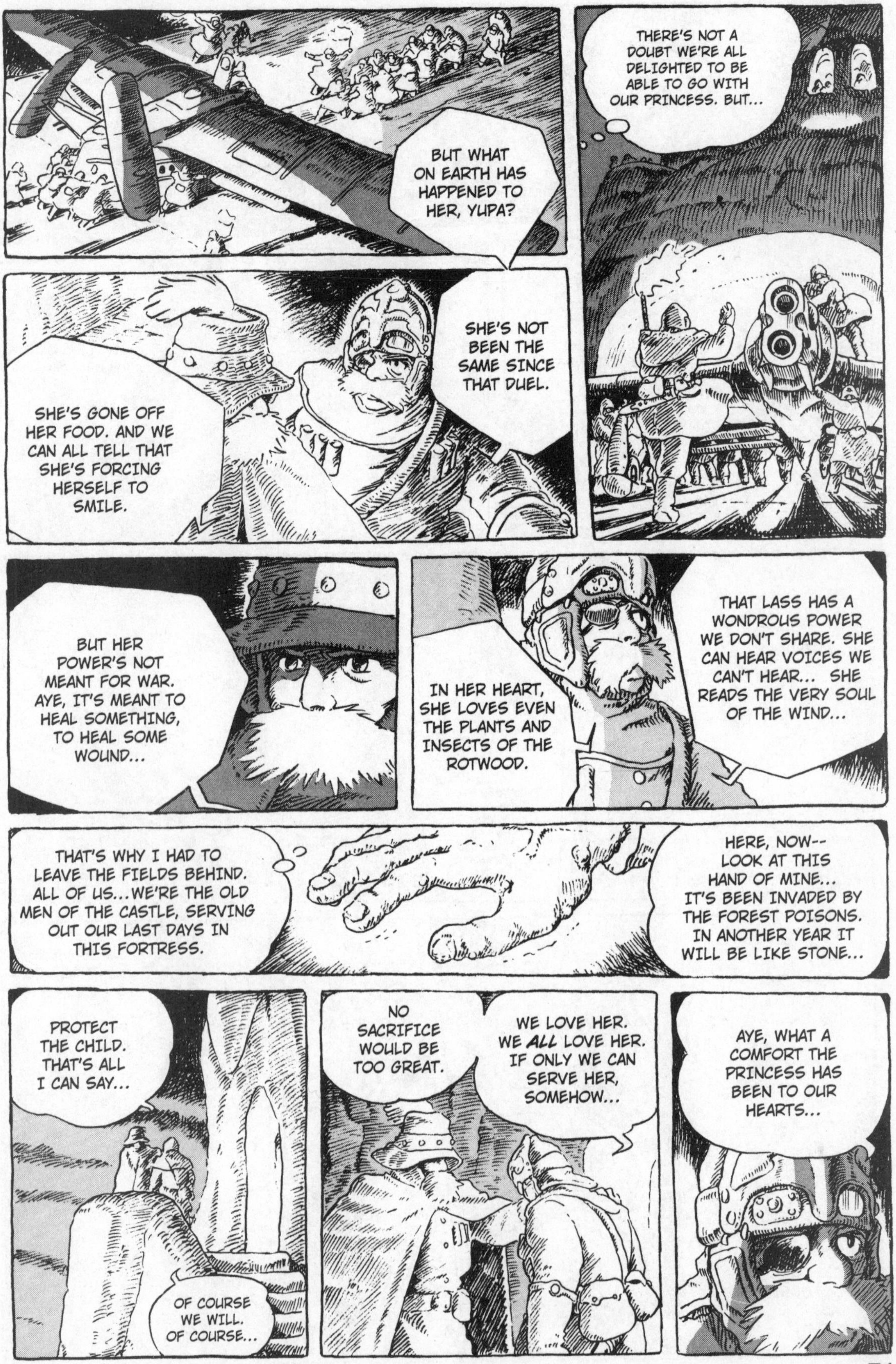
THERE'S NOT A DOUBT WE'RE ALL DELIGHTED TO BE ABLE TO GO WITH OUR PRINCESS. BUT...
BUT WHAT ON EARTH HAS HAPPENED TO HER, YUPA?
SHE'S NOT BEEN THE SAME SINCE THAT DUEL.
SHE'S GONE OFF HER FOOD. AND WE CAN ALL TELL THAT SHE'S FORCING HERSELF TO SMILE.
THAT LASS HAS A WONDROUS POWER WE DON'T SHARE. SHE CAN HEAR VOICES WE CAN'T HEAR... SHE READS THE VERY SOUL OF THE WIND...
IN HER HEART, SHE LOVES EVEN THE PLANTS AND INSECTS OF THE ROTWOOD.
BUT HER POWER'S NOT MEANT FOR WAR. AYE, IT'S MEANT TO HEAL SOMETHING, TO HEAL SOME WOUND...
HERE, NOW-- LOOK AT THIS HAND OF MINE... IT'S BEEN INVADED BY THE FOREST POISONS. IN ANOTHER YEAR IT WILL BE LIKE STONE...
THAT'S WHY I HAD TO LEAVE THE FIELDS BEHIND. ALL OF US...WE'RE THE OLD MEN OF THE CASTLE, SERVING OUT OUR LAST DAYS IN THIS FORTRESS.
AYE, WHAT A COMFORT THE PRINCESS HAS BEEN TO OUR HEARTS...
WE LOVE HER. WE *ALL* LOVE HER. IF ONLY WE CAN SERVE HER, SOMEHOW...
NO SACRIFICE WOULD BE TOO GREAT.
PROTECT THE CHILD. THAT'S ALL I CAN SAY...
OF COURSE WE WILL. OF COURSE...

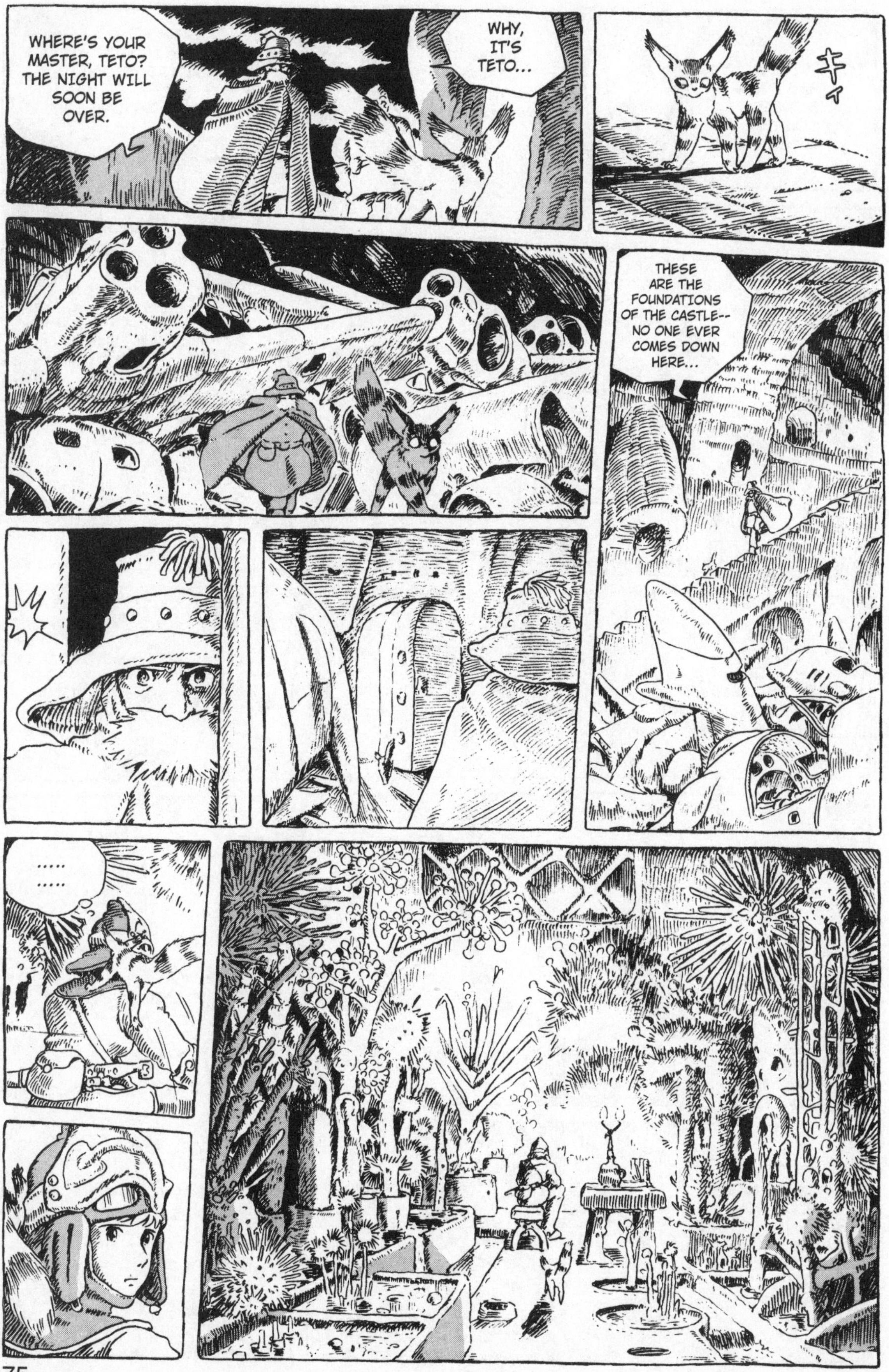
キィ
WHY, IT'S TETO...
WHERE'S YOUR MASTER, TETO? THE NIGHT WILL SOON BE OVER.
THESE ARE THE FOUNDATIONS OF THE CASTLE--NO ONE EVER COMES DOWN HERE...
......
......

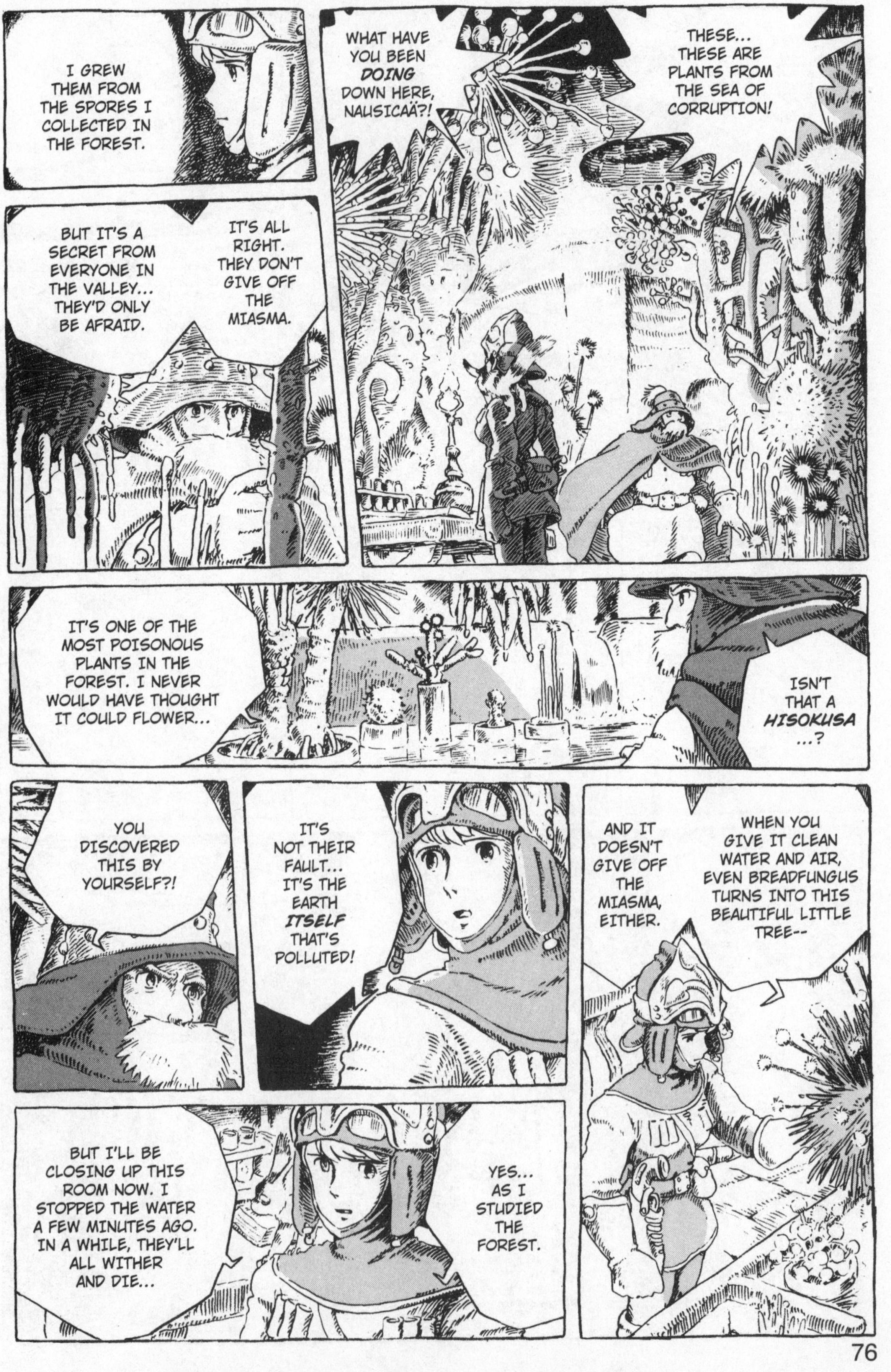
THESE... THESE ARE PLANTS FROM THE SEA OF CORRUPTION!
WHAT HAVE YOU BEEN *DOING* DOWN HERE, NAUSICAÄ?!
I GREW THEM FROM THE SPORES I COLLECTED IN THE FOREST.
IT'S ALL RIGHT. THEY DON'T GIVE OFF THE MIASMA.
BUT IT'S A SECRET FROM EVERYONE IN THE VALLEY... THEY'D ONLY BE AFRAID.
ISN'T THAT A *HISOKUSA* ...?
IT'S ONE OF THE MOST POISONOUS PLANTS IN THE FOREST. I NEVER WOULD HAVE THOUGHT IT COULD FLOWER...
WHEN YOU GIVE IT CLEAN WATER AND AIR, EVEN BREADFUNGUS TURNS INTO THIS BEAUTIFUL LITTLE TREE--
AND IT DOESN'T GIVE OFF THE MIASMA, EITHER.
IT'S NOT THEIR FAULT... IT'S THE EARTH *ITSELF* THAT'S POLLUTED!
YOU DISCOVERED THIS BY YOURSELF?!
YES... AS I STUDIED THE FOREST.
BUT I'LL BE CLOSING UP THIS ROOM NOW. I STOPPED THE WATER A FEW MINUTES AGO. IN A WHILE, THEY'LL ALL WITHER AND DIE...

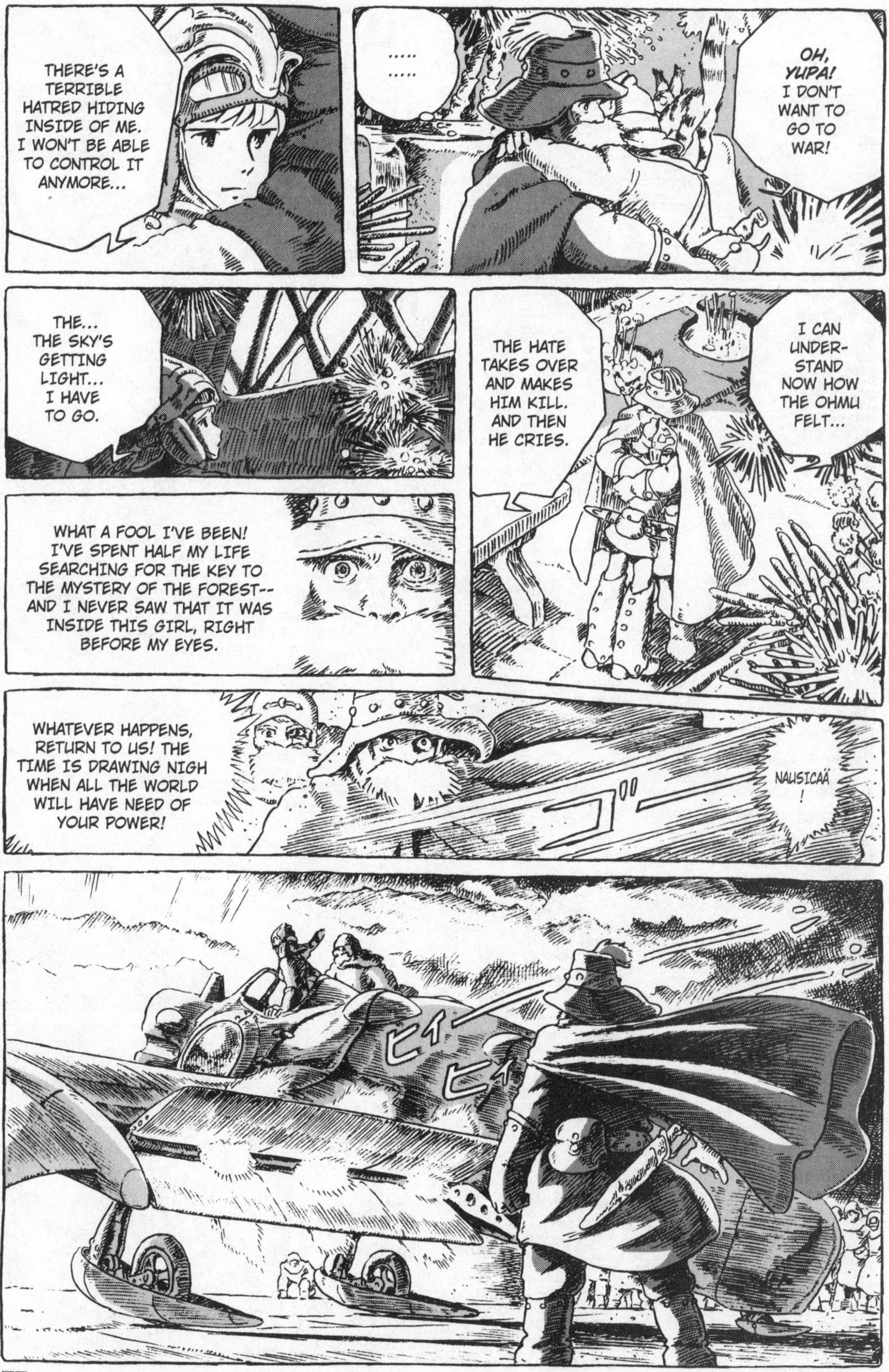
OH, YUPA! I DON'T WANT TO GO TO WAR!
.....
.....
THERE'S A TERRIBLE HATRED HIDING INSIDE OF ME. I WON'T BE ABLE TO CONTROL IT ANYMORE...
I CAN UNDER-STAND NOW HOW THE OHMU FELT...
THE HATE TAKES OVER AND MAKES HIM KILL. AND THEN HE CRIES.
THE... THE SKY'S GETTING LIGHT... I HAVE TO GO.
WHAT A FOOL I'VE BEEN! I'VE SPENT HALF MY LIFE SEARCHING FOR THE KEY TO THE MYSTERY OF THE FOREST-- AND I NEVER SAW THAT IT WAS INSIDE THIS GIRL, RIGHT BEFORE MY EYES.
NAUSICAÄ!
ゴー
WHATEVER HAPPENS, RETURN TO US! THE TIME IS DRAWING NIGH WHEN ALL THE WORLD WILL HAVE NEED OF YOUR POWER!
ヒィ
ヒィ

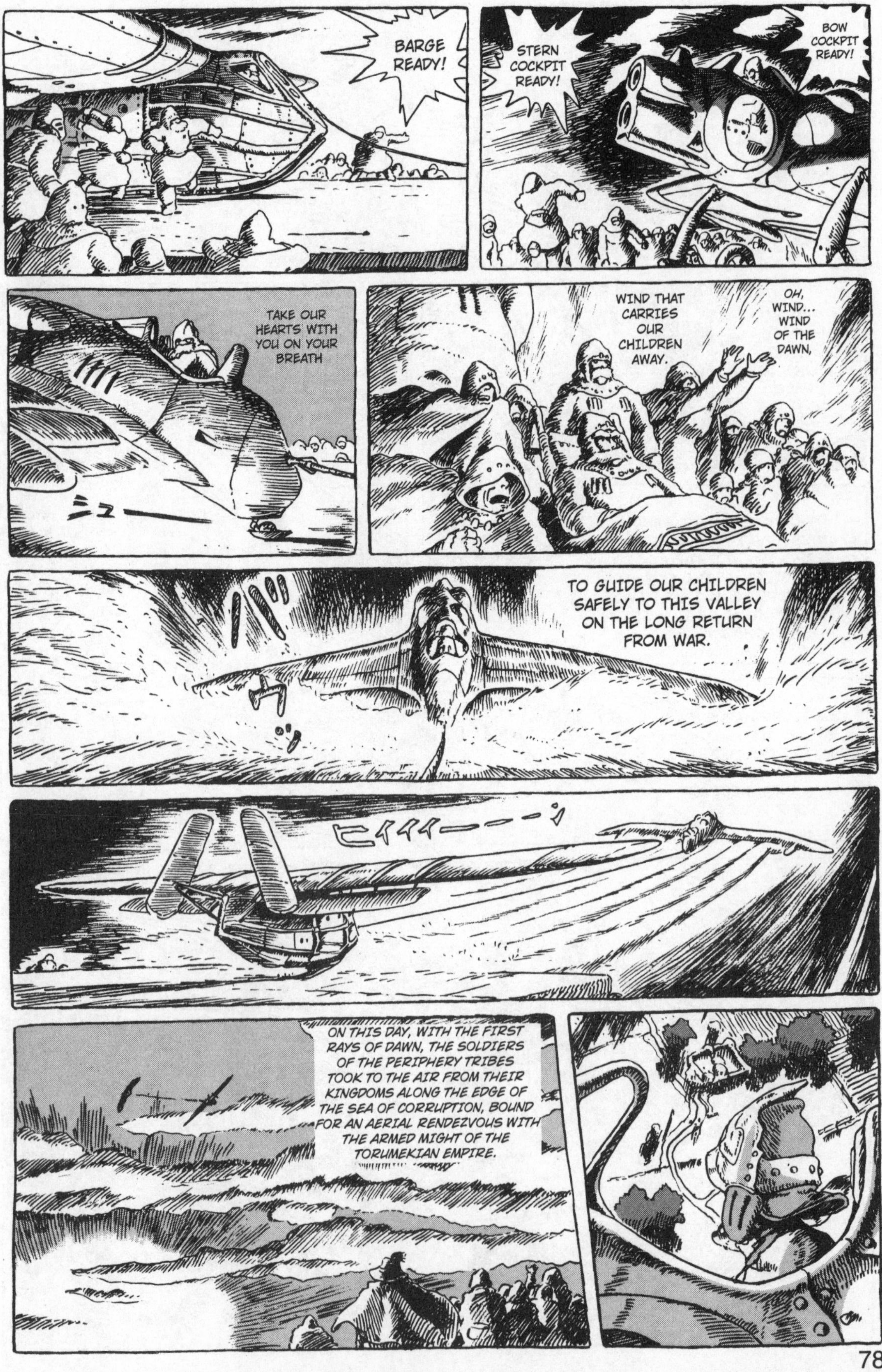
BOW COCKPIT READY!
STERN COCKPIT READY!
BARGE READY!
OH, WIND... WIND OF THE DAWN,
WIND THAT CARRIES OUR CHILDREN AWAY.
TAKE OUR HEARTS WITH YOU ON YOUR BREATH
シュー
TO GUIDE OUR CHILDREN SAFELY TO THIS VALLEY ON THE LONG RETURN FROM WAR.
ON THIS DAY, WITH THE FIRST RAYS OF DAWN, THE SOLDIERS OF THE PERIPHERY TRIBES TOOK TO THE AIR FROM THEIR KINGDOMS ALONG THE EDGE OF THE SEA OF CORRUPTION, BOUND FOR AN AERIAL RENDEZVOUS WITH THE ARMED MIGHT OF THE TORUMEKIAN EMPIRE.

ヒイ

ハハハハハ

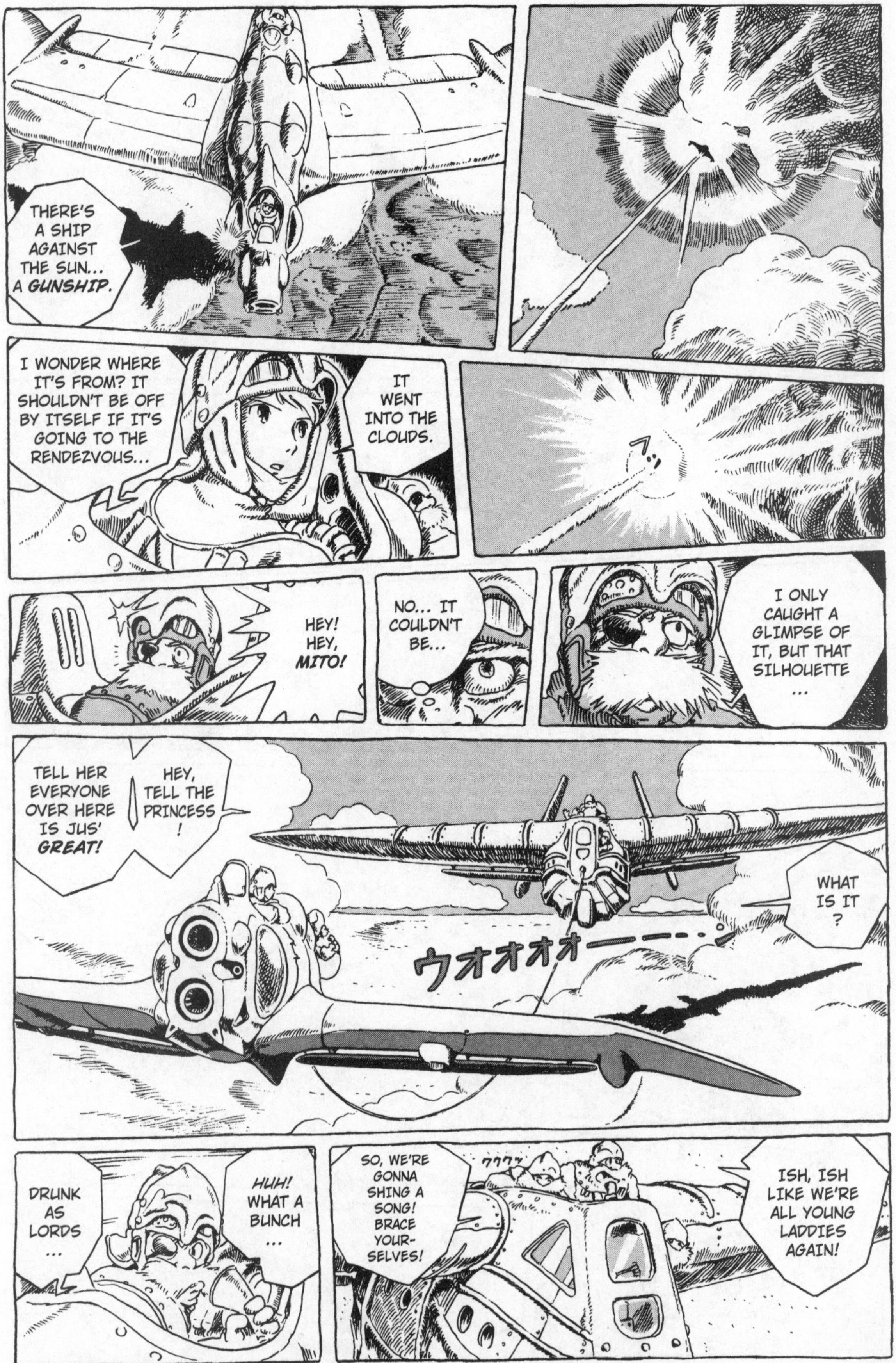
THERE'S A SHIP AGAINST THE SUN... A **GUNSHIP**.
IT WENT INTO THE CLOUDS.
I WONDER WHERE IT'S FROM? IT SHOULDN'T BE OFF BY ITSELF IF IT'S GOING TO THE RENDEZVOUS...
I ONLY CAUGHT A GLIMPSE OF IT, BUT THAT SILHOUETTE ...
NO... IT COULDN'T BE...
HEY! HEY, ***MITO!***
HEY, TELL THE PRINCESS !
WHAT IS IT ?
TELL HER EVERYONE OVER HERE IS JUS' ***GREAT!***
ウオオオオー
ISH, ISH LIKE WE'RE ALL YOUNG LADDIES AGAIN!
SO, WE'RE GONNA SHING A SONG! BRACE YOUR-SELVES!
***HUH!*** WHAT A BUNCH ...
DRUNK AS LORDS ...

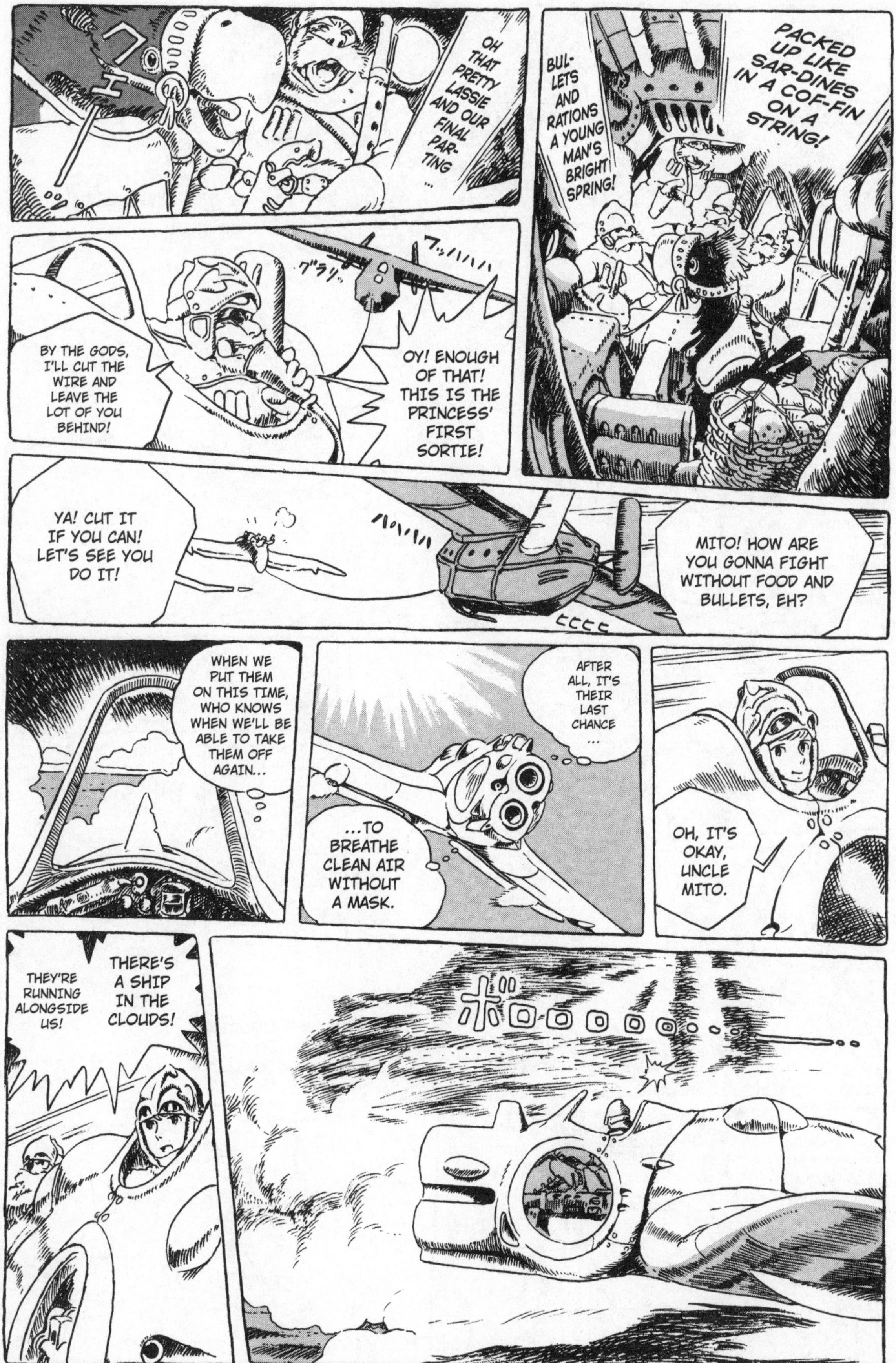

OH THAT PRETTY LASSIE AND OUR FINAL PAR-TING ...
BUL-LETS AND RATIONS A YOUNG MAN'S BRIGHT SPRING!
PACKED UP LIKE SAR-DINES IN A COF-FIN ON A STRING!
BY THE GODS, I'LL CUT THE WIRE AND LEAVE THE LOT OF YOU BEHIND!
OY! ENOUGH OF THAT! THIS IS THE PRINCESS' FIRST SORTIE!
YA! CUT IT IF YOU CAN! LET'S SEE YOU DO IT!
MITO! HOW ARE YOU GONNA FIGHT WITHOUT FOOD AND BULLETS, EH?
WHEN WE PUT THEM ON THIS TIME, WHO KNOWS WHEN WE'LL BE ABLE TO TAKE THEM OFF AGAIN...
AFTER ALL, IT'S THEIR LAST CHANCE ...
...TO BREATHE CLEAN AIR WITHOUT A MASK.
OH, IT'S OKAY, UNCLE MITO.
THERE'S A SHIP IN THE CLOUDS!
THEY'RE RUNNING ALONGSIDE US!

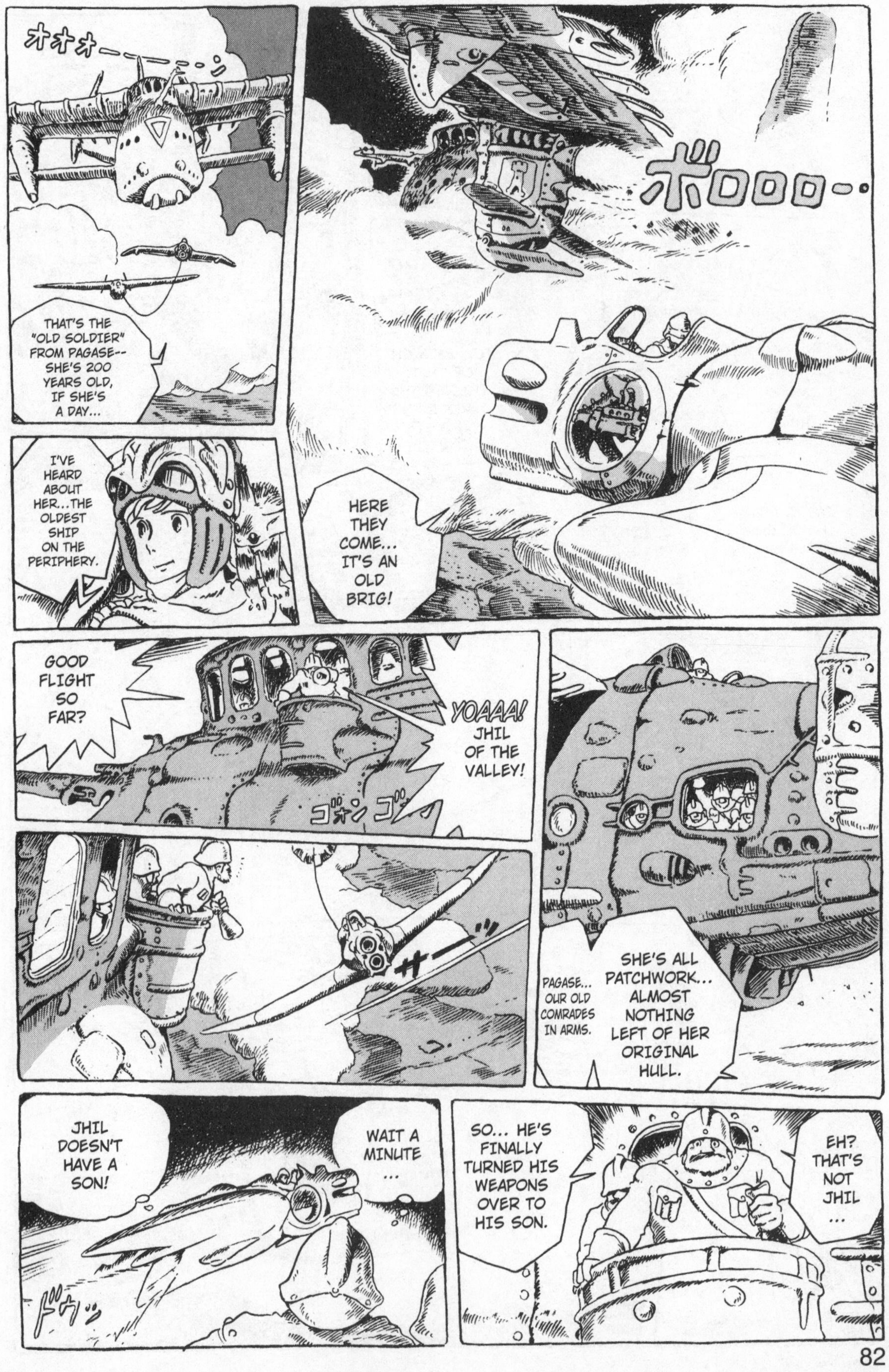
ボロロロ‥
HERE THEY COME... IT'S AN OLD BRIG!
オオオーーーーーン
THAT'S THE "OLD SOLDIER" FROM PAGASE-- SHE'S 200 YEARS OLD, IF SHE'S A DAY...
I'VE HEARD ABOUT HER... THE OLDEST SHIP ON THE PERIPHERY.
SHE'S ALL PATCHWORK... ALMOST NOTHING LEFT OF HER ORIGINAL HULL.
PAGASE... OUR OLD COMRADES IN ARMS.
YOAAA! JHIL OF THE VALLEY!
GOOD FLIGHT SO FAR?
ゴォンゴ
サーッ
EH? THAT'S NOT JHIL...
SO... HE'S FINALLY TURNED HIS WEAPONS OVER TO HIS SON.
WAIT A MINUTE...
JHIL DOESN'T HAVE A SON!
ドウッ

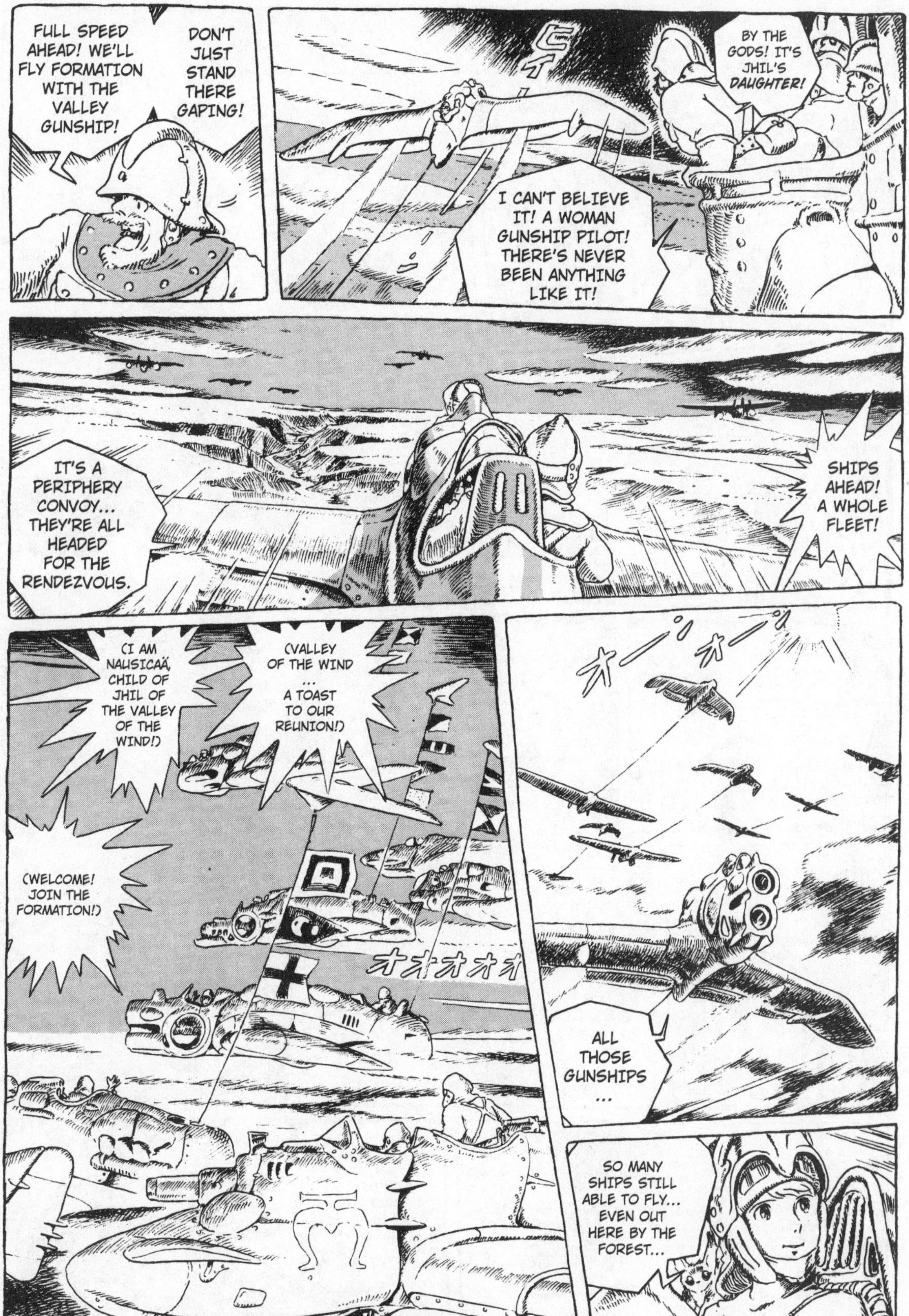
BY THE GODS! IT'S JHIL'S DAUGHTER!
I CAN'T BELIEVE IT! A WOMAN GUNSHIP PILOT! THERE'S NEVER BEEN ANYTHING LIKE IT!
DON'T JUST STAND THERE GAPING!
FULL SPEED AHEAD! WE'LL FLY FORMATION WITH THE VALLEY GUNSHIP!
SHIPS AHEAD! A WHOLE FLEET!
IT'S A PERIPHERY CONVOY... THEY'RE ALL HEADED FOR THE RENDEZVOUS.
ALL THOSE GUNSHIPS ...
SO MANY SHIPS STILL ABLE TO FLY... EVEN OUT HERE BY THE FOREST...
(VALLEY OF THE WIND ... A TOAST TO OUR REUNION!)
(I AM NAUSICAÄ, CHILD OF JHIL OF THE VALLEY OF THE WIND!)
(WELCOME! JOIN THE FORMATION!)
オオオオオ

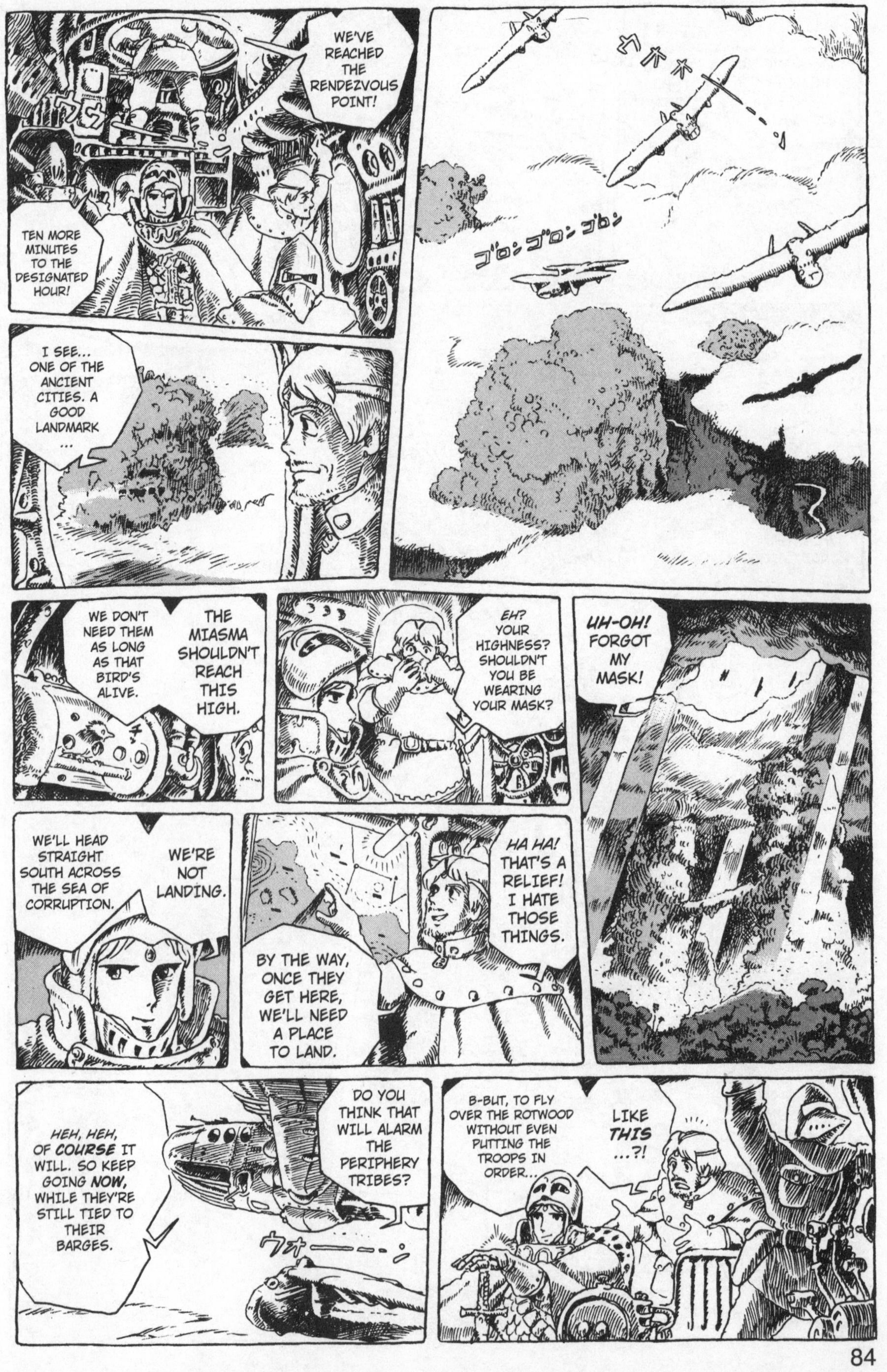
ウホホー
ゴロンゴロンゴロン
WE'VE REACHED THE RENDEZVOUS POINT!
TEN MORE MINUTES TO THE DESIGNATED HOUR!
I SEE... ONE OF THE ANCIENT CITIES. A GOOD LANDMARK ...
UH-OH! FORGOT MY MASK!
EH? YOUR HIGHNESS? SHOULDN'T YOU BE WEARING YOUR MASK?
THE MIASMA SHOULDN'T REACH THIS HIGH.
WE DON'T NEED THEM AS LONG AS THAT BIRD'S ALIVE.
HA HA! THAT'S A RELIEF! I HATE THOSE THINGS.
BY THE WAY, ONCE THEY GET HERE, WE'LL NEED A PLACE TO LAND.
WE'RE NOT LANDING.
WE'LL HEAD STRAIGHT SOUTH ACROSS THE SEA OF CORRUPTION.
LIKE *THIS* ...?!
B-BUT, TO FLY OVER THE ROTWOOD WITHOUT EVEN PUTTING THE TROOPS IN ORDER...
DO YOU THINK THAT WILL ALARM THE PERIPHERY TRIBES?
*HEH, HEH,* OF ***COURSE*** IT WILL. SO KEEP GOING ***NOW,*** WHILE THEY'RE STILL TIED TO THEIR BARGES.
ウォーー

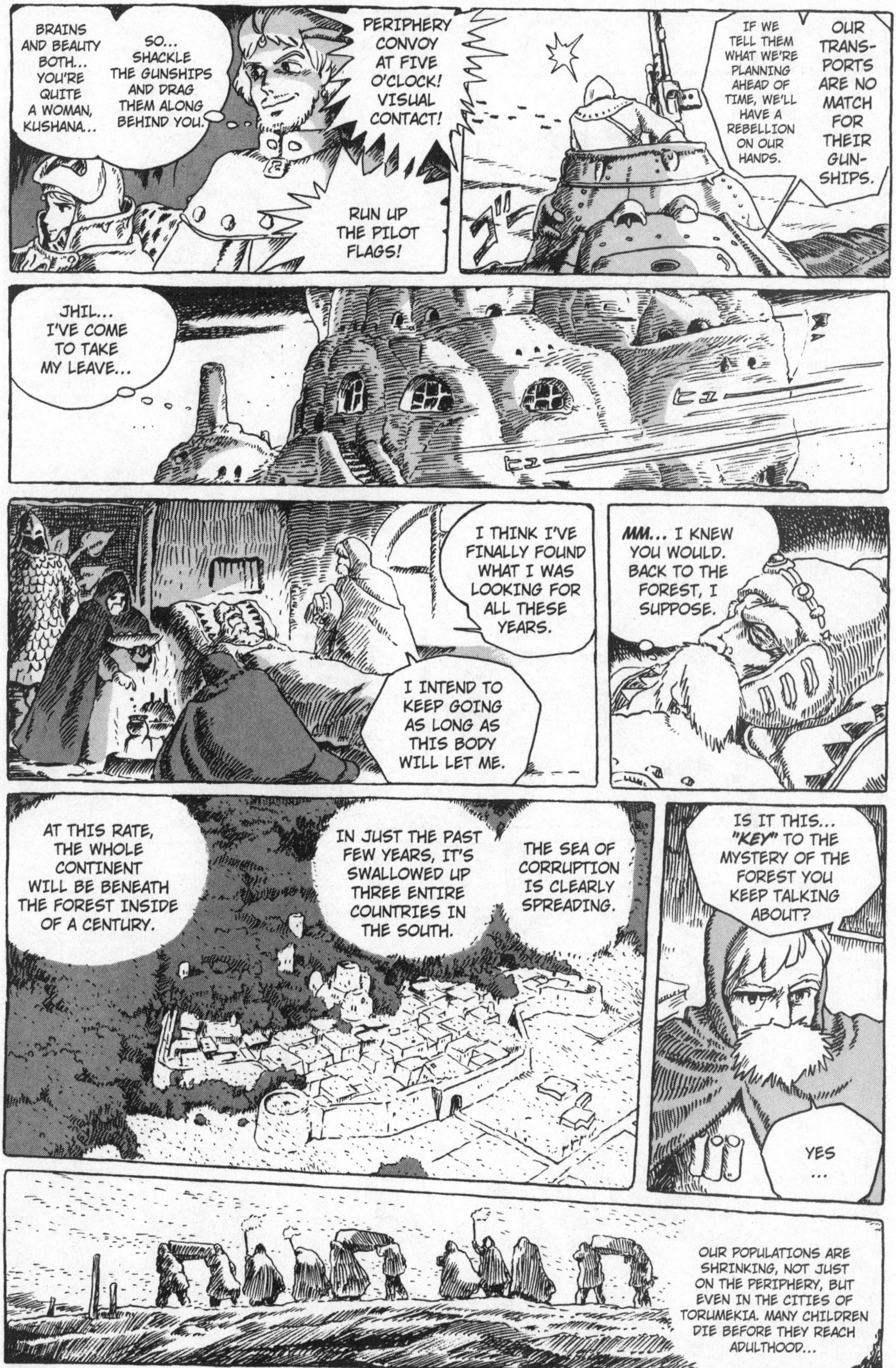
OUR TRANSPORTS ARE NO MATCH FOR THEIR GUNSHIPS.
IF WE TELL THEM WHAT WE'RE PLANNING AHEAD OF TIME, WE'LL HAVE A REBELLION ON OUR HANDS.
PERIPHERY CONVOY AT FIVE O'CLOCK! VISUAL CONTACT!
SO... SHACKLE THE GUNSHIPS AND DRAG THEM ALONG BEHIND YOU.
BRAINS AND BEAUTY BOTH... YOU'RE QUITE A WOMAN, KUSHANA...
RUN UP THE PILOT FLAGS!
JHIL... I'VE COME TO TAKE MY LEAVE...
MM... I KNEW YOU WOULD. BACK TO THE FOREST, I SUPPOSE.
I THINK I'VE FINALLY FOUND WHAT I WAS LOOKING FOR ALL THESE YEARS.
I INTEND TO KEEP GOING AS LONG AS THIS BODY WILL LET ME.
IS IT THIS... "KEY" TO THE MYSTERY OF THE FOREST YOU KEEP TALKING ABOUT?
YES ...
THE SEA OF CORRUPTION IS CLEARLY SPREADING.
IN JUST THE PAST FEW YEARS, IT'S SWALLOWED UP THREE ENTIRE COUNTRIES IN THE SOUTH.
AT THIS RATE, THE WHOLE CONTINENT WILL BE BENEATH THE FOREST INSIDE OF A CENTURY.
OUR POPULATIONS ARE SHRINKING, NOT JUST ON THE PERIPHERY, BUT EVEN IN THE CITIES OF TORUMEKIA. MANY CHILDREN DIE BEFORE THEY REACH ADULTHOOD...

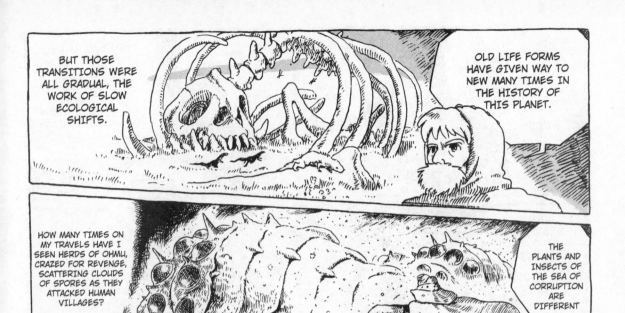

OLD LIFE FORMS HAVE GIVEN WAY TO NEW MANY TIMES IN THE HISTORY OF THIS PLANET.
BUT THOSE TRANSITIONS WERE ALL GRADUAL, THE WORK OF SLOW ECOLOGICAL SHIFTS.
THE PLANTS AND INSECTS OF THE SEA OF CORRUPTION ARE DIFFERENT ...
HOW MANY TIMES ON MY TRAVELS HAVE I SEEN HERDS OF OHMU, CRAZED FOR REVENGE, SCATTERING CLOUDS OF SPORES AS THEY ATTACKED HUMAN VILLAGES?
THE LIFE FORMS OF THE FOREST ALMOST SEEM BENT ON DESTROYING THE PLANTS AND ANIMALS OF THE OLD WORLD.
THE PRIESTS OF TORUMEKIA SAY IT'S THE WRATH OF HEAVEN -- GOD'S PUNISHMENT FOR OUR POLLUTION OF THE WORLD DURING THE SEVEN DAYS OF FIRE.
BUT CAN THAT REALLY BE SO ...?
IF THE FOREST IS GOD'S PUNISHMENT FOR MAN'S POLLUTION OF OUR WORLD, THEN WHAT REASON IS THERE TO DESTROY THE PLANTS AND BIRDS? THEY'VE BEEN HERE FAR LONGER THAN WE.
WHEN I WAS STILL A YOUNG MAN, I PENETRATED-- JUST ONCE-- ALL THE WAY TO THE HEART OF THE FOREST. "A BARREN DESERT OF SAND, BURNED AND CORRUPT WITH POISONS." THAT'S WHAT THE OLD CHRONICLES SAID ABOUT THOSE LANDS...
BUT WHEN I GOT THERE, IT WAS A *CLIMAX FOREST*, THE FINAL STAGE OF GROWTH IN THE SEA OF CORRUPTION.

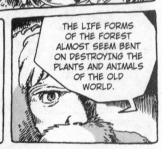

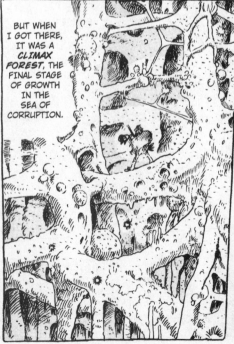

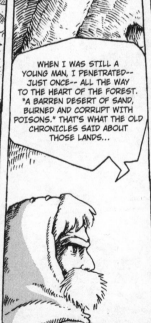

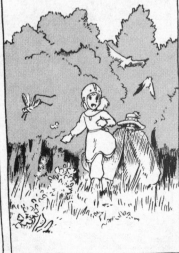

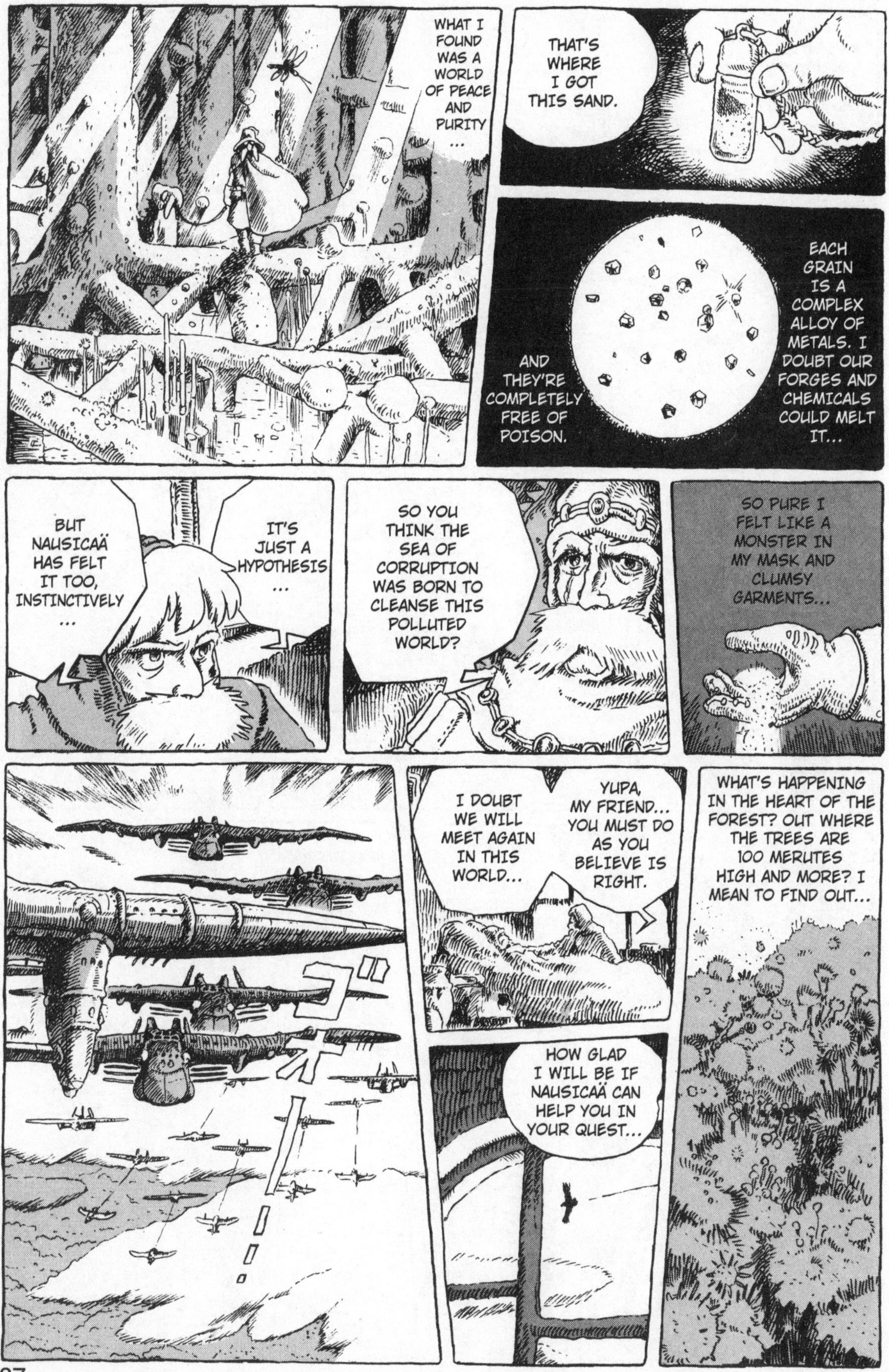
THAT'S WHERE I GOT THIS SAND.
EACH GRAIN IS A COMPLEX ALLOY OF METALS. I DOUBT OUR FORGES AND CHEMICALS COULD MELT IT...
AND THEY'RE COMPLETELY FREE OF POISON.
WHAT I FOUND WAS A WORLD OF PEACE AND PURITY...
SO PURE I FELT LIKE A MONSTER IN MY MASK AND CLUMSY GARMENTS...
SO YOU THINK THE SEA OF CORRUPTION WAS BORN TO CLEANSE THIS POLLUTED WORLD?
IT'S JUST A HYPOTHESIS...
BUT NAUSICAÄ HAS FELT IT TOO, INSTINCTIVELY...
WHAT'S HAPPENING IN THE HEART OF THE FOREST? OUT WHERE THE TREES ARE 100 MERUTES HIGH AND MORE? I MEAN TO FIND OUT...
YUPA, MY FRIEND... YOU MUST DO AS YOU BELIEVE IS RIGHT.
I DOUBT WE WILL MEET AGAIN IN THIS WORLD...
HOW GLAD I WILL BE IF NAUSICAÄ CAN HELP YOU IN YOUR QUEST...
ゴオ

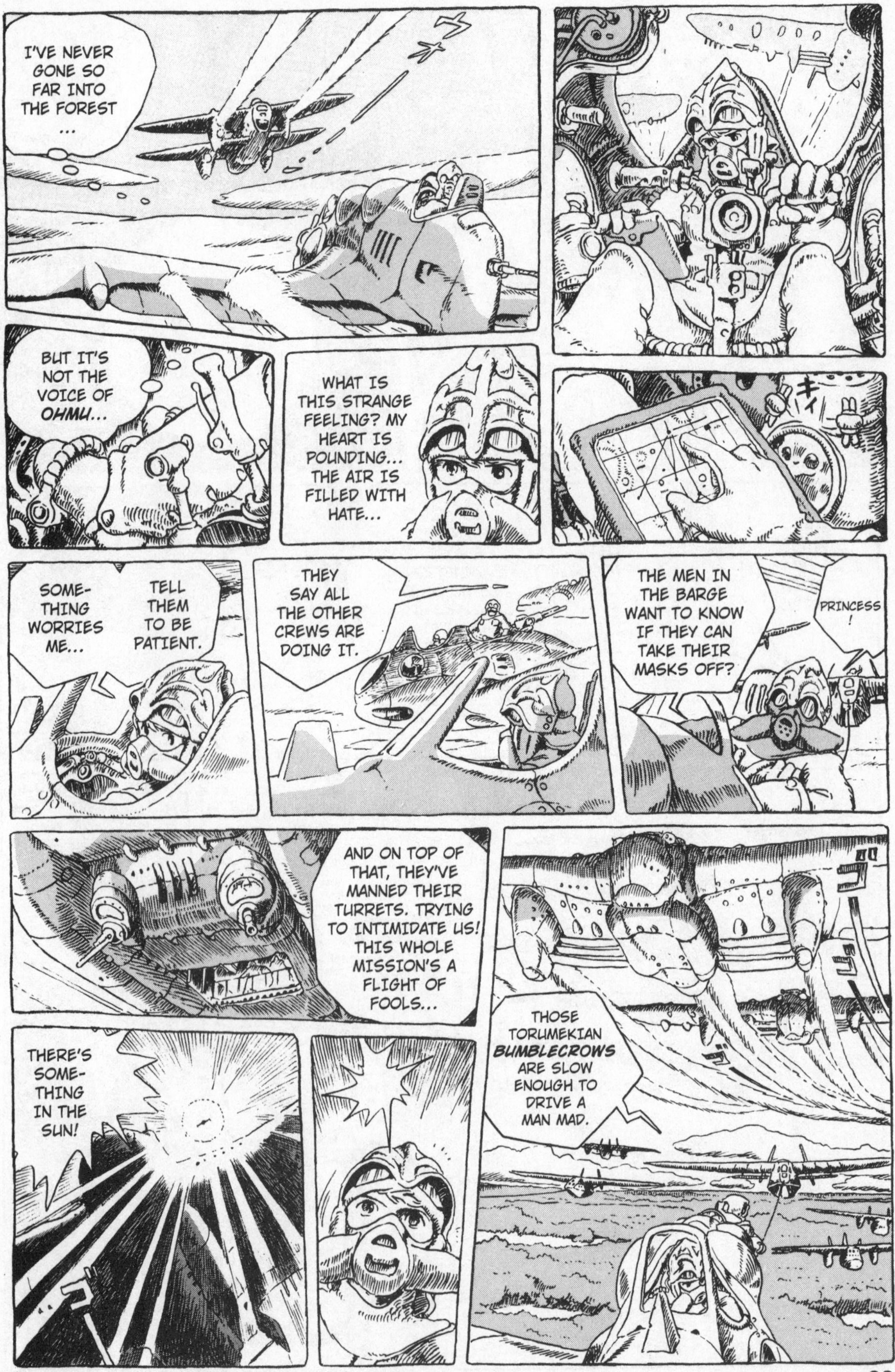
I'VE NEVER GONE SO FAR INTO THE FOREST ...
WHAT IS THIS STRANGE FEELING? MY HEART IS POUNDING... THE AIR IS FILLED WITH HATE...
BUT IT'S NOT THE VOICE OF ***OHMU***...
PRINCESS!
THE MEN IN THE BARGE WANT TO KNOW IF THEY CAN TAKE THEIR MASKS OFF?
THEY SAY ALL THE OTHER CREWS ARE DOING IT.
TELL THEM TO BE PATIENT.
SOME-THING WORRIES ME...
THOSE TORUMEKIAN ***BUMBLECROWS*** ARE SLOW ENOUGH TO DRIVE A MAN MAD.
AND ON TOP OF THAT, THEY'VE MANNED THEIR TURRETS. TRYING TO INTIMIDATE US! THIS WHOLE MISSION'S A FLIGHT OF FOOLS...
THERE'S SOME-THING IN THE SUN!

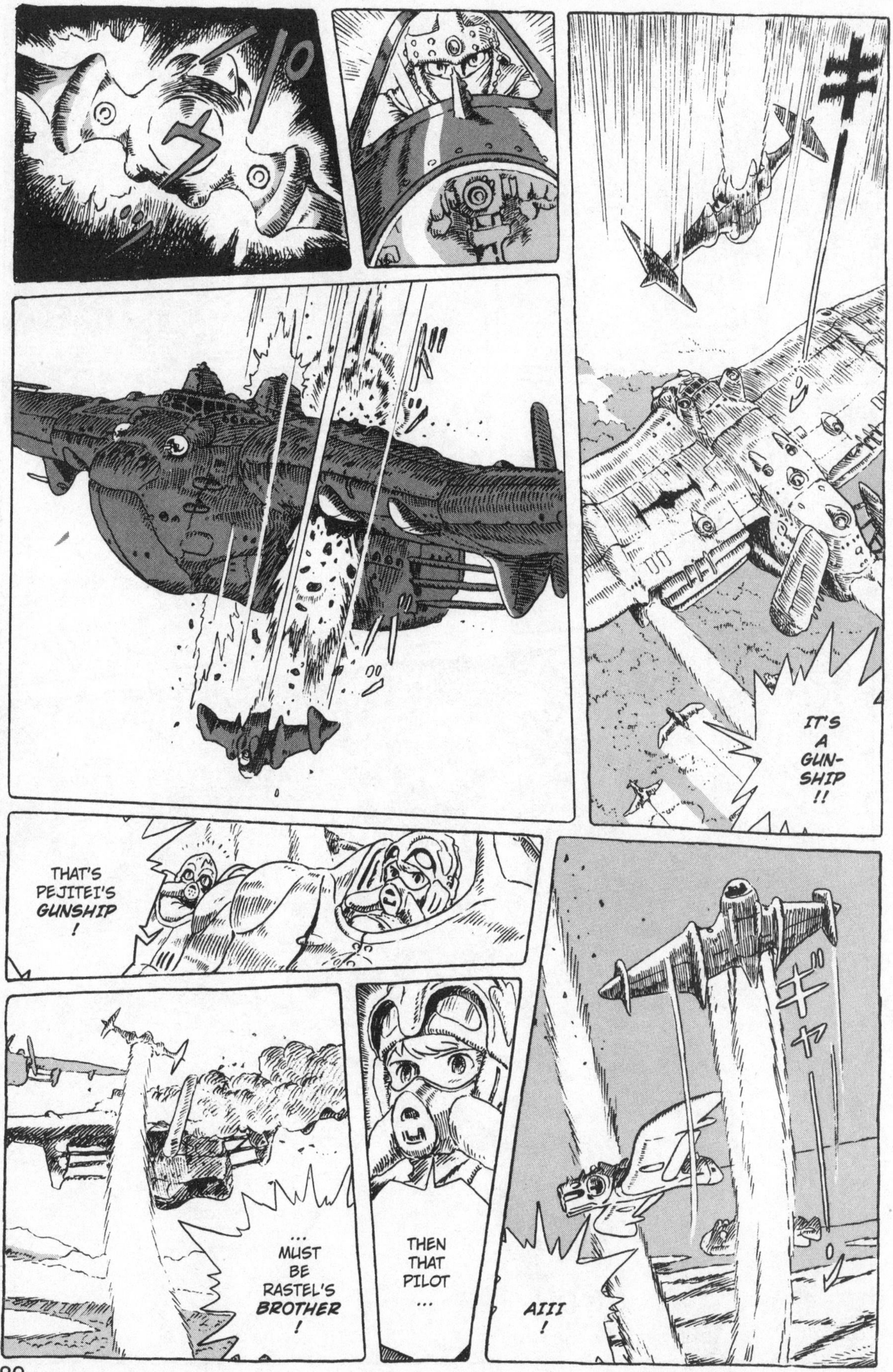
IT'S A GUN-SHIP !!
AIII !
THAT'S PEJITEI'S GUNSHIP !
THEN THAT PILOT ...
... MUST BE RASTEL'S BROTHER !

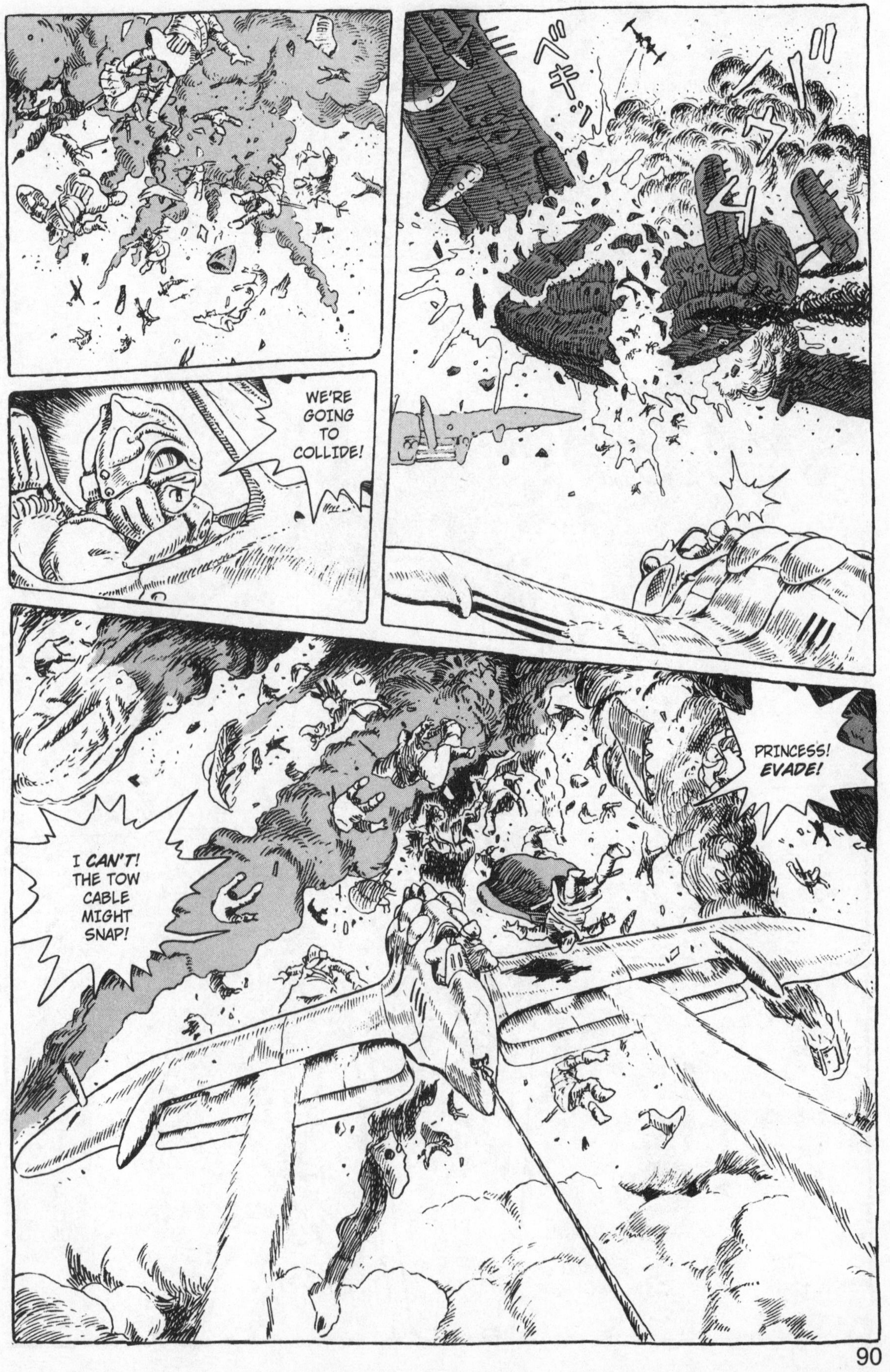
WE'RE GOING TO COLLIDE!
PRINCESS! **EVADE!**
I ***CAN'T!*** THE TOW CABLE MIGHT SNAP!

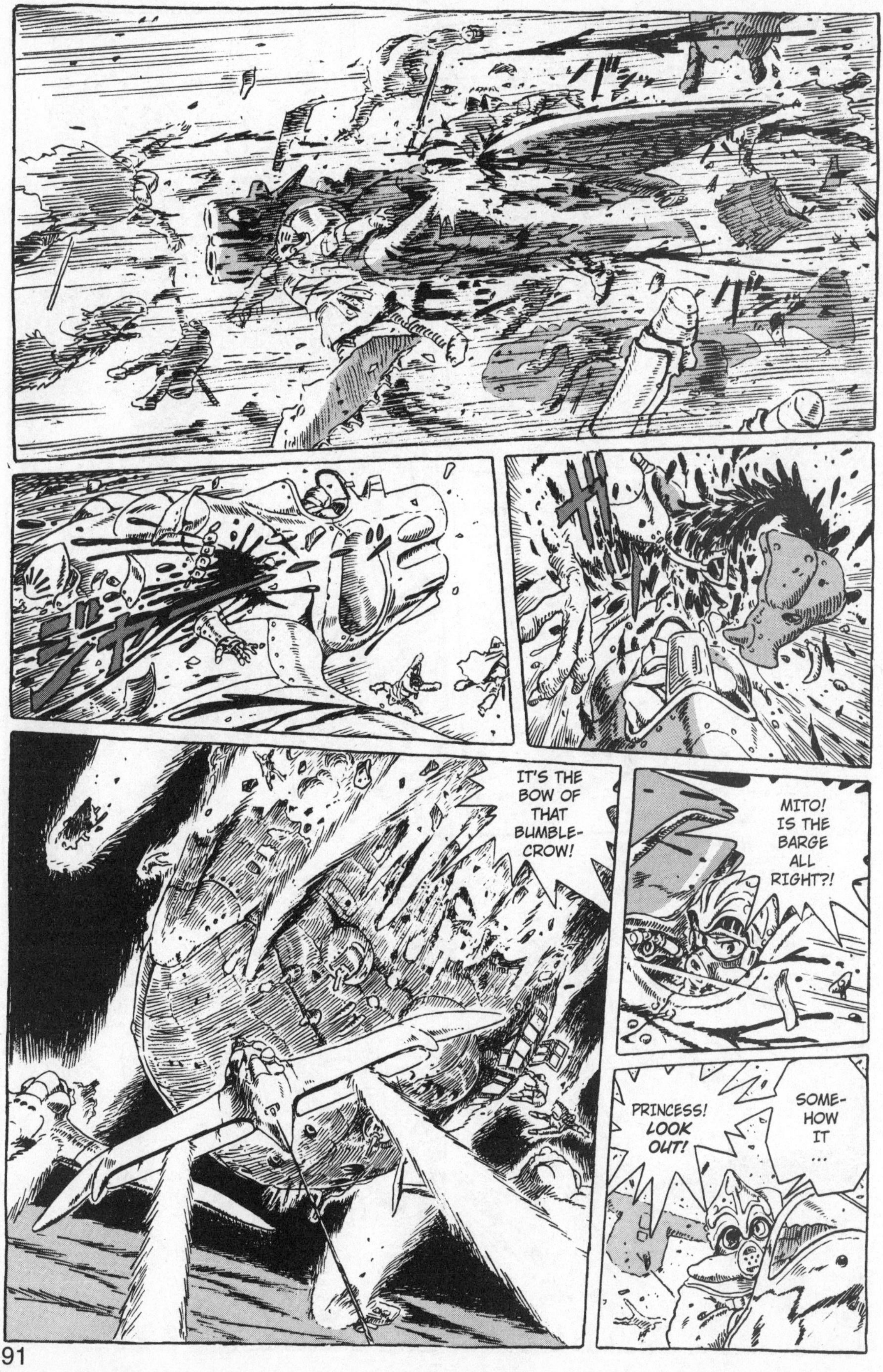

MITO! IS THE BARGE ALL RIGHT?!
SOME-HOW IT ...
PRINCESS! LOOK OUT!
IT'S THE BOW OF THAT BUMBLE-CROW!

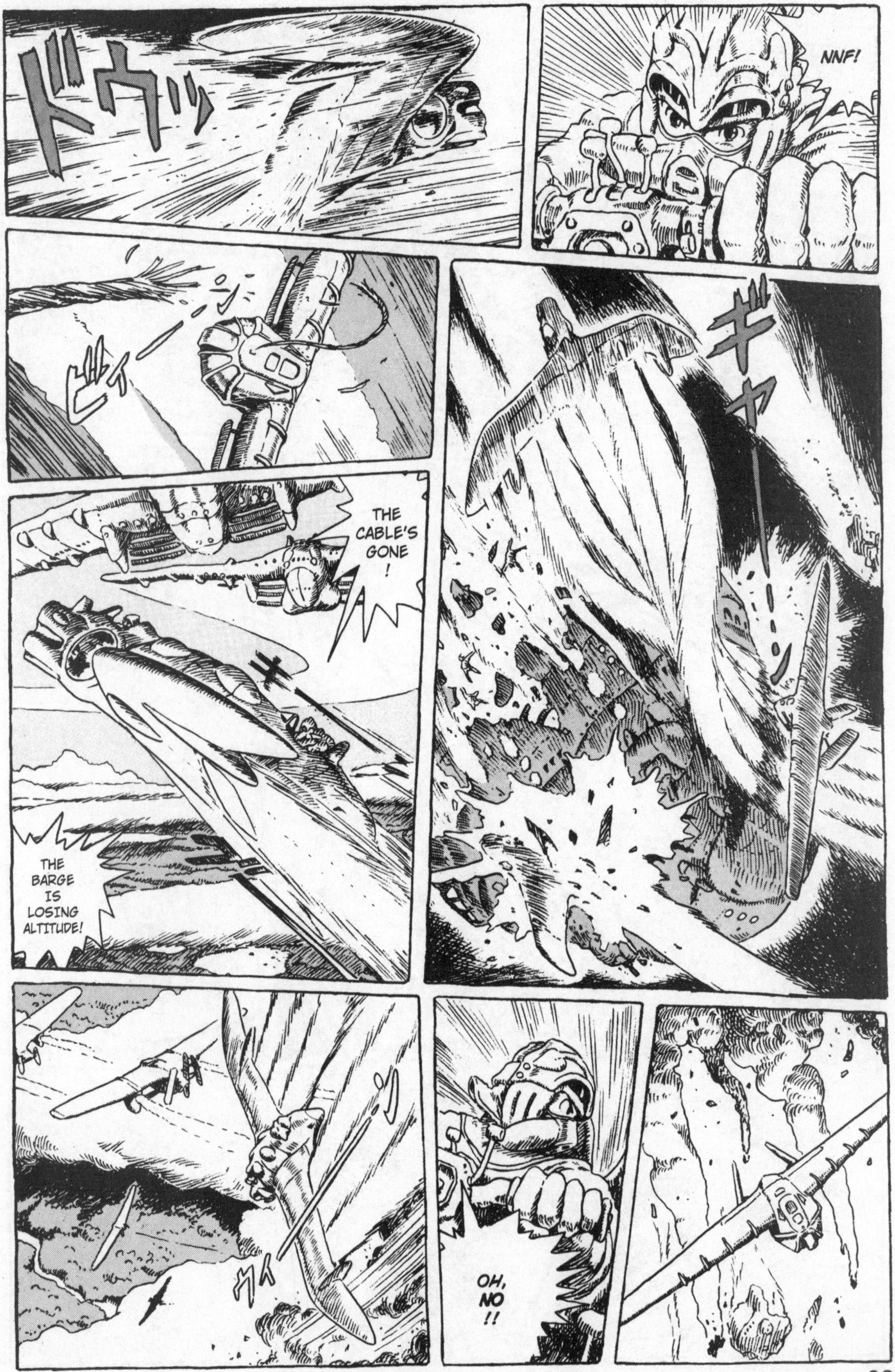
NNF!
THE CABLE'S GONE!
THE BARGE IS LOSING ALTITUDE!
OH, NO!!

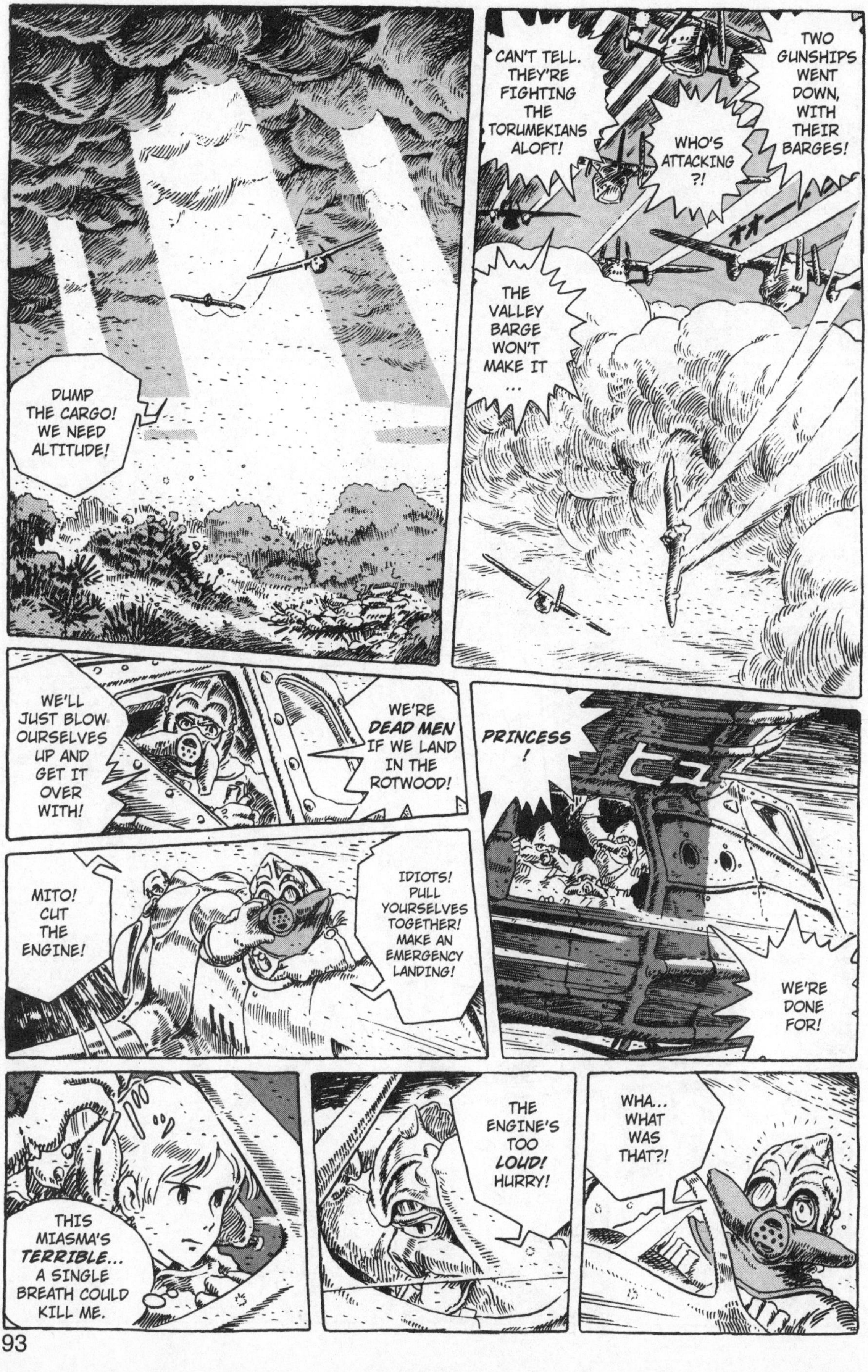
TWO GUNSHIPS WENT DOWN, WITH THEIR BARGES!
WHO'S ATTACKING ?!
CAN'T TELL. THEY'RE FIGHTING THE TORUMEKIANS ALOFT!
オオー
THE VALLEY BARGE WON'T MAKE IT ...
DUMP THE CARGO! WE NEED ALTITUDE!
PRINCESS !
ヒュ
WE'RE DONE FOR!
WE'RE *DEAD MEN* IF WE LAND IN THE ROTWOOD!
WE'LL JUST BLOW OURSELVES UP AND GET IT OVER WITH!
IDIOTS! PULL YOURSELVES TOGETHER! MAKE AN EMERGENCY LANDING!
MITO! CUT THE ENGINE!
WHA... WHAT WAS THAT?!
THE ENGINE'S TOO *LOUD!* HURRY!
THIS MIASMA'S *TERRIBLE*... A SINGLE BREATH COULD KILL ME.

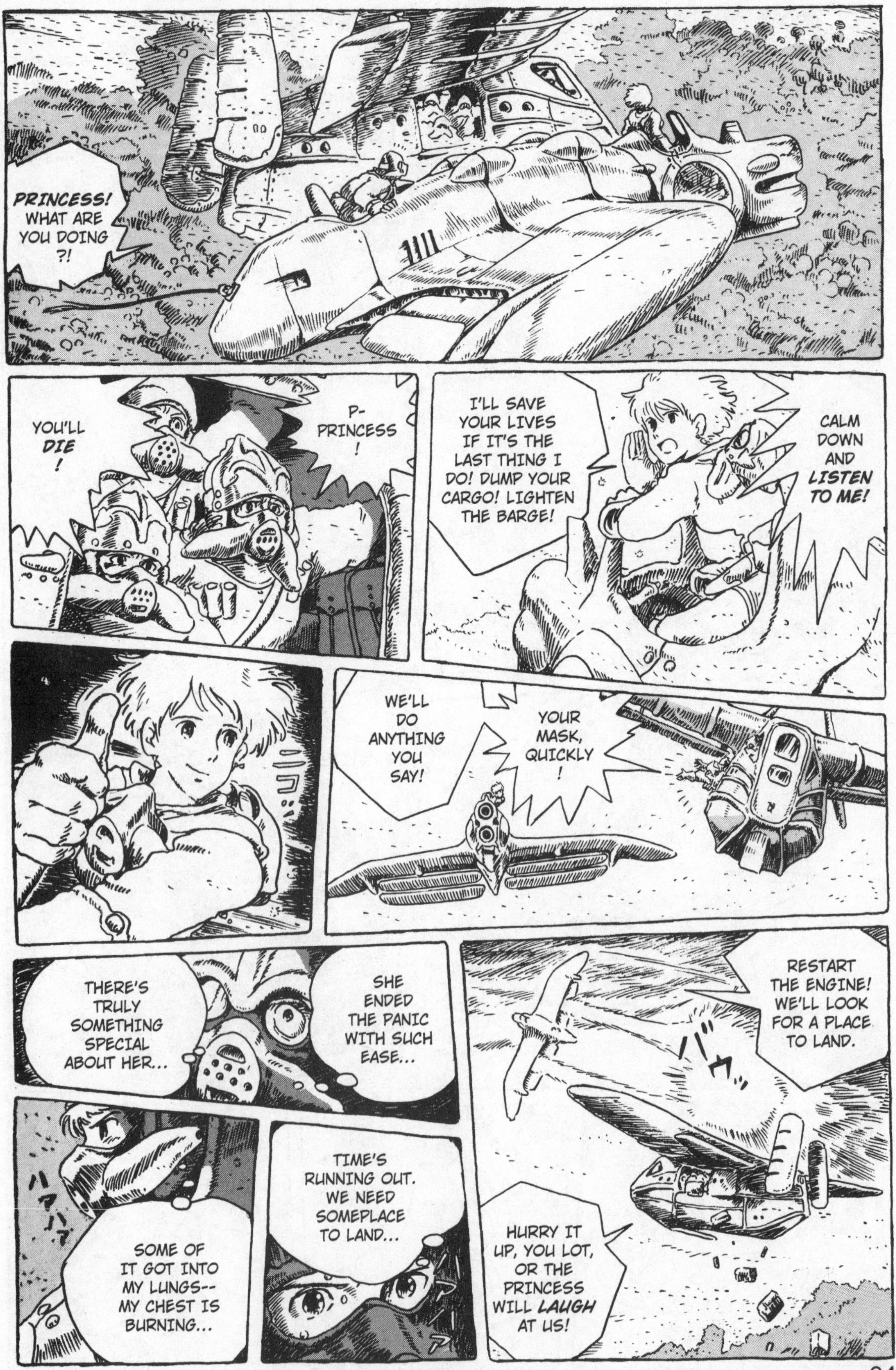

**PRINCESS!** WHAT ARE YOU DOING ?!
CALM DOWN AND ***LISTEN TO ME!***
I'LL SAVE YOUR LIVES IF IT'S THE LAST THING I DO! DUMP YOUR CARGO! LIGHTEN THE BARGE!
P-PRINCESS!
YOU'LL ***DIE!***
YOUR MASK, QUICKLY!
WE'LL DO ANYTHING YOU SAY!
ニコッ
RESTART THE ENGINE! WE'LL LOOK FOR A PLACE TO LAND.
HURRY IT UP, YOU LOT, OR THE PRINCESS WILL ***LAUGH*** AT US!
SHE ENDED THE PANIC WITH SUCH EASE...
THERE'S TRULY SOMETHING SPECIAL ABOUT HER...
TIME'S RUNNING OUT. WE NEED SOMEPLACE TO LAND...
ハァハァ
SOME OF IT GOT INTO MY LUNGS-- MY CHEST IS BURNING...

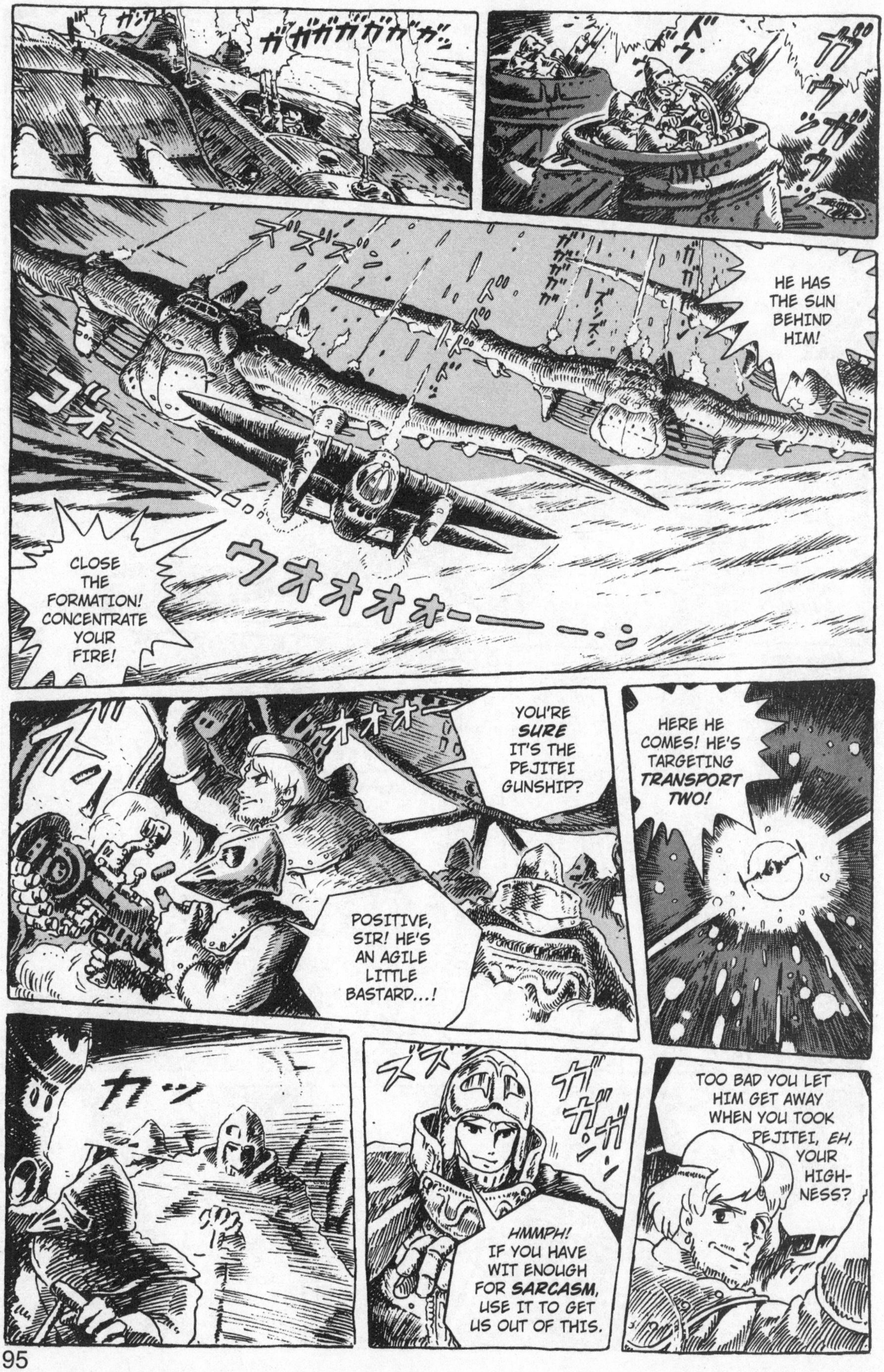
HE HAS THE SUN BEHIND HIM!
CLOSE THE FORMATION! CONCENTRATE YOUR FIRE!
HERE HE COMES! HE'S TARGETING *TRANSPORT TWO!*
YOU'RE *SURE* IT'S THE PEJITEI GUNSHIP?
POSITIVE, SIR! HE'S AN AGILE LITTLE BASTARD...!
TOO BAD YOU LET HIM GET AWAY WHEN YOU TOOK PEJITEI, *EH,* YOUR HIGH-NESS?
*HMMPH!* IF YOU HAVE WIT ENOUGH FOR **SARCASM**, USE IT TO GET US OUT OF THIS.

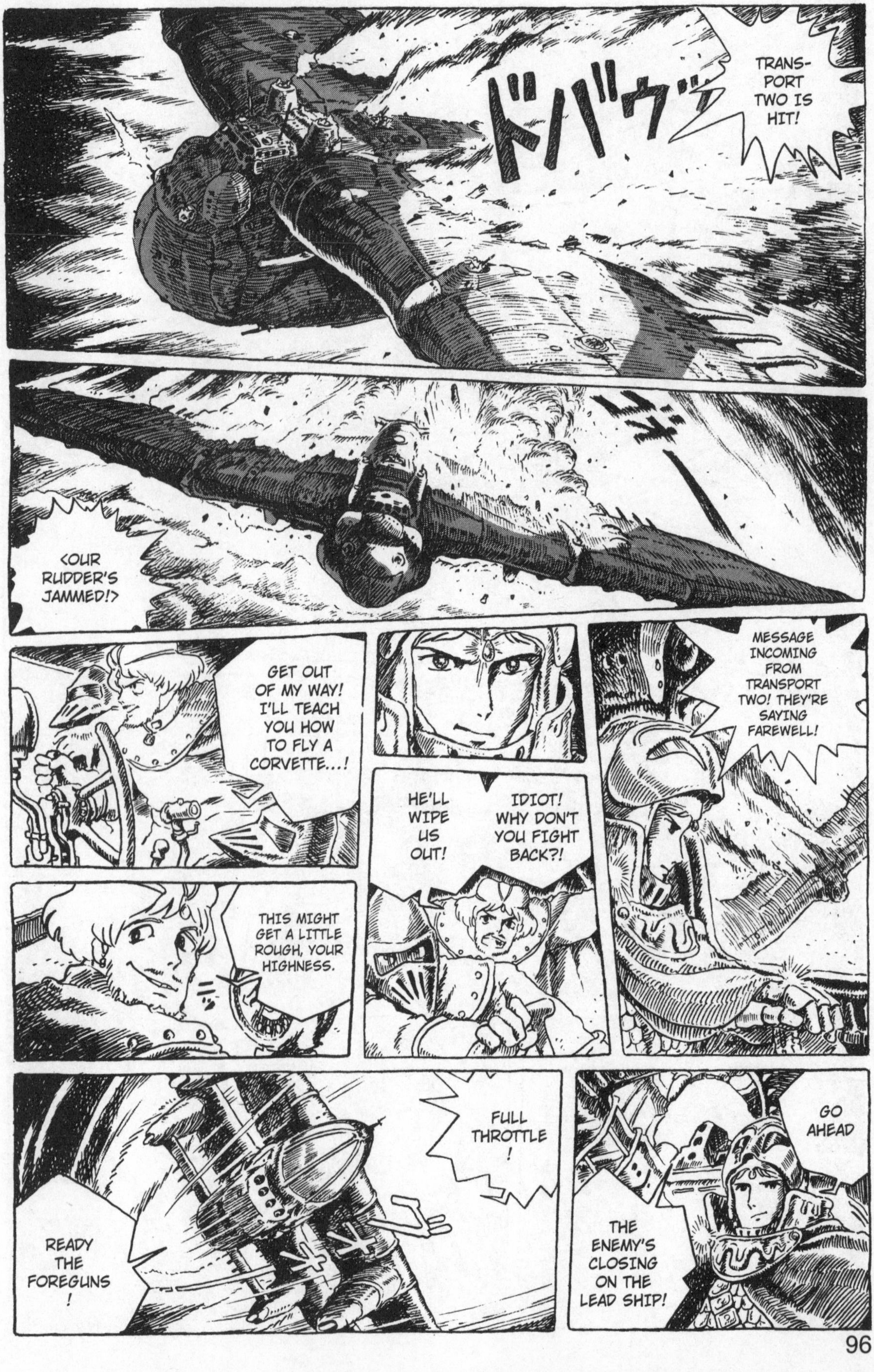
ドバヴ
TRANS-PORT TWO IS HIT!
<OUR RUDDER'S JAMMED!>
MESSAGE INCOMING FROM TRANSPORT TWO! THEY'RE SAYING FAREWELL!
IDIOT! WHY DON'T YOU FIGHT BACK?!
HE'LL WIPE US OUT!
GET OUT OF MY WAY! I'LL TEACH YOU HOW TO FLY A CORVETTE...!
THIS MIGHT GET A LITTLE ROUGH, YOUR HIGHNESS.
GO AHEAD
THE ENEMY'S CLOSING ON THE LEAD SHIP!
FULL THROTTLE!
READY THE FOREGUNS!

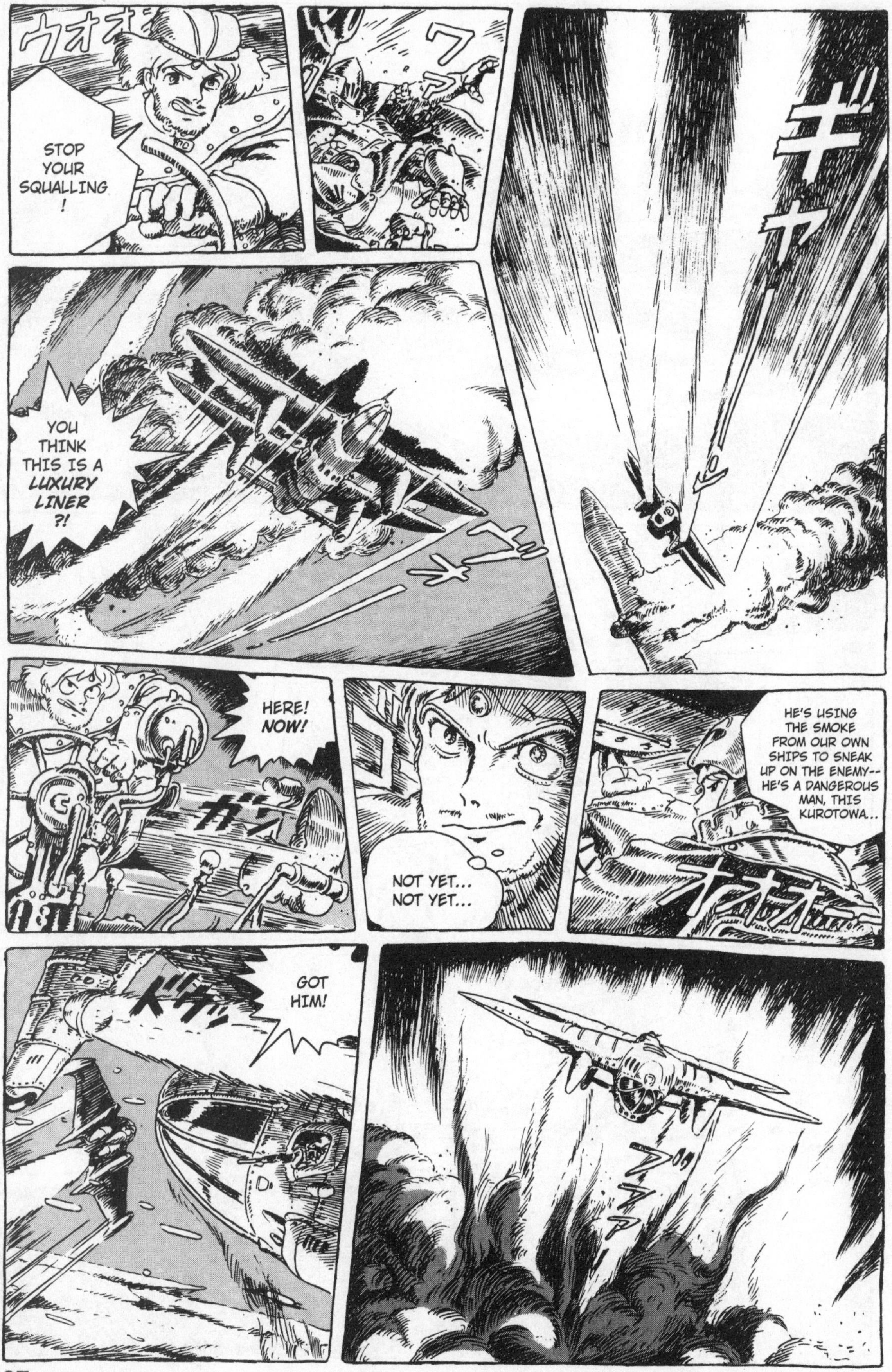
STOP YOUR SQUALLING !
YOU THINK THIS IS A *LUXURY LINER* ?!
HE'S USING THE SMOKE FROM OUR OWN SHIPS TO SNEAK UP ON THE ENEMY-- HE'S A DANGEROUS MAN, THIS KUROTOWA...
NOT YET... NOT YET...
HERE! *NOW!*
GOT HIM!

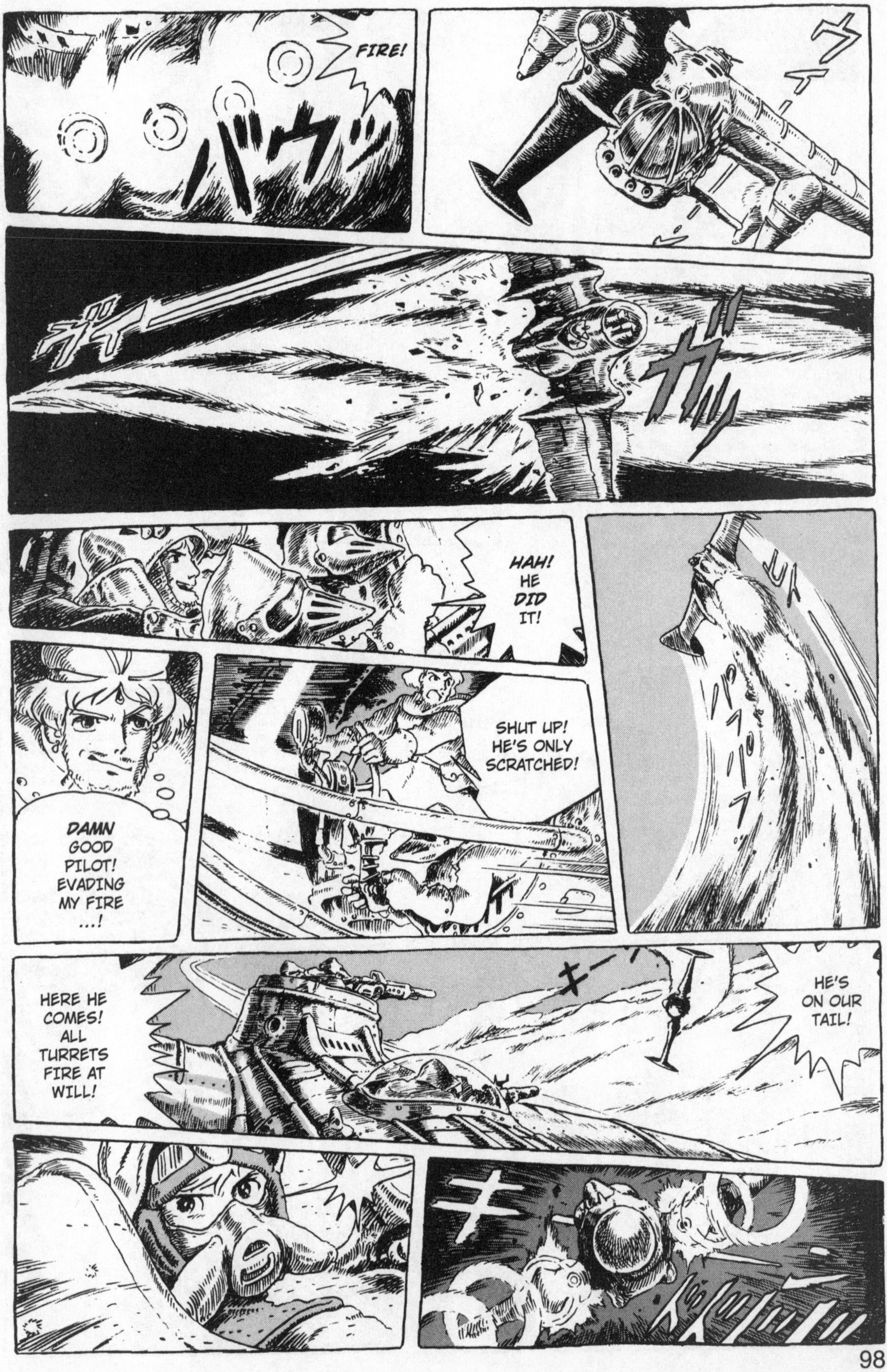
FIRE!
HAH! HE DID IT!
SHUT UP! HE'S ONLY SCRATCHED!
DAMN GOOD PILOT! EVADING MY FIRE ...!
HE'S ON OUR TAIL!
HERE HE COMES! ALL TURRETS FIRE AT WILL!

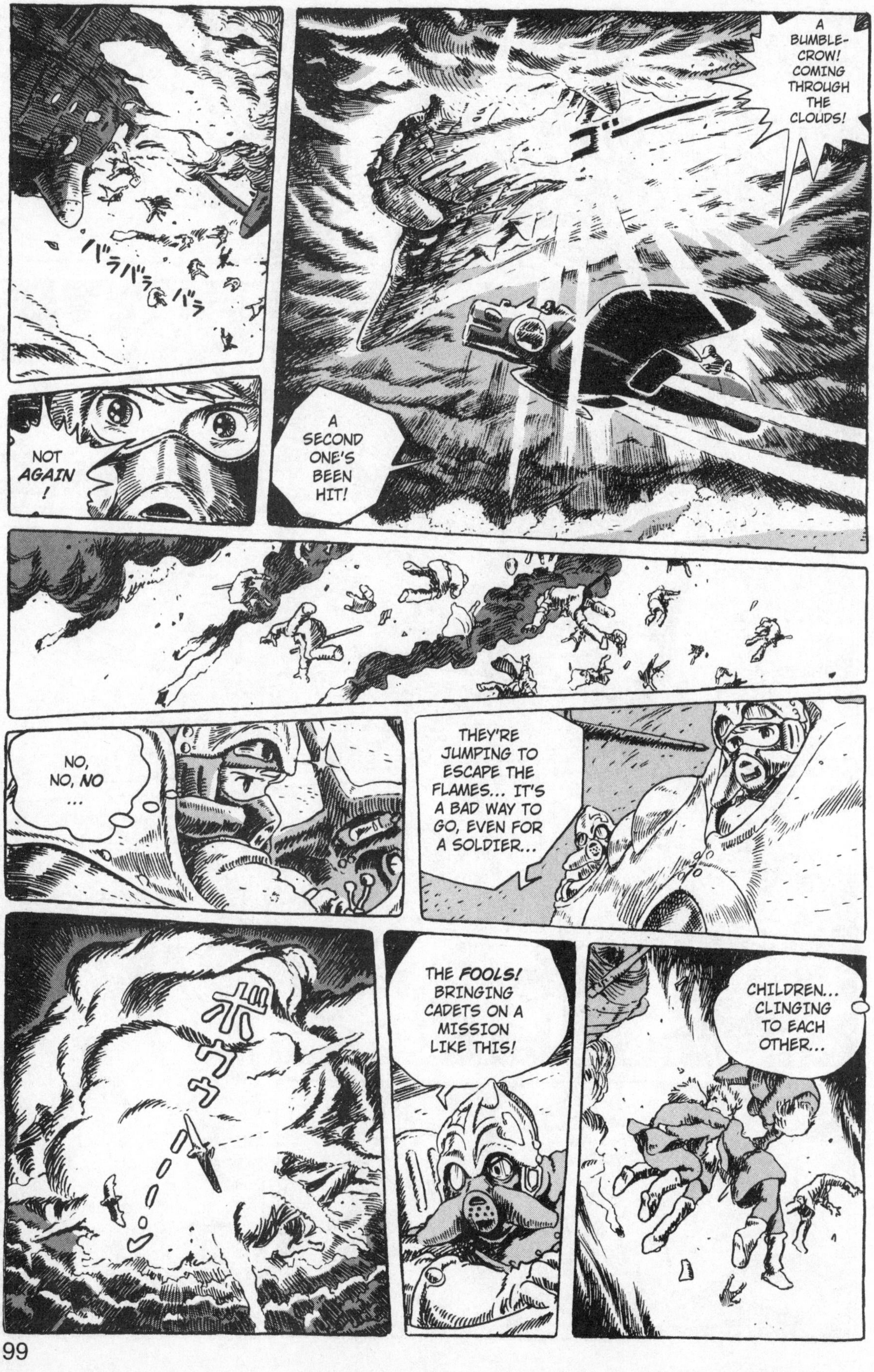
A BUMBLE-CROW! COMING THROUGH THE CLOUDS!
ゴー
A SECOND ONE'S BEEN HIT!
バラバラバラ
NOT *AGAIN*!
THEY'RE JUMPING TO ESCAPE THE FLAMES... IT'S A BAD WAY TO GO, EVEN FOR A SOLDIER...
NO, NO, *NO*...
CHILDREN... CLINGING TO EACH OTHER...
THE *FOOLS!* BRINGING CADETS ON A MISSION LIKE THIS!
ボウゥ

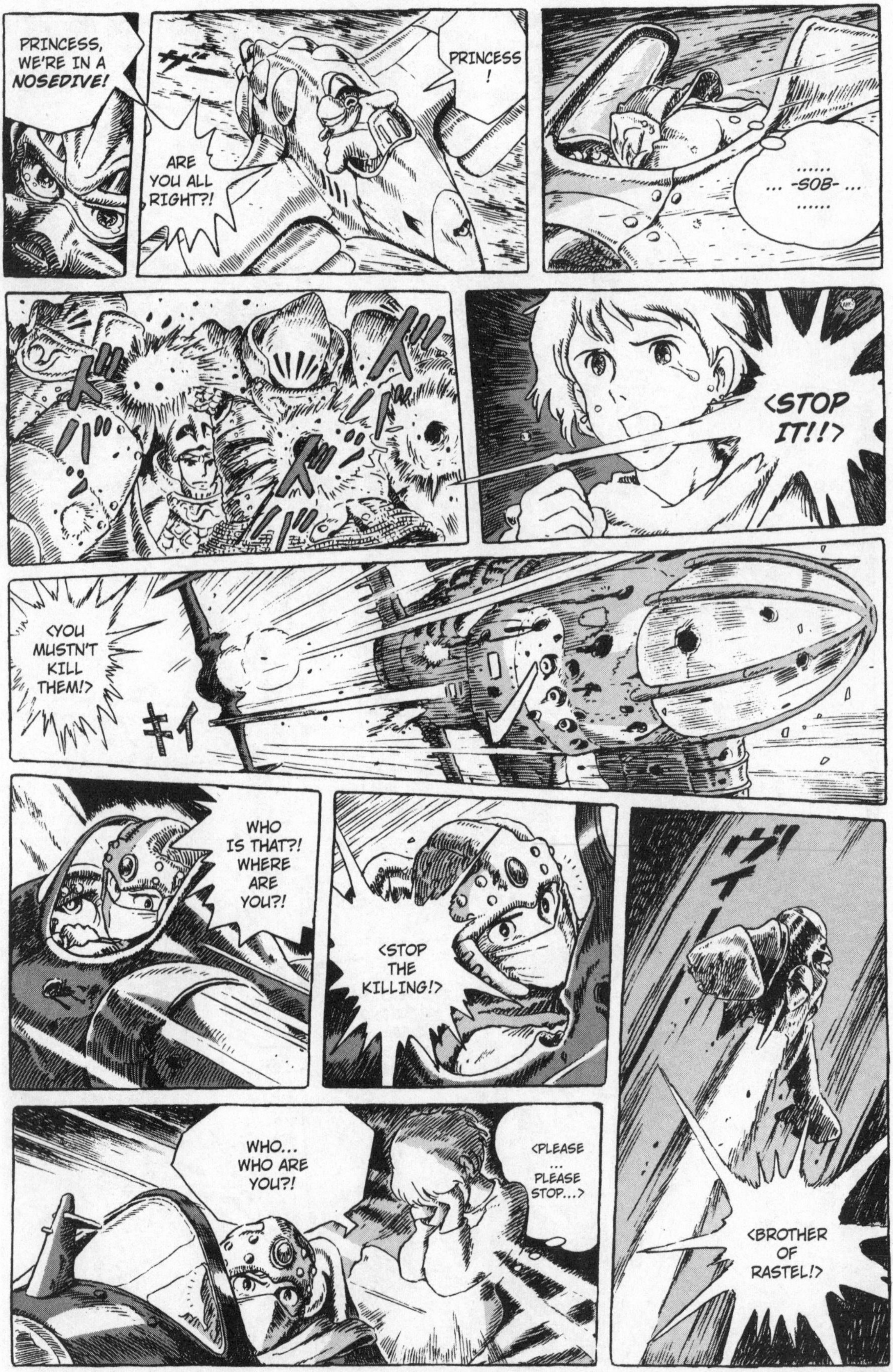
......
... -SOB- ...
......
PRINCESS!
ARE YOU ALL RIGHT?!
PRINCESS, WE'RE IN A ***NOSEDIVE!***
***<STOP IT!!>***
<YOU MUSTN'T KILL THEM!>
キイ
ヴィー
<BROTHER OF RASTEL!>
<STOP THE KILLING!>
WHO IS THAT?! WHERE ARE YOU?!
<PLEASE ... PLEASE STOP...>
WHO... WHO ARE YOU?!

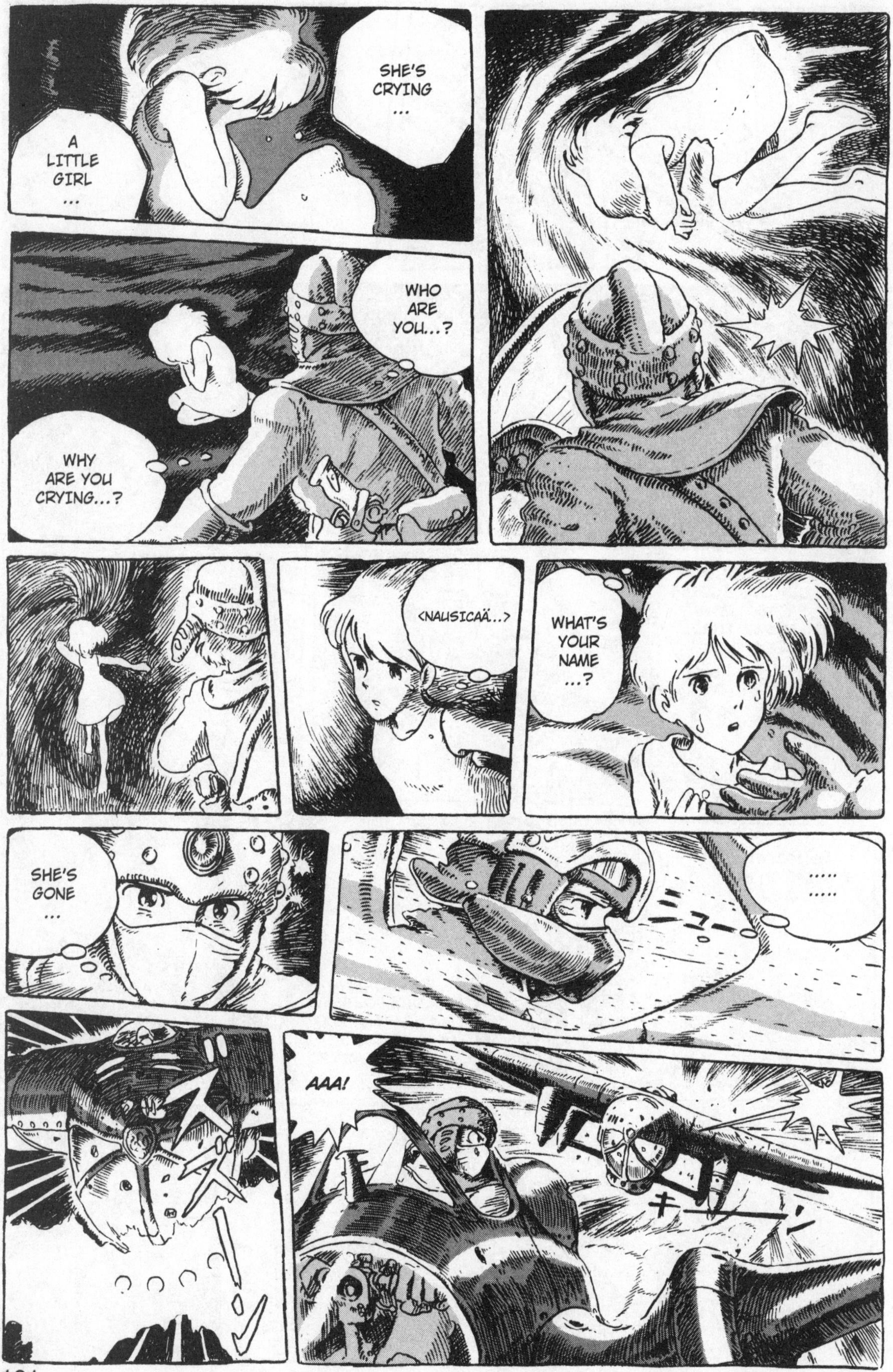
SHE'S CRYING ...
A LITTLE GIRL ...
WHO ARE YOU...?
WHY ARE YOU CRYING...?
WHAT'S YOUR NAME ...?
<NAUSICAÄ...>
.....
.....
SHE'S GONE ...
AAA!

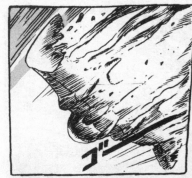

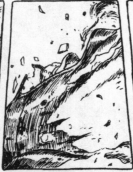

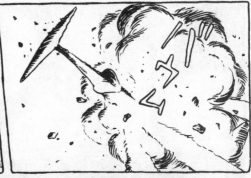

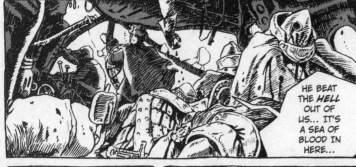

GOT HIM!
オオオーーーン
WHEW! THAT WAS TOO DAMNED CLOSE!
HE BEAT THE HELL OUT OF US... IT'S A SEA OF BLOOD IN HERE...
....
....
YOU MADE A SHIELD OF YOUR OWN BODIES TO PROTECT ME-- I WILL NEVER FORGET YOUR LOYALTY...
YOUR HIGHNESS ...
WE'VE TAKEN SEVERE LOSSES. SHALL WE SCRUB THE OPERATION AND PULL BACK?
NO! GET THE FORMATION BACK IN ORDER. WE HEAD SOUTH, JUST AS PLANNED.
WE'LL BURY THE DEAD AT THE ENCAMPMENT.
YES, COMMANDER!
NO... IT CAN'T BE. THE WOMAN'S NOT CRYING, IS SHE?
RUN UP A SIGNAL FLAG! GET THE FLOTILLA BACK INTO FORMATION!
ウオオー

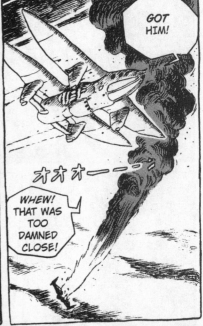

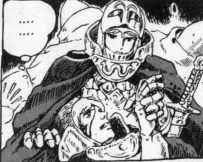

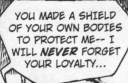

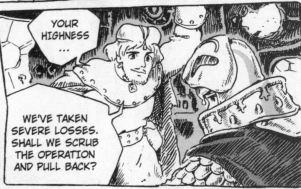

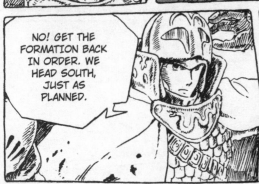

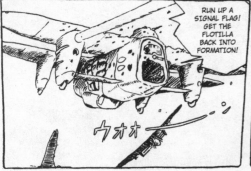

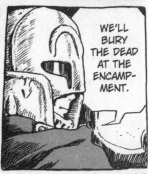

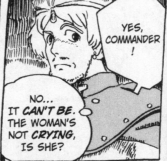

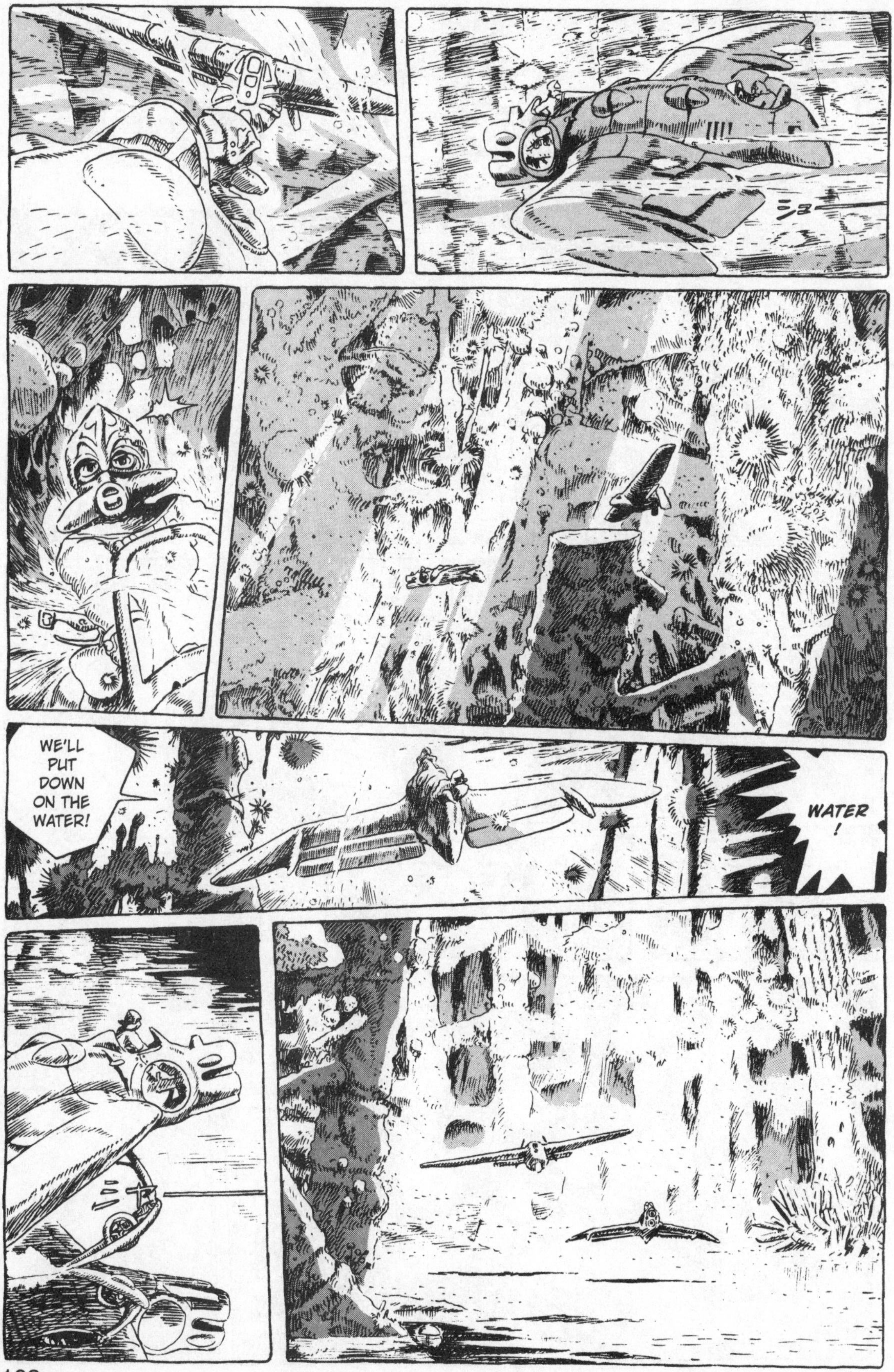
WATER!
WE'LL PUT DOWN ON THE WATER!

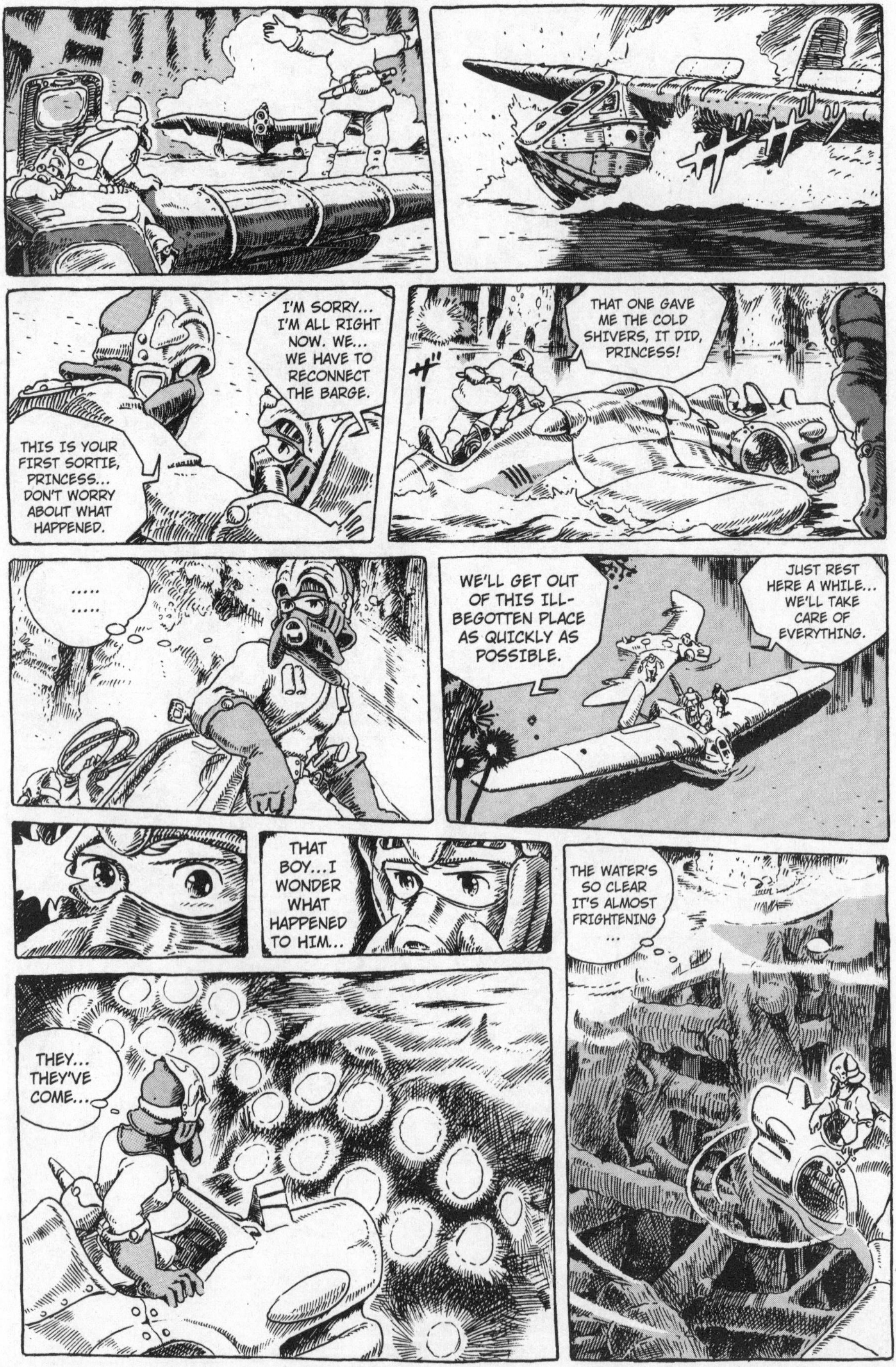
THAT ONE GAVE ME THE COLD SHIVERS, IT DID, PRINCESS!
I'M SORRY... I'M ALL RIGHT NOW. WE... WE HAVE TO RECONNECT THE BARGE.
THIS IS YOUR FIRST SORTIE, PRINCESS... DON'T WORRY ABOUT WHAT HAPPENED.
JUST REST HERE A WHILE... WE'LL TAKE CARE OF EVERYTHING.
WE'LL GET OUT OF THIS ILL-BEGOTTEN PLACE AS QUICKLY AS POSSIBLE.
..... .....
THE WATER'S SO CLEAR IT'S ALMOST FRIGHTENING ...
THAT BOY...I WONDER WHAT HAPPENED TO HIM...
THEY... THEY'VE COME...

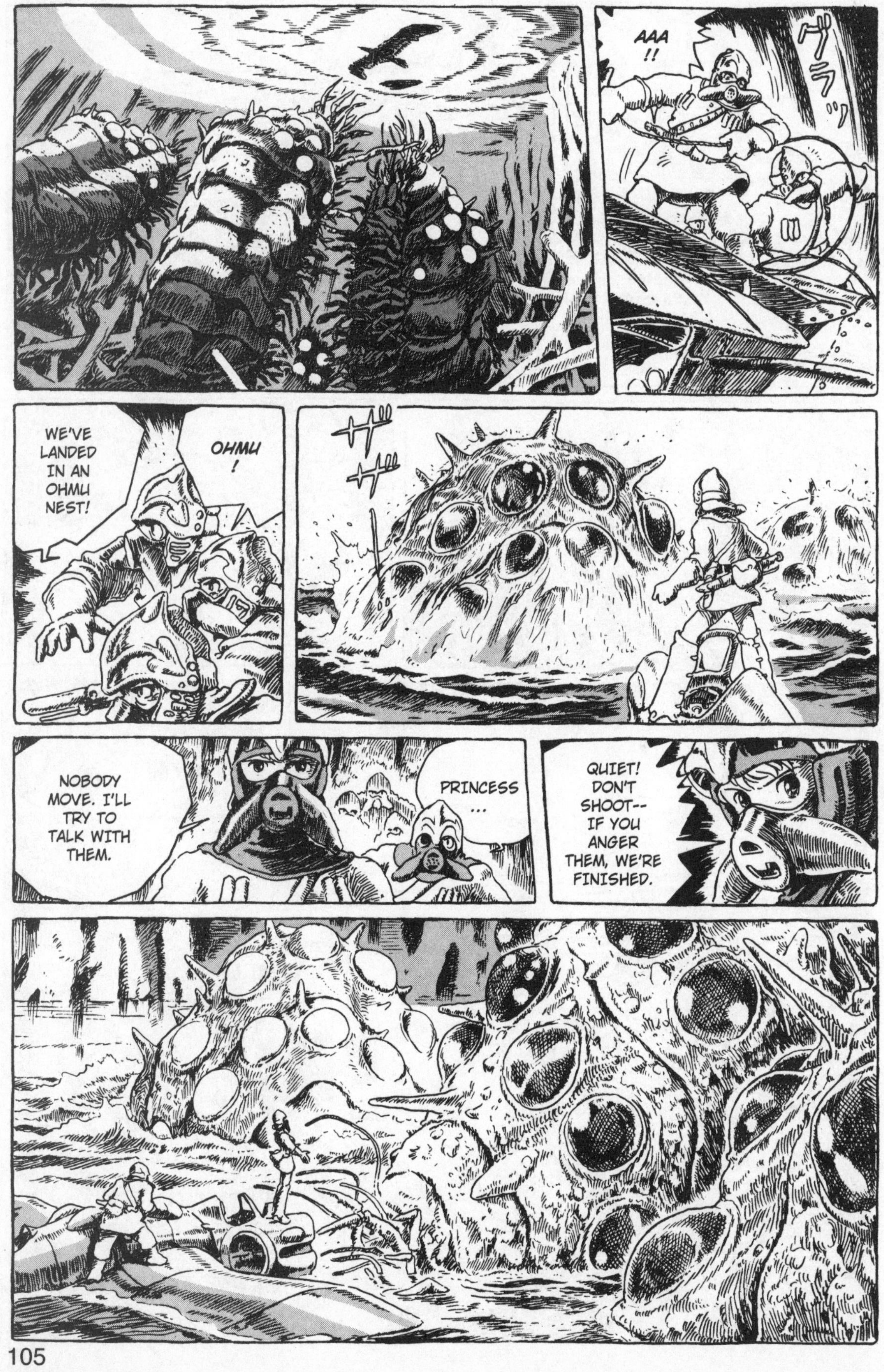
AAA !!
グラッ
OHMU !
WE'VE LANDED IN AN OHMU NEST!
QUIET! DON'T SHOOT-- IF YOU ANGER THEM, WE'RE FINISHED.
PRINCESS ...
NOBODY MOVE. I'LL TRY TO TALK WITH THEM.

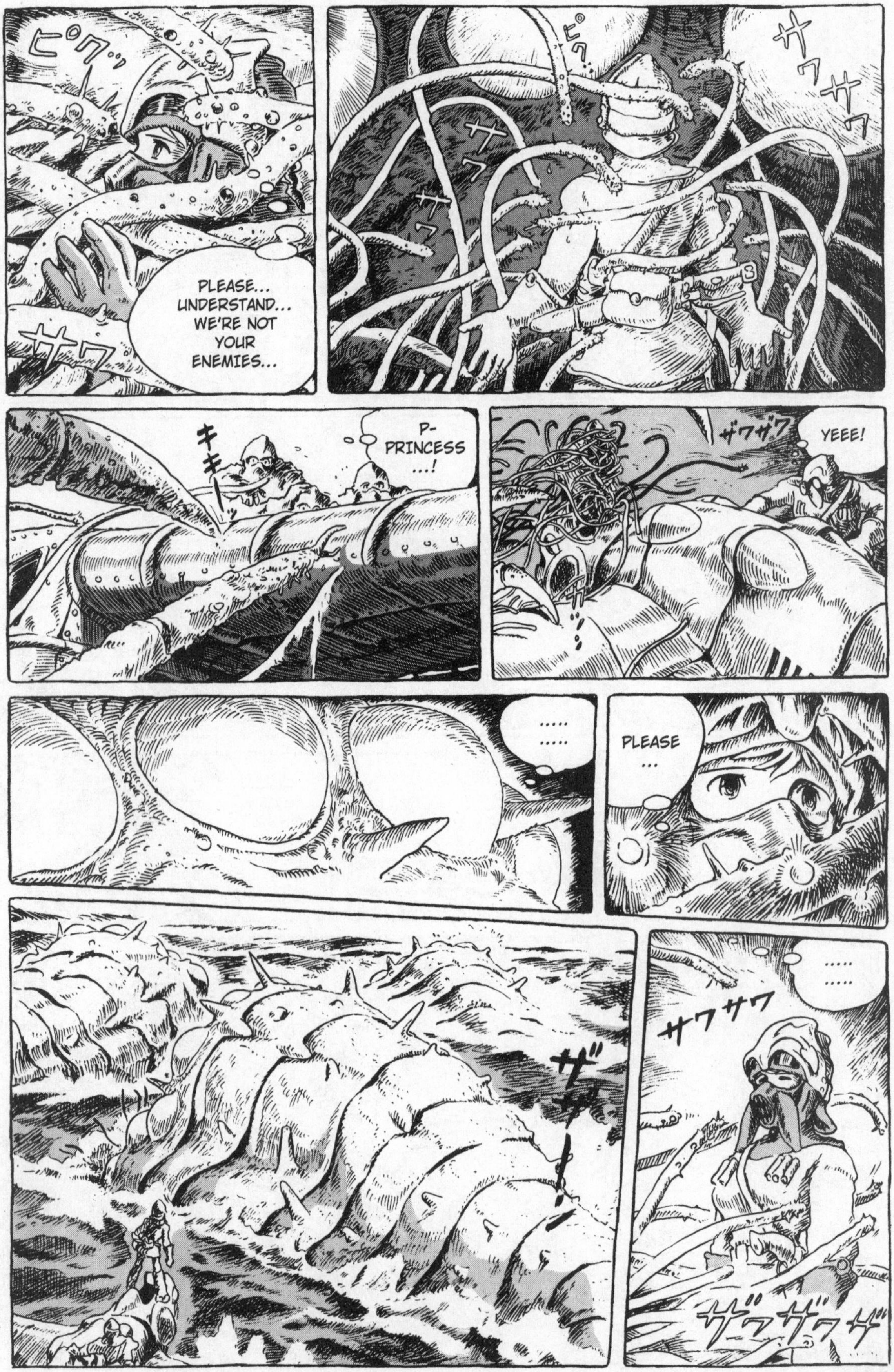
ザワザワ
ピク
ザワザワ
ピクッ
PLEASE... UNDERSTAND... WE'RE NOT YOUR ENEMIES...
ザワ
ザワザワ
YEEE!
P- PRINCESS ...!
キキー
PLEASE ...
.....
.....
.....
.....
サワサワ
ザワザワザ
ザザー

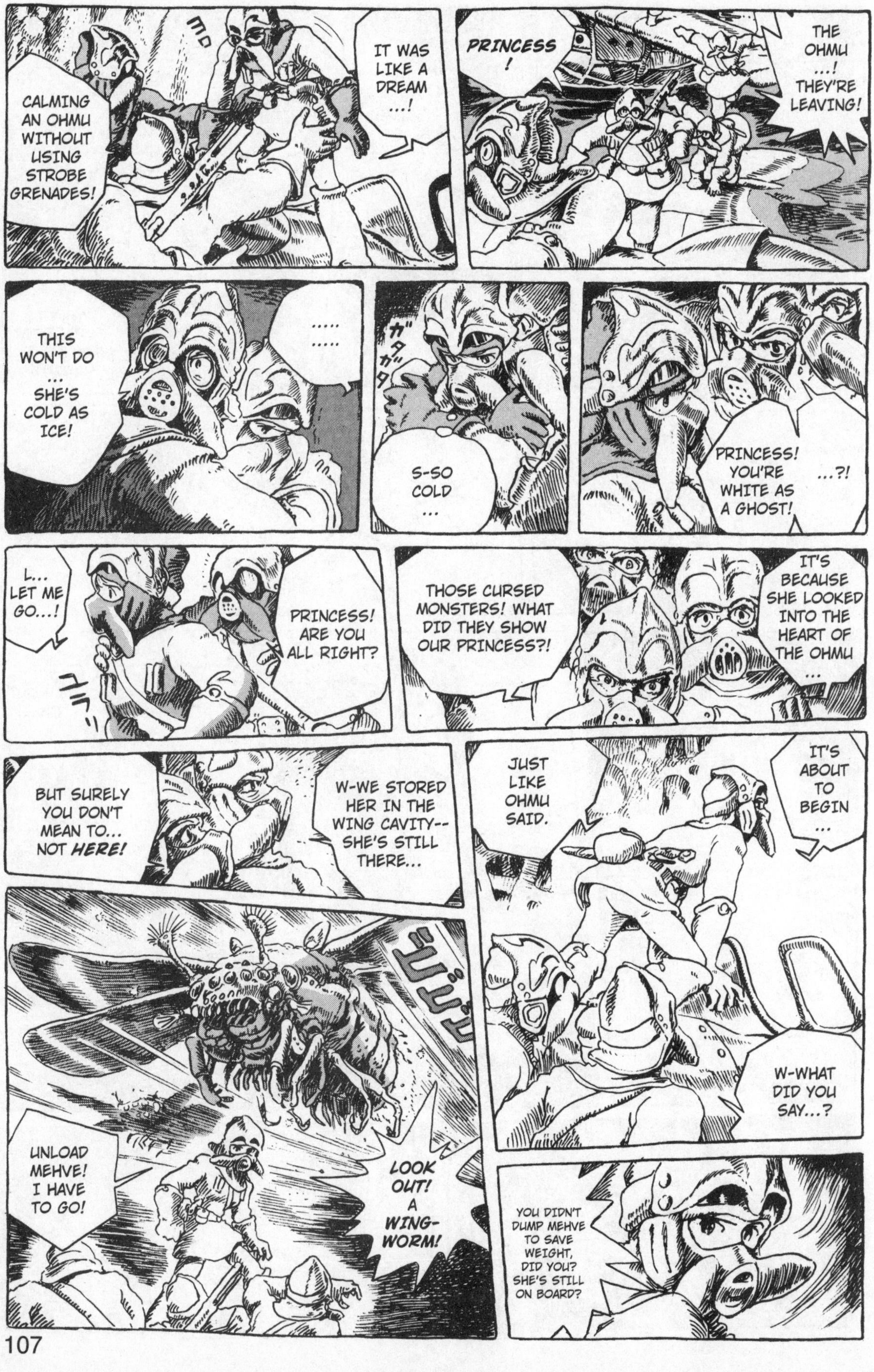

THE OHMU ...! THEY'RE LEAVING!
PRINCESS !
IT WAS LIKE A DREAM ...!
CALMING AN OHMU WITHOUT USING STROBE GRENADES!
...?!
PRINCESS! YOU'RE WHITE AS A GHOST!
S-SO COLD ...
..... .....
THIS WON'T DO ... SHE'S COLD AS ICE!
IT'S BECAUSE SHE LOOKED INTO THE HEART OF THE OHMU ...
THOSE CURSED MONSTERS! WHAT DID THEY SHOW OUR PRINCESS?!
PRINCESS! ARE YOU ALL RIGHT?
L... LET ME GO...!
YOU DIDN'T DUMP MEHVE TO SAVE WEIGHT, DID YOU? SHE'S STILL ON BOARD?
W-WE STORED HER IN THE WING CAVITY-- SHE'S STILL THERE...
BUT SURELY YOU DON'T MEAN TO... NOT *HERE!*
IT'S ABOUT TO BEGIN ...
JUST LIKE OHMU SAID.
W-WHAT DID YOU SAY...?
LOOK OUT! A *WING-WORM!*
UNLOAD MEHVE! I HAVE TO GO!

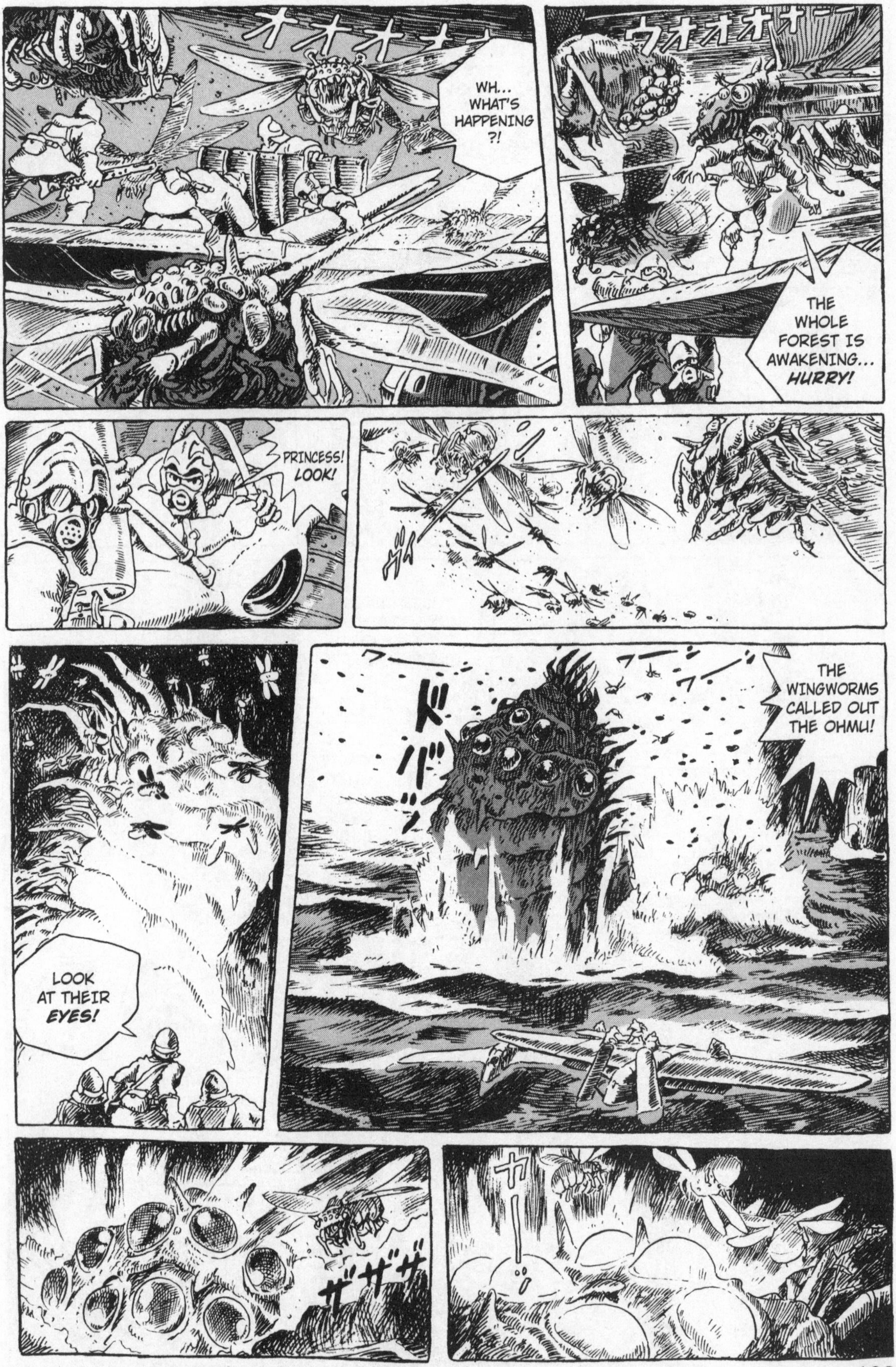
ウオオオオー
THE WHOLE FOREST IS AWAKENING... ***HURRY!***
オオオオオ
WH... WHAT'S HAPPENING ?!
PRINCESS! ***LOOK!***
THE WINGWORMS CALLED OUT THE OHMU!
LOOK AT THEIR ***EYES!***
ザザザ

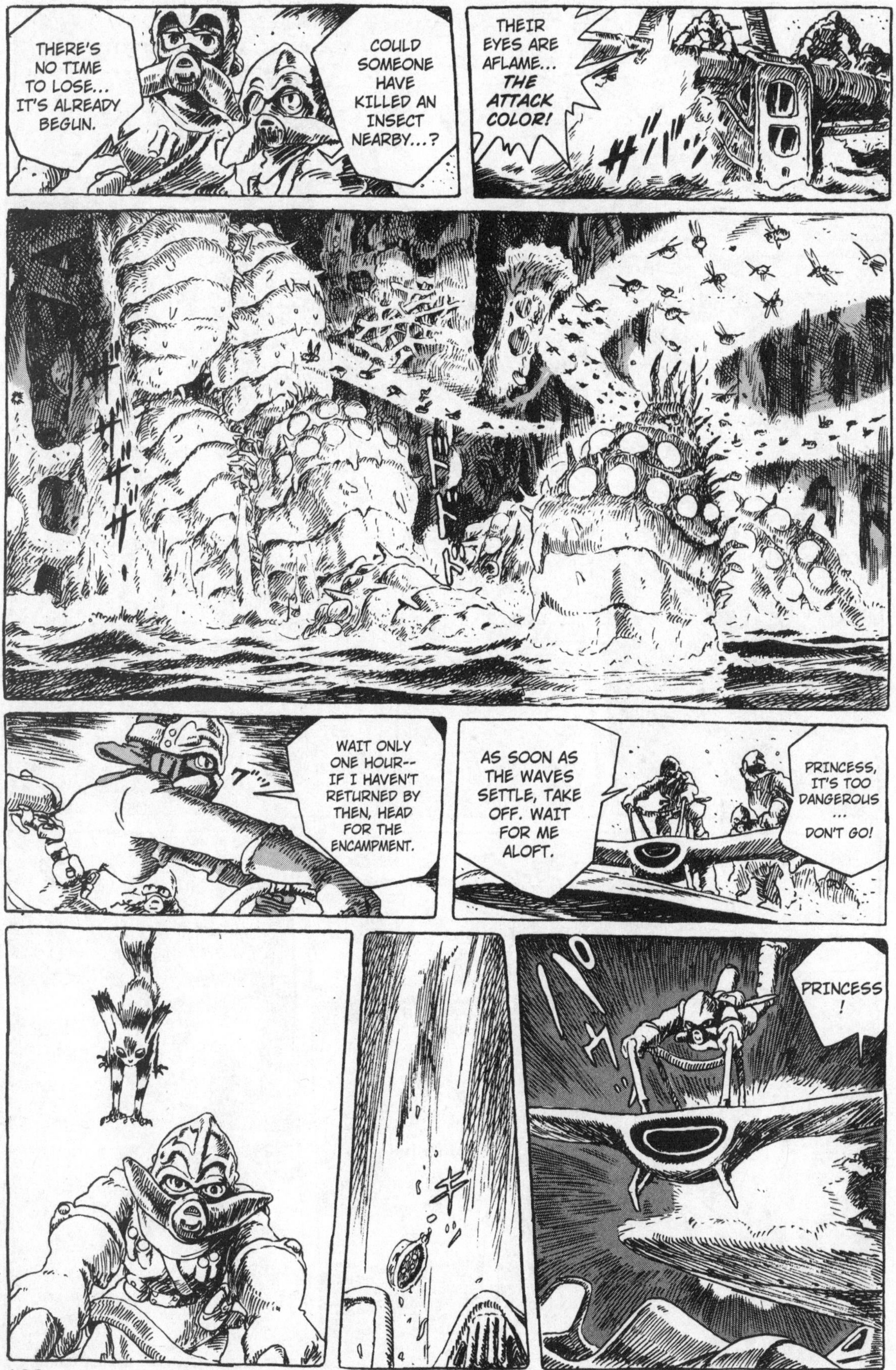
THEIR EYES ARE AFLAME... THE ATTACK COLOR!
COULD SOMEONE HAVE KILLED AN INSECT NEARBY...?
THERE'S NO TIME TO LOSE... IT'S ALREADY BEGUN.
PRINCESS, IT'S TOO DANGEROUS ... DON'T GO!
AS SOON AS THE WAVES SETTLE, TAKE OFF. WAIT FOR ME ALOFT.
WAIT ONLY ONE HOUR-- IF I HAVEN'T RETURNED BY THEN, HEAD FOR THE ENCAMPMENT.
PRINCESS !

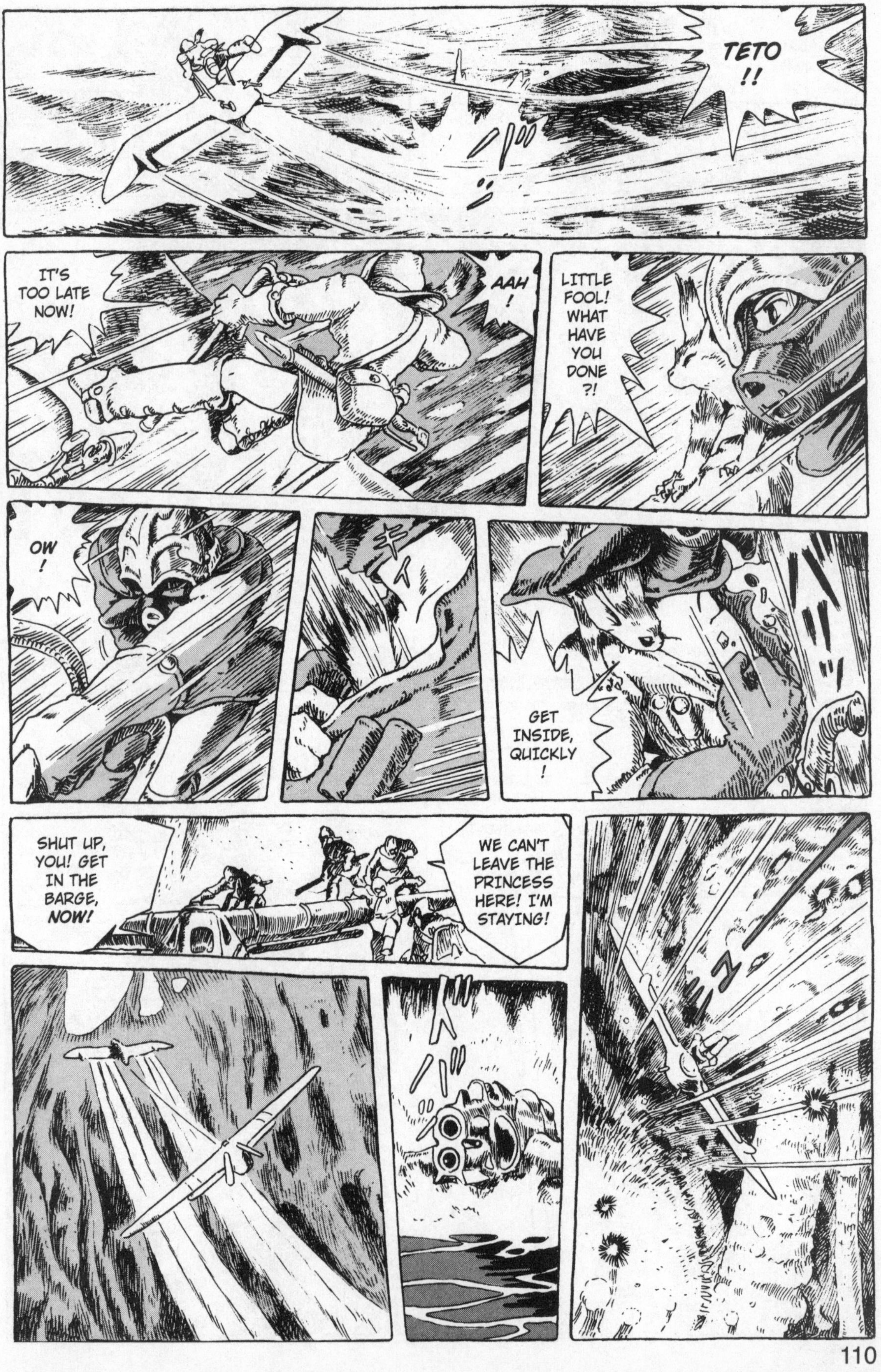
TETO !!
LITTLE FOOL! WHAT HAVE YOU DONE ?!
AAH !
IT'S TOO LATE NOW!
GET INSIDE, QUICKLY !
OW !
WE CAN'T LEAVE THE PRINCESS HERE! I'M STAYING!
SHUT UP, YOU! GET IN THE BARGE, NOW!

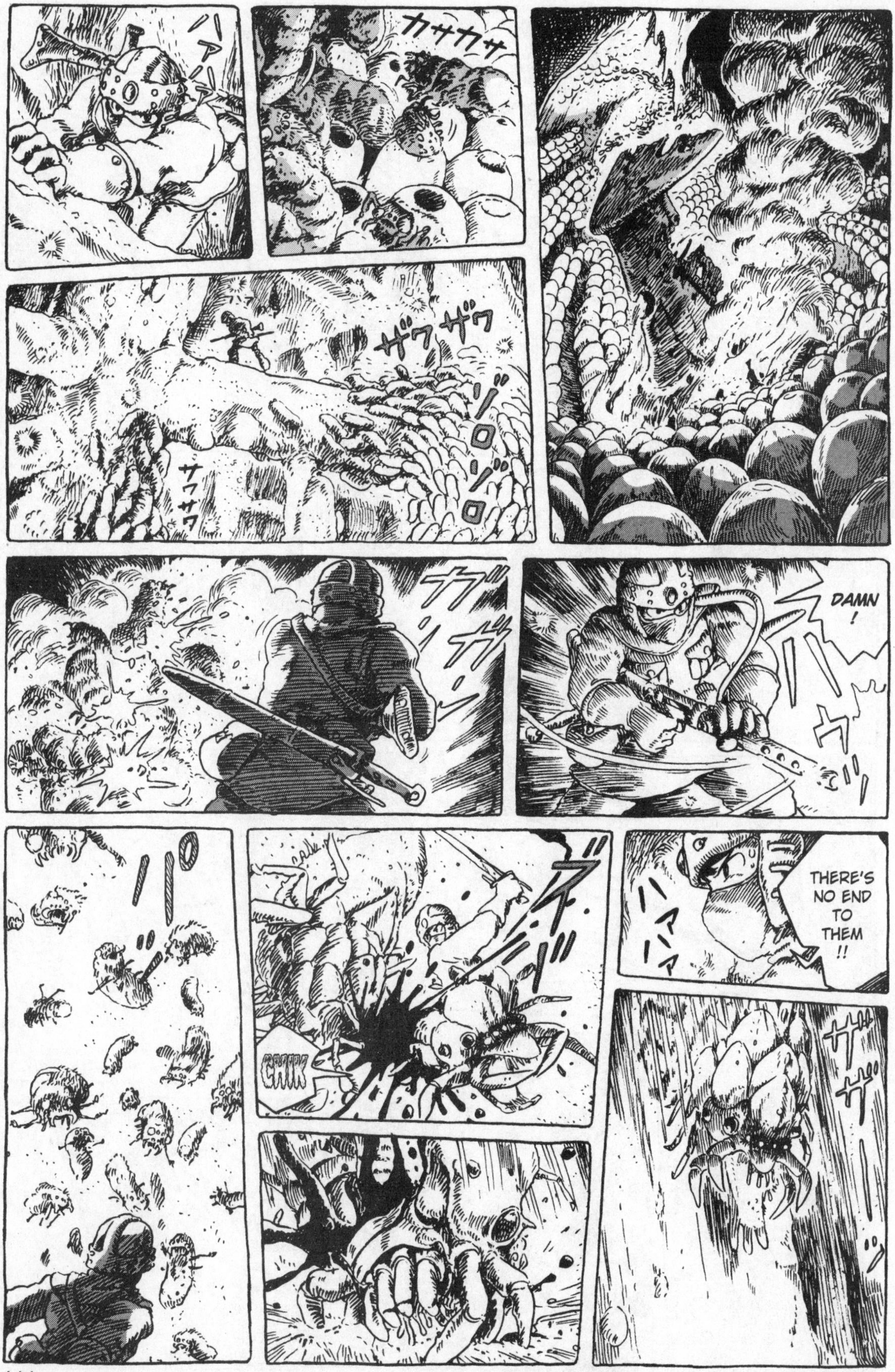
カサカサ
ザワザワ
ゾロゾロ
サワサワ
DAMN!
THERE'S NO END TO THEM!!
CHIK

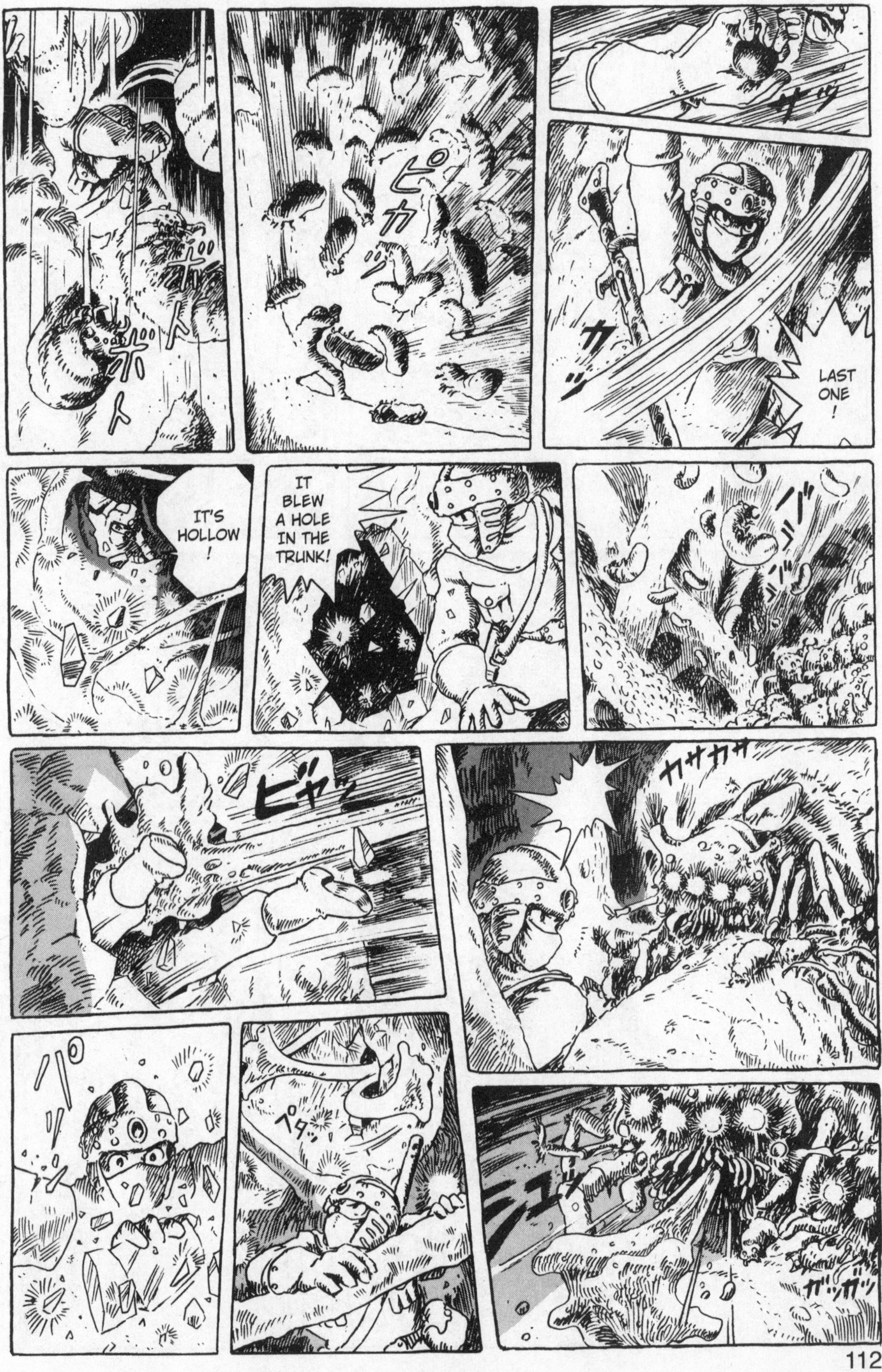
LAST ONE !
IT BLEW A HOLE IN THE TRUNK!
IT'S HOLLOW !

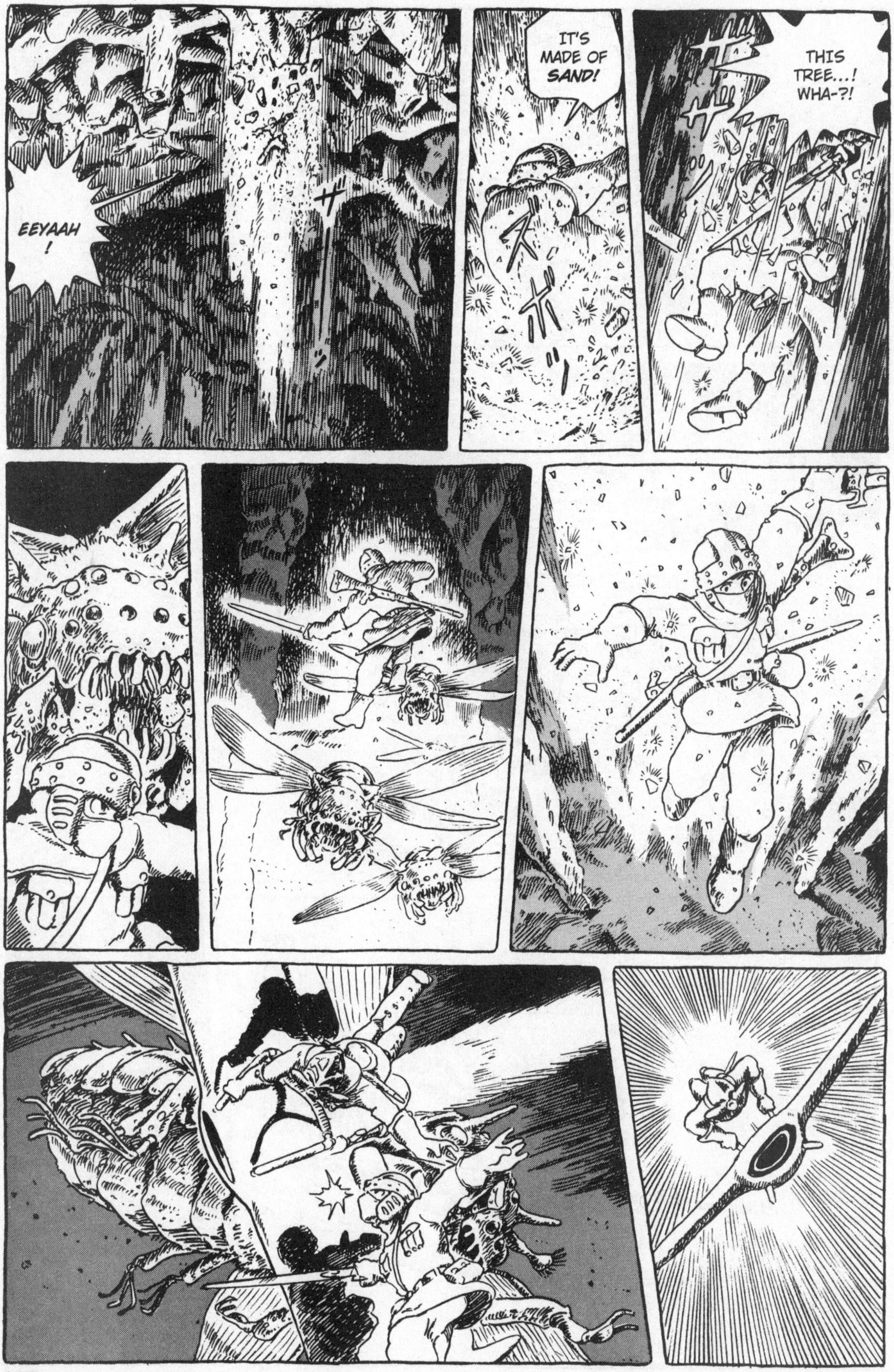
THIS TREE...! WHA-?!
IT'S MADE OF SAND!
EEYAAH!

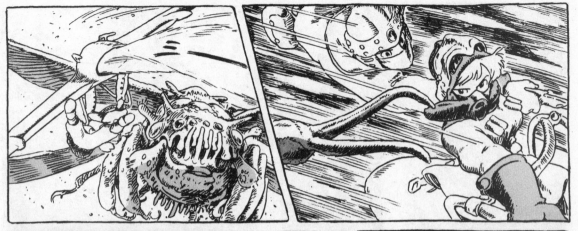

SHE CAN'T HANDLE TWO PEOPLE!

QUICKLY!

THERE'S A WORM-FLUTE IN MY POUCH-- GET IT OUT!

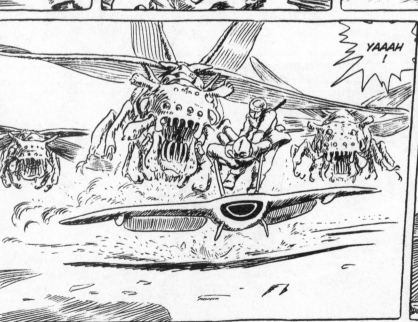

YAAAH!

THIS STONE ...!

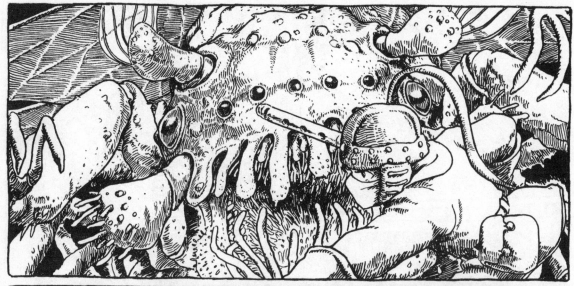

STOP! DON'T USE YOUR GUN!!

DAMN IT!

WHY DID YOU DO *THAT*?!

HOLD ON! I'M GOING TO VERTICAL THRUST!

UHKK!

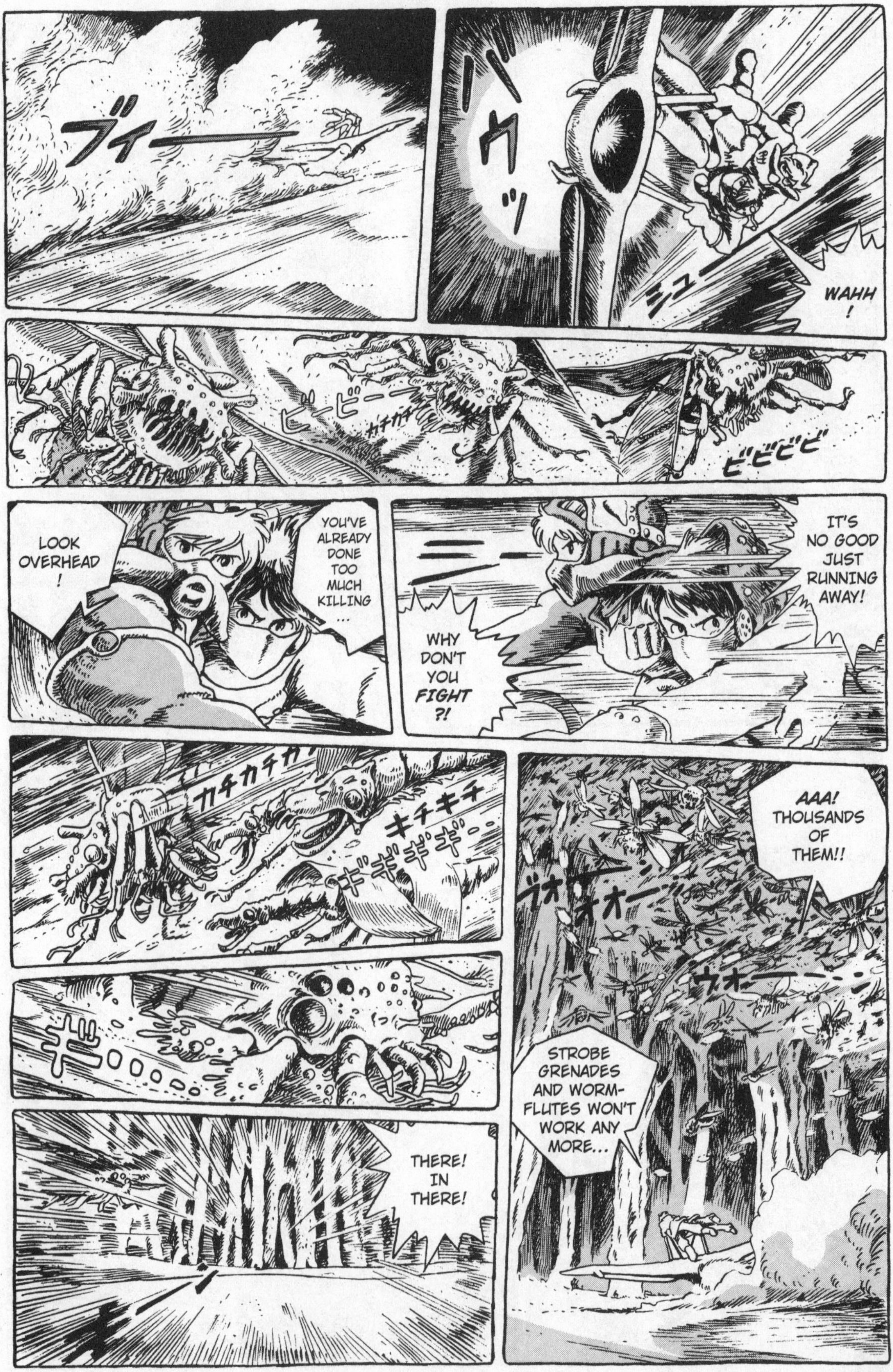

ハウッ
シュー
WAHH!
ブィー
ビビビビ
ビービー
カチカチ
IT'S NO GOOD JUST RUNNING AWAY!
WHY DON'T YOU *FIGHT*?!
LOOK OVERHEAD!
YOU'VE ALREADY DONE TOO MUCH KILLING...
*AAA!* THOUSANDS OF THEM!!
ヴォオー
ウォー
STROBE GRENADES AND WORM-FLUTES WON'T WORK ANY MORE...
カチカチカ
キチキチ
ギギギー
THERE! IN THERE!

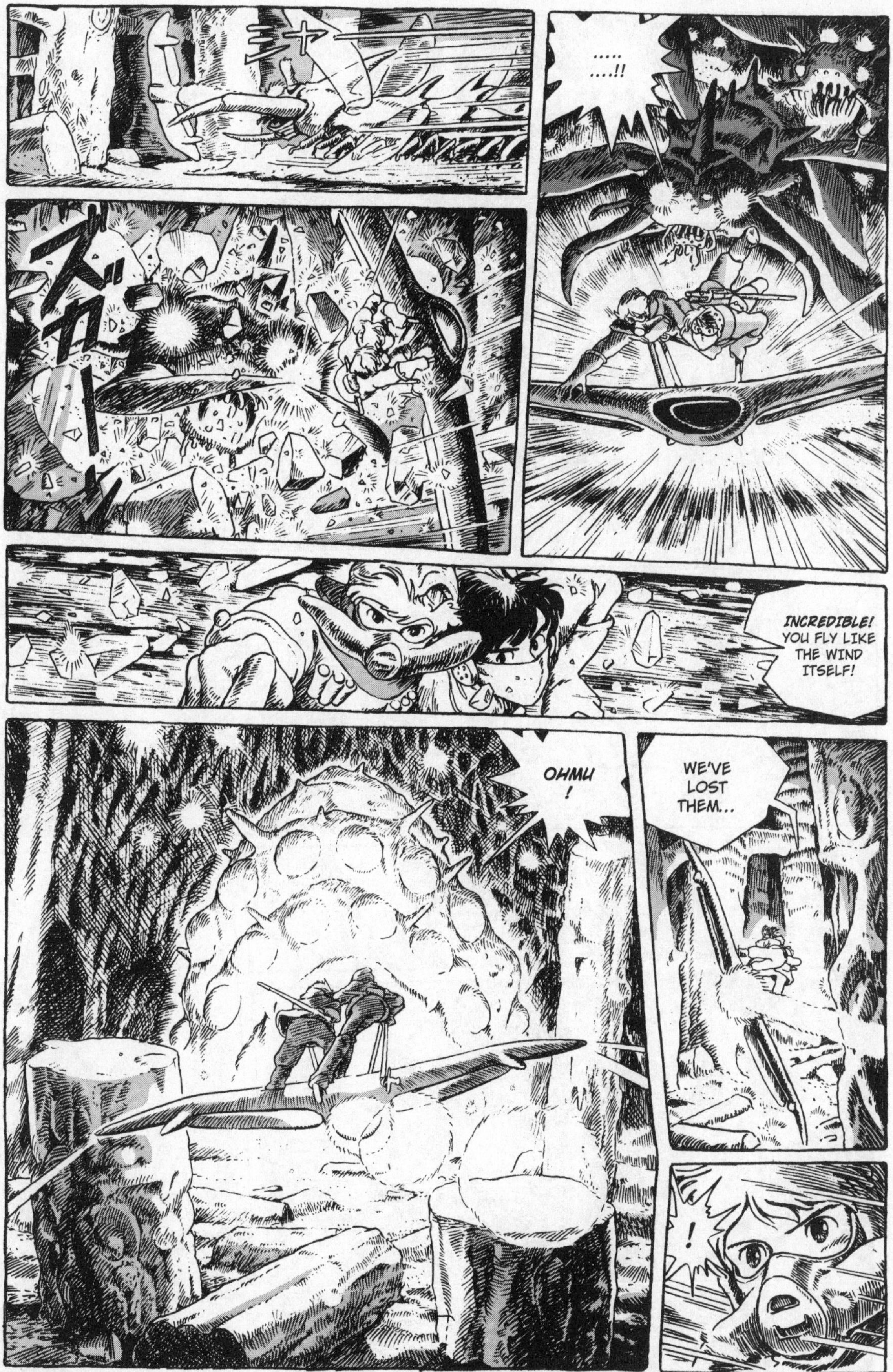
.....
....!!
INCREDIBLE! YOU FLY LIKE THE WIND ITSELF!
WE'VE LOST THEM...
!
OHMU !

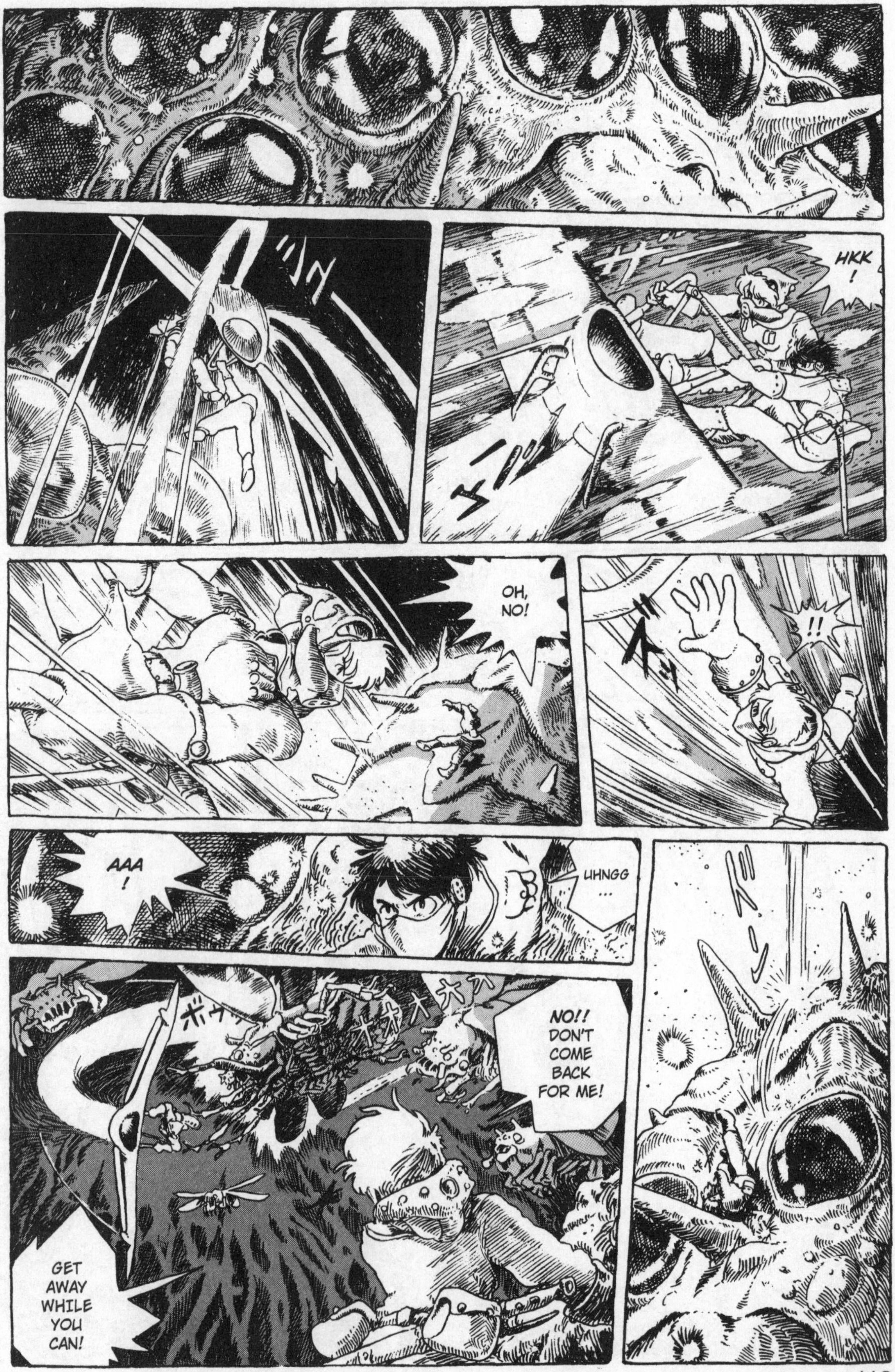
HKK !
!!
OH, NO!
UHNGG ...
AAA !
NO!! DON'T COME BACK FOR ME!
GET AWAY WHILE YOU CAN!

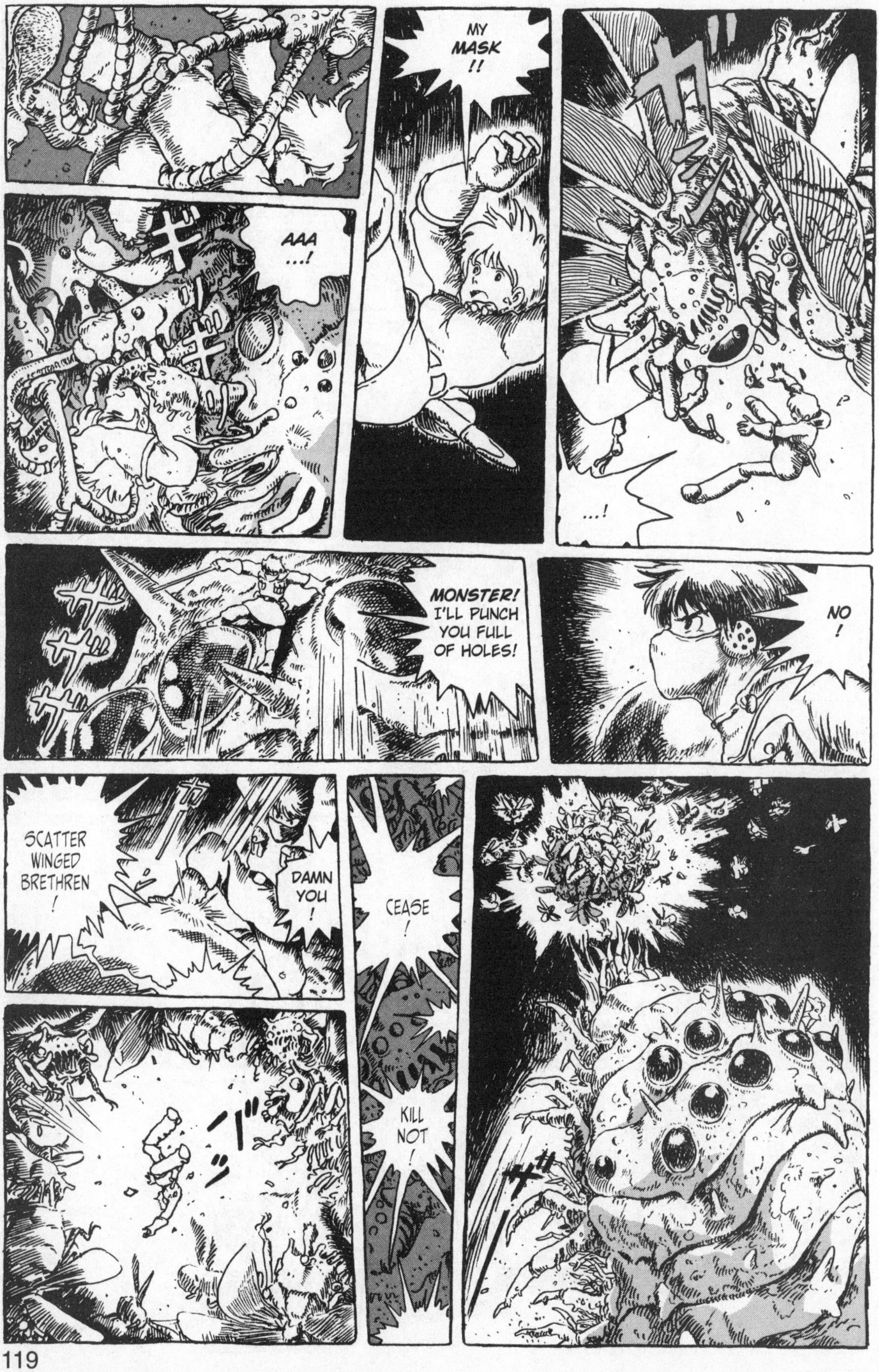

...!
MY MASK !!
AAA ...!
NO !
MONSTER! I'LL PUNCH YOU FULL OF HOLES!
CEASE !
KILL NOT !
DAMN YOU !
SCATTER WINGED BRETHREN !

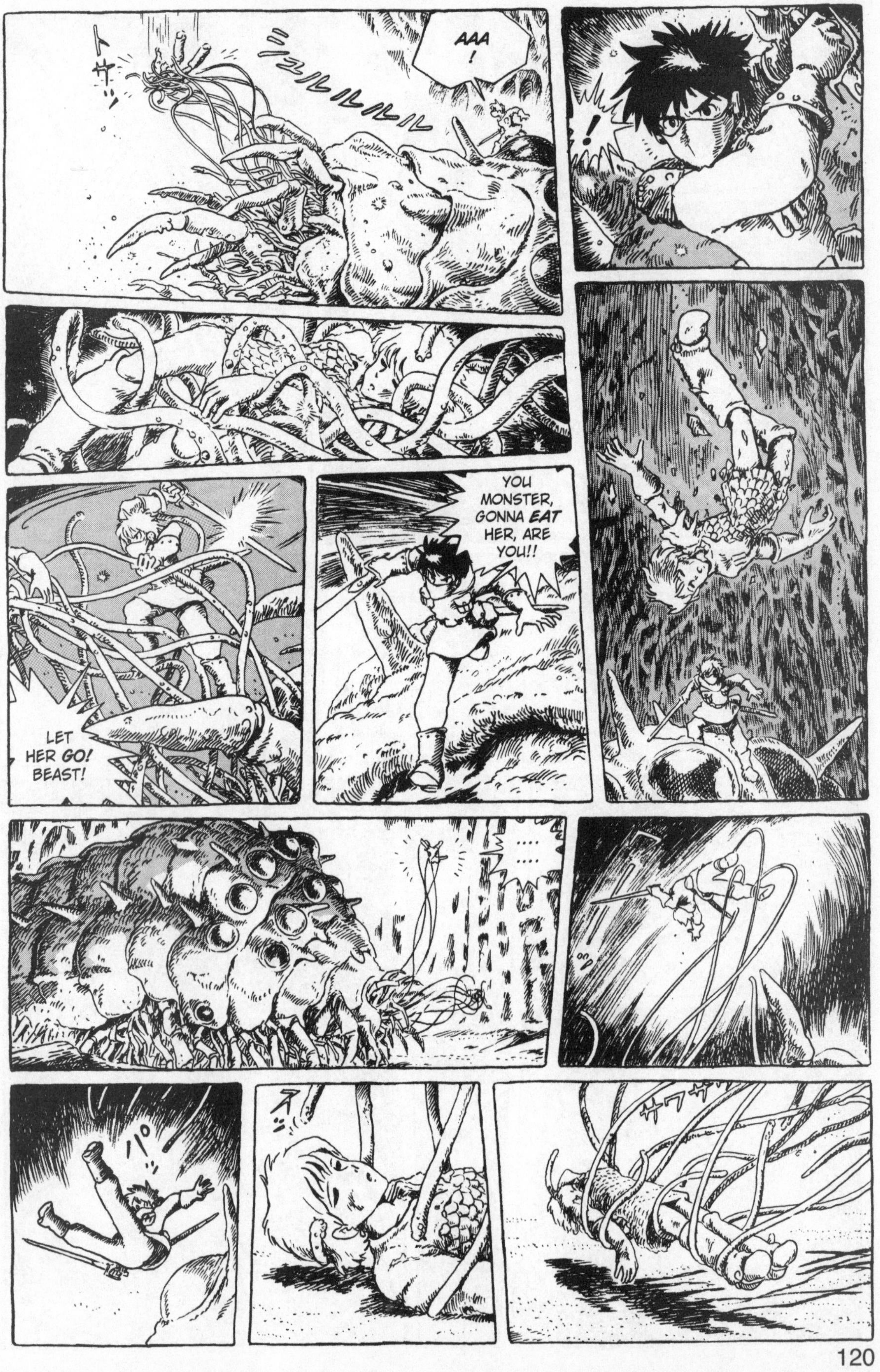
AAA!
YOU MONSTER, GONNA EAT HER, ARE YOU!!
LET HER GO! BEAST!
....
....

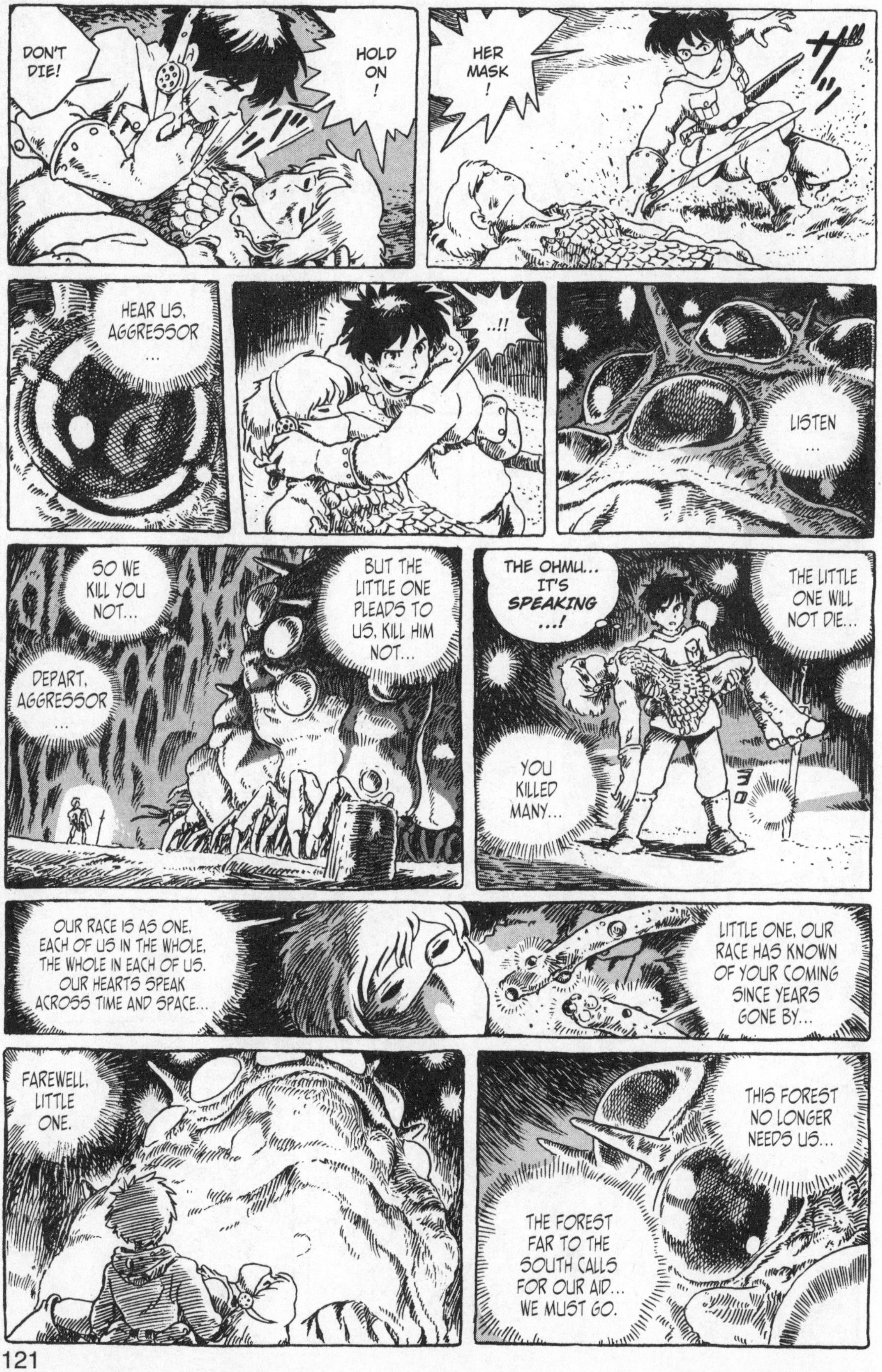
HER MASK!
HOLD ON!
DON'T DIE!
LISTEN...
..!!
HEAR US, AGGRESSOR...
THE LITTLE ONE WILL NOT DIE...
THE OHMU... IT'S SPEAKING...!
YOU KILLED MANY...
BUT THE LITTLE ONE PLEADS TO US, KILL HIM NOT...
SO WE KILL YOU NOT...
DEPART, AGGRESSOR...
LITTLE ONE, OUR RACE HAS KNOWN OF YOUR COMING SINCE YEARS GONE BY...
OUR RACE IS AS ONE, EACH OF US IN THE WHOLE, THE WHOLE IN EACH OF US. OUR HEARTS SPEAK ACROSS TIME AND SPACE...
THIS FOREST NO LONGER NEEDS US...
THE FOREST FAR TO THE SOUTH CALLS FOR OUR AID... WE MUST GO.
FAREWELL, LITTLE ONE.

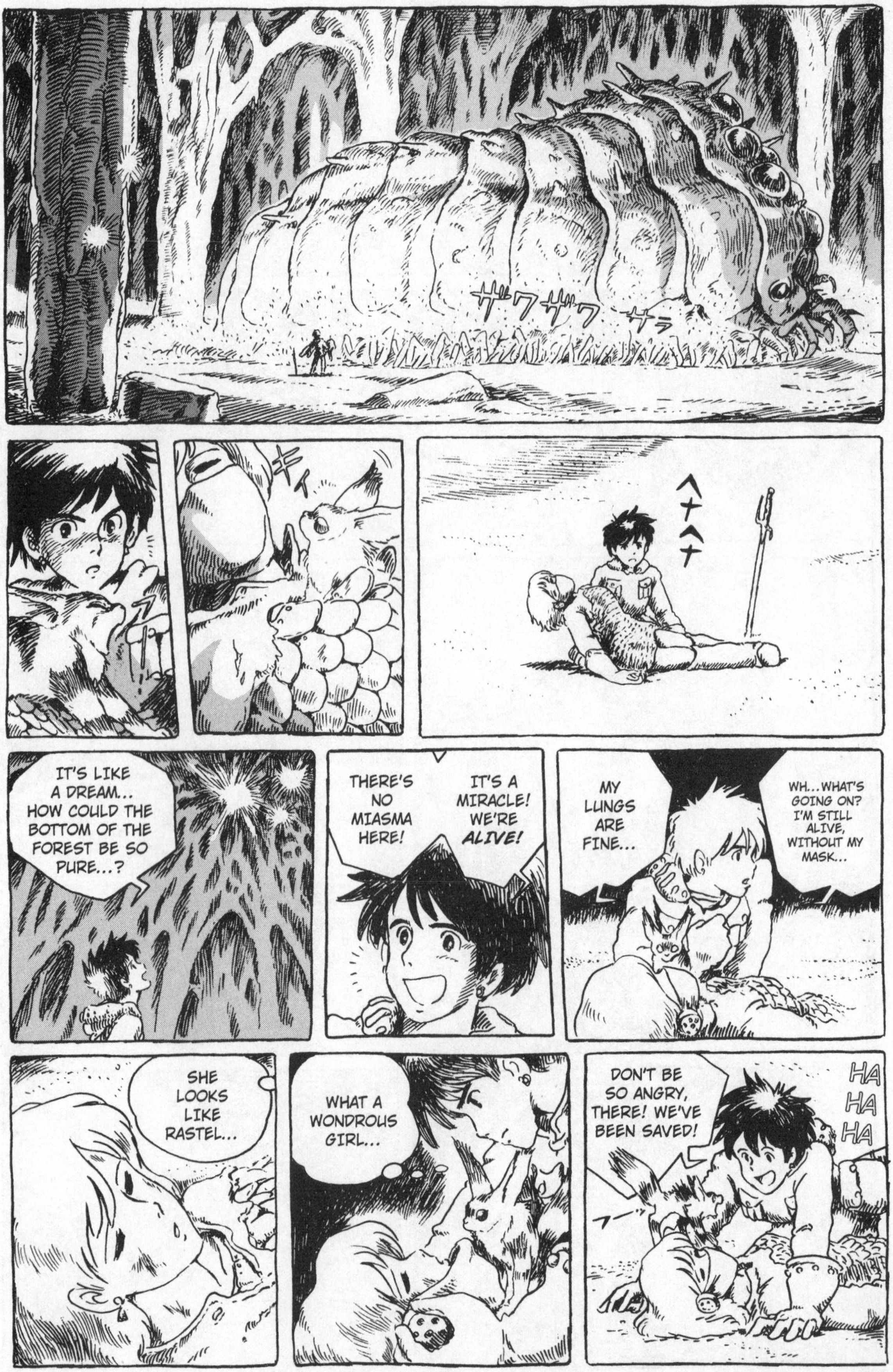
ザワザワ
サラ
ヘナヘナ
キィ
WH...WHAT'S GOING ON? I'M STILL ALIVE, WITHOUT MY MASK...
MY LUNGS ARE FINE...
IT'S A MIRACLE! WE'RE *ALIVE!*
THERE'S NO MIASMA HERE!
IT'S LIKE A DREAM... HOW COULD THE BOTTOM OF THE FOREST BE SO PURE...?
HA HA HA
DON'T BE SO ANGRY, THERE! WE'VE BEEN SAVED!
フーッ
WHAT A WONDROUS GIRL...
SHE LOOKS LIKE RASTEL...

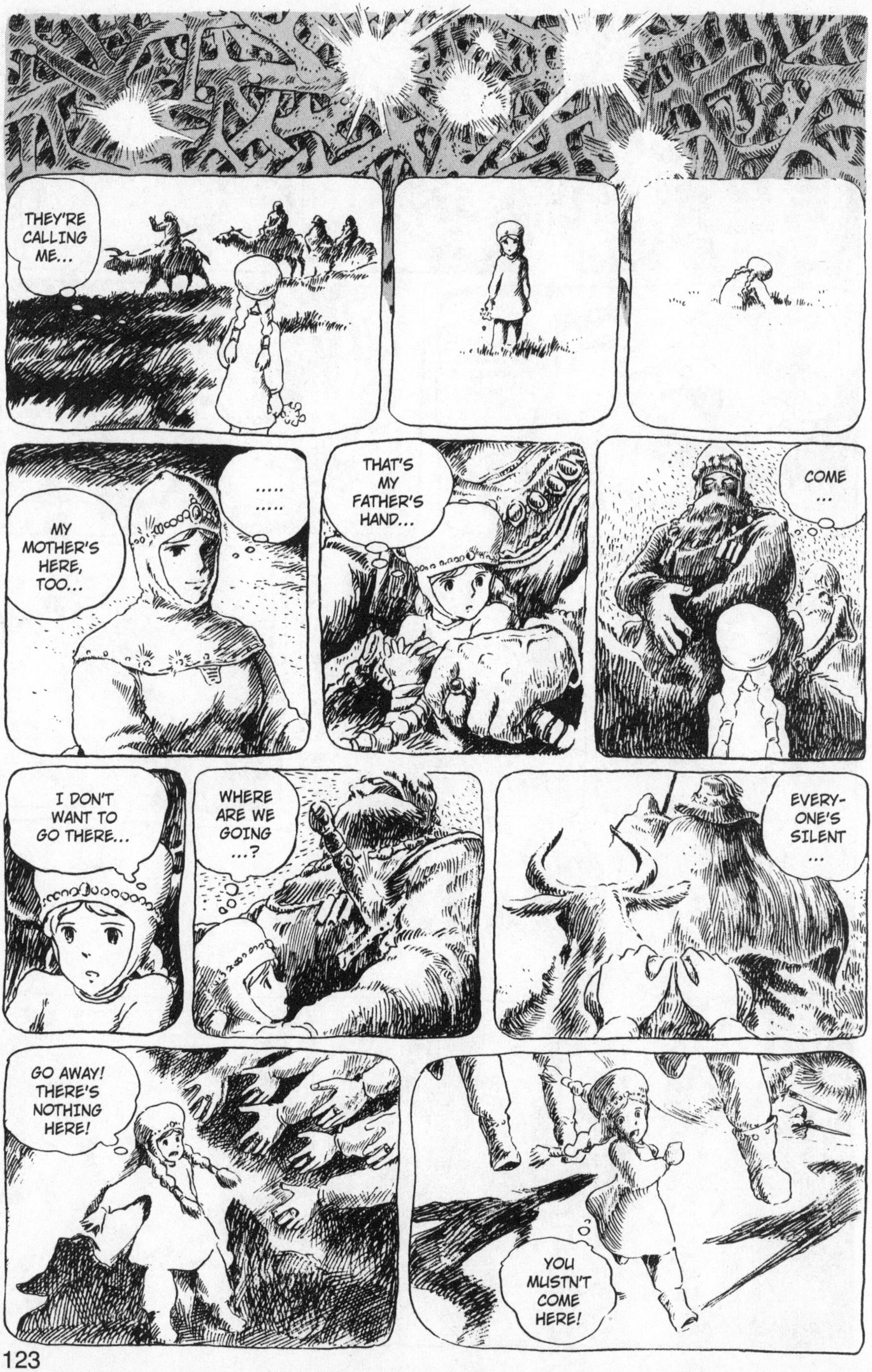
THEY'RE CALLING ME...
COME ...
THAT'S MY FATHER'S HAND...
..... .....
MY MOTHER'S HERE, TOO...
EVERY-ONE'S SILENT ...
WHERE ARE WE GOING ...?
I DON'T WANT TO GO THERE...
YOU MUSTN'T COME HERE!
GO AWAY! THERE'S NOTHING HERE!

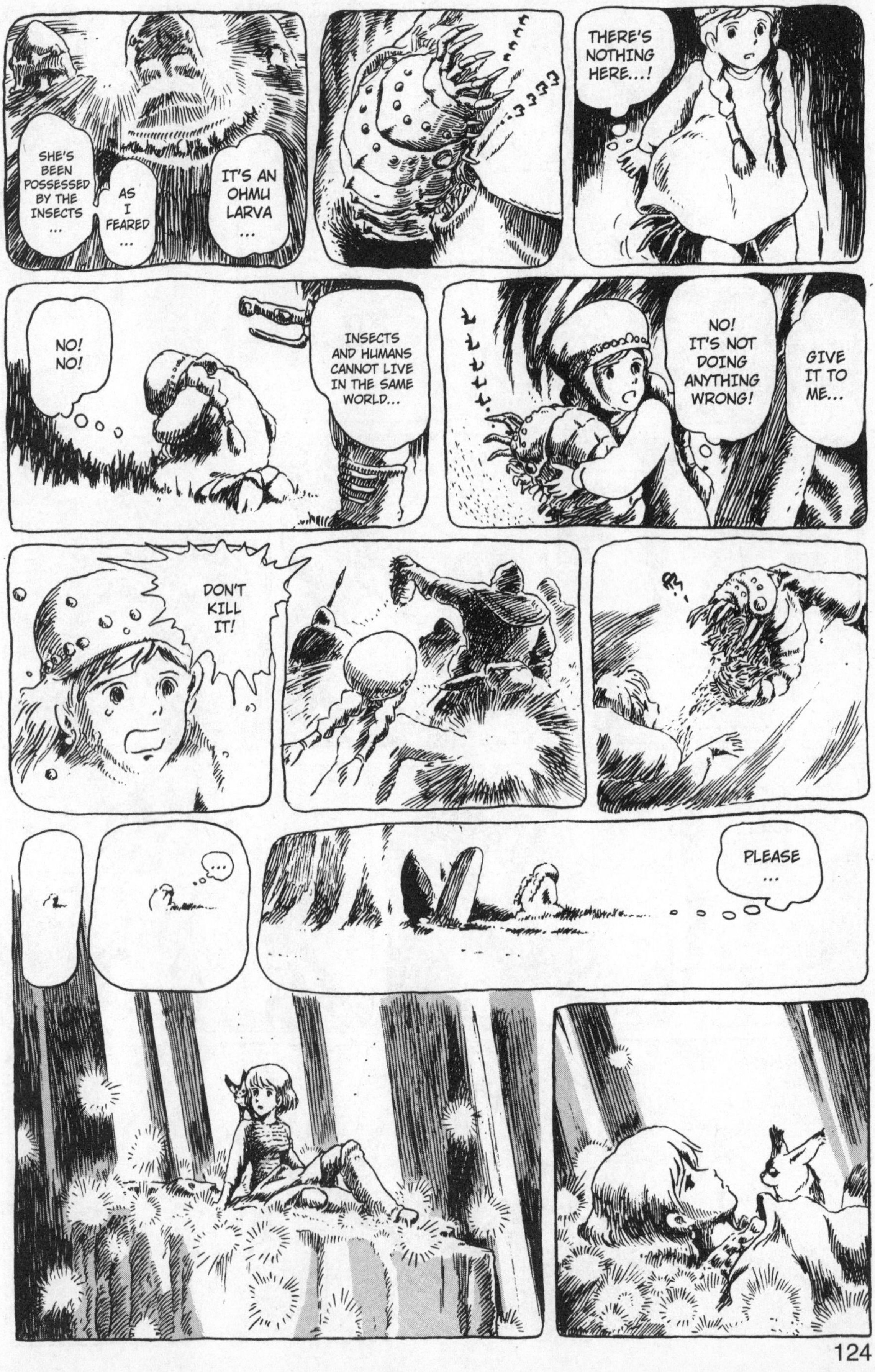
THERE'S NOTHING HERE...!
IT'S AN OHMU LARVA ...
AS I FEARED ...
SHE'S BEEN POSSESSED BY THE INSECTS ...
GIVE IT TO ME...
NO! IT'S NOT DOING ANYTHING WRONG!
INSECTS AND HUMANS CANNOT LIVE IN THE SAME WORLD...
NO! NO!
DON'T KILL IT!
PLEASE ...
...

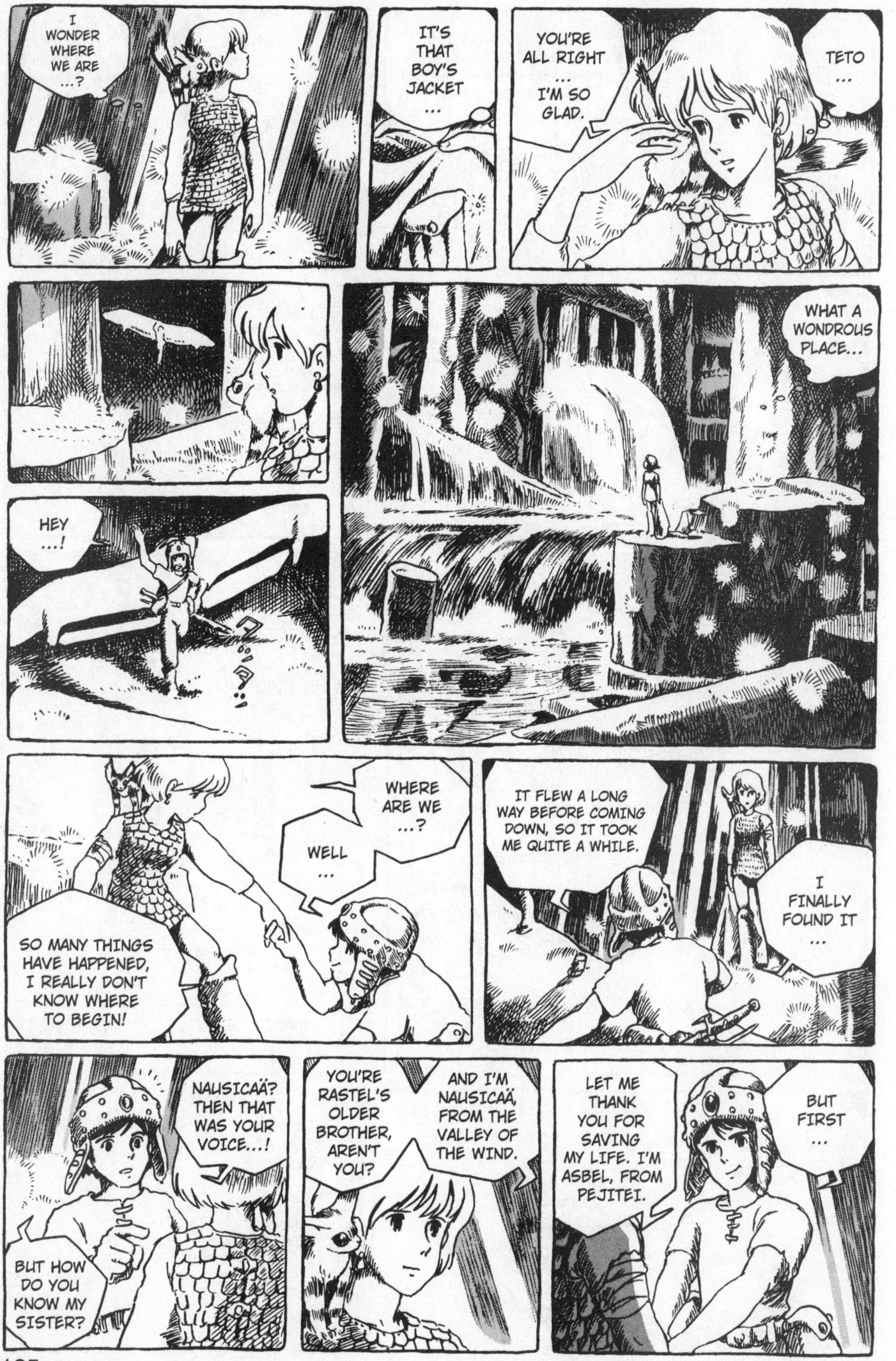
TETO ...
YOU'RE ALL RIGHT ... I'M SO GLAD.
IT'S THAT BOY'S JACKET ...
I WONDER WHERE WE ARE ...?
WHAT A WONDROUS PLACE...
HEY ...!
I FINALLY FOUND IT ...
IT FLEW A LONG WAY BEFORE COMING DOWN, SO IT TOOK ME QUITE A WHILE.
WHERE ARE WE ...?
WELL ...
SO MANY THINGS HAVE HAPPENED, I REALLY DON'T KNOW WHERE TO BEGIN!
BUT FIRST ...
LET ME THANK YOU FOR SAVING MY LIFE. I'M ASBEL, FROM PEJITEI.
YOU'RE RASTEL'S OLDER BROTHER, AREN'T YOU?
AND I'M NAUSICAÄ, FROM THE VALLEY OF THE WIND.
NAUSICAÄ? THEN THAT WAS YOUR VOICE...!
BUT HOW DO YOU KNOW MY SISTER?

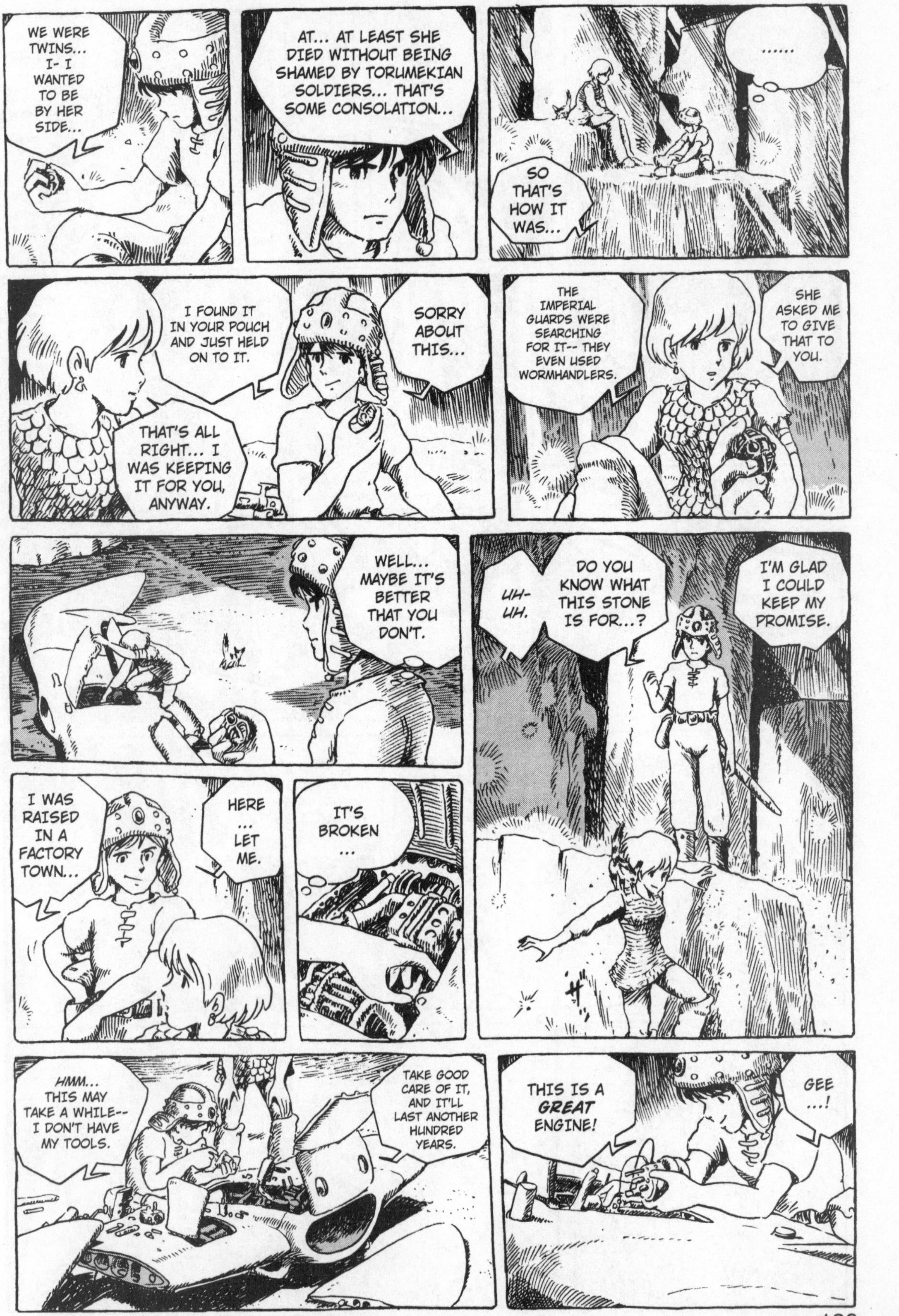
......
SO THAT'S HOW IT WAS...
AT... AT LEAST SHE DIED WITHOUT BEING SHAMED BY TORUMEKIAN SOLDIERS... THAT'S SOME CONSOLATION...
WE WERE TWINS... I- I WANTED TO BE BY HER SIDE...
SHE ASKED ME TO GIVE THAT TO YOU.
THE IMPERIAL GUARDS WERE SEARCHING FOR IT-- THEY EVEN USED WORMHANDLERS.
SORRY ABOUT THIS...
I FOUND IT IN YOUR POUCH AND JUST HELD ON TO IT.
THAT'S ALL RIGHT... I WAS KEEPING IT FOR YOU, ANYWAY.
I'M GLAD I COULD KEEP MY PROMISE.
DO YOU KNOW WHAT THIS STONE IS FOR...?
UH-UH.
WELL... MAYBE IT'S BETTER THAT YOU DON'T.
IT'S BROKEN ...
HERE ... LET ME.
I WAS RAISED IN A FACTORY TOWN...
GEE ...!
THIS IS A *GREAT* ENGINE!
TAKE GOOD CARE OF IT, AND IT'LL LAST ANOTHER HUNDRED YEARS.
*HMM...* THIS MAY TAKE A WHILE-- I DON'T HAVE MY TOOLS.

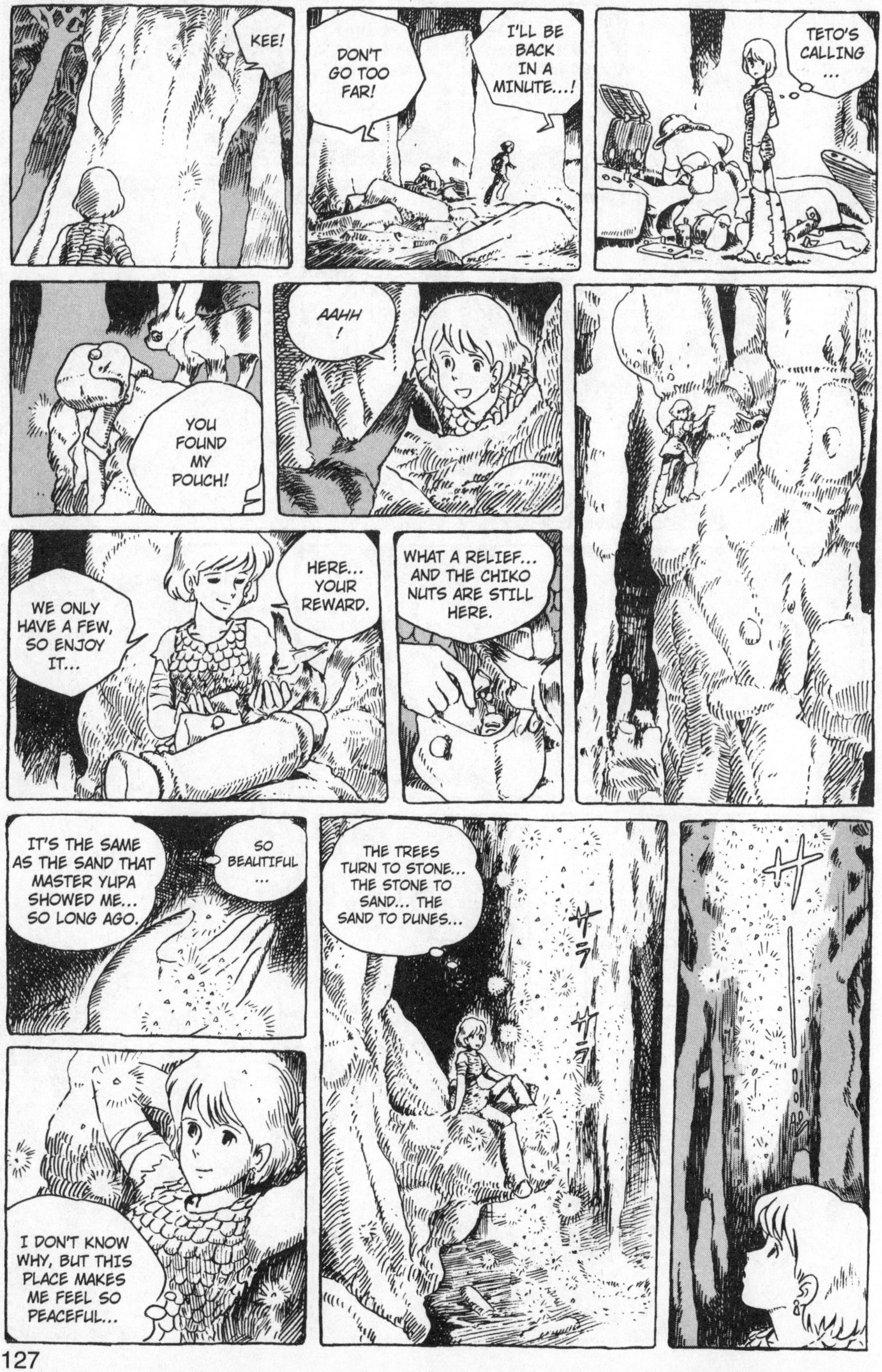

TETO'S CALLING ...
I'LL BE BACK IN A MINUTE...!
DON'T GO TOO FAR!
KEE!
AAHH!
YOU FOUND MY POUCH!
WHAT A RELIEF... AND THE CHIKO NUTS ARE STILL HERE.
HERE... YOUR REWARD.
WE ONLY HAVE A FEW, SO ENJOY IT...
THE TREES TURN TO STONE... THE STONE TO SAND... THE SAND TO DUNES...
サラ
サラ
SO BEAUTIFUL ...
IT'S THE SAME AS THE SAND THAT MASTER YUPA SHOWED ME... SO LONG AGO.
I DON'T KNOW WHY, BUT THIS PLACE MAKES ME FEEL SO PEACEFUL...

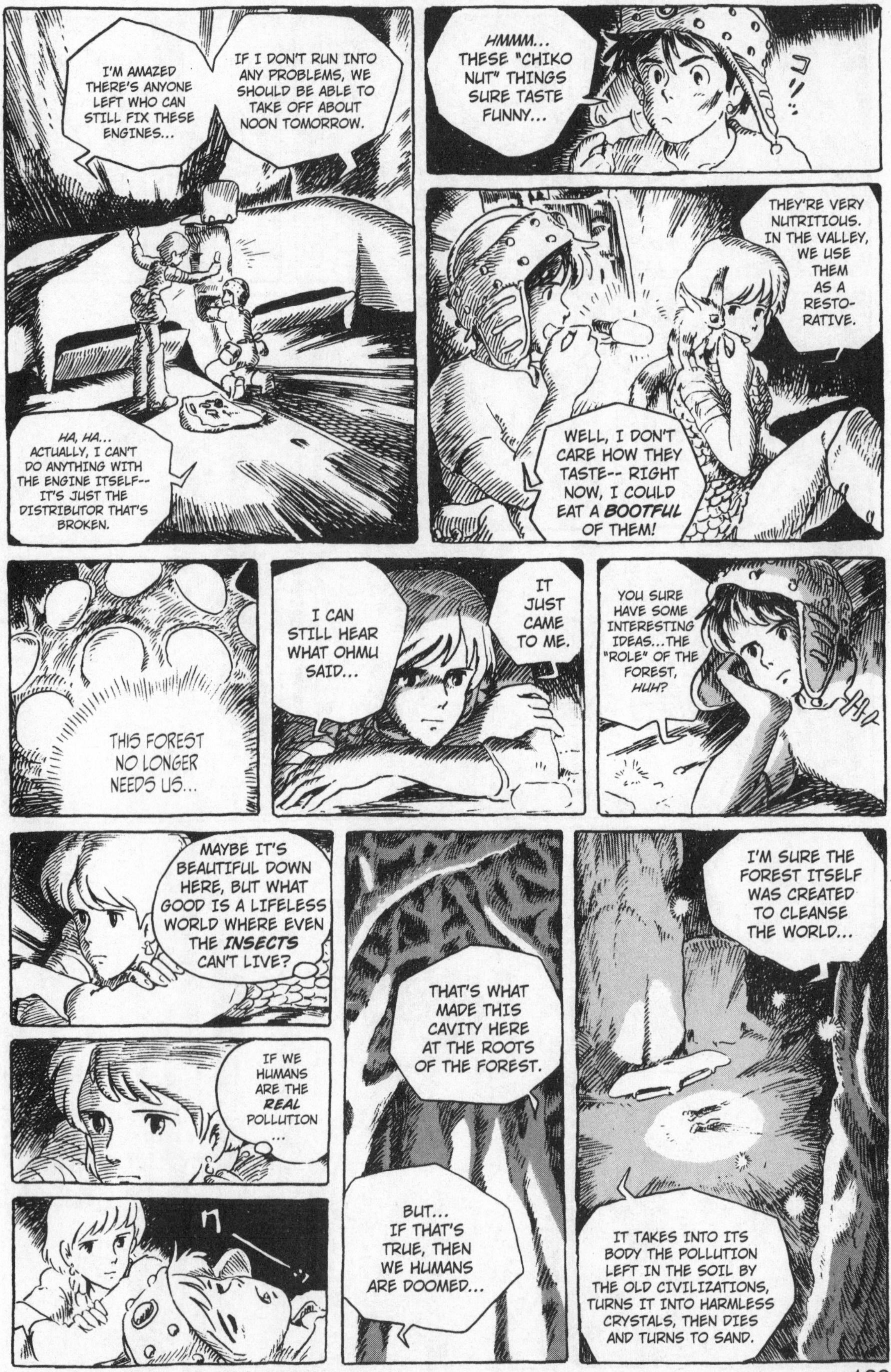
HMMM... THESE "CHIKO NUT" THINGS SURE TASTE FUNNY...
THEY'RE VERY NUTRITIOUS. IN THE VALLEY, WE USE THEM AS A RESTO-RATIVE.
WELL, I DON'T CARE HOW THEY TASTE-- RIGHT NOW, I COULD EAT A BOOTFUL OF THEM!
IF I DON'T RUN INTO ANY PROBLEMS, WE SHOULD BE ABLE TO TAKE OFF ABOUT NOON TOMORROW.
I'M AMAZED THERE'S ANYONE LEFT WHO CAN STILL FIX THESE ENGINES...
HA, HA... ACTUALLY, I CAN'T DO ANYTHING WITH THE ENGINE ITSELF-- IT'S JUST THE DISTRIBUTOR THAT'S BROKEN.
YOU SURE HAVE SOME INTERESTING IDEAS...THE "ROLE" OF THE FOREST, HUH?
IT JUST CAME TO ME.
I CAN STILL HEAR WHAT OHMU SAID...
THIS FOREST NO LONGER NEEDS US...
I'M SURE THE FOREST ITSELF WAS CREATED TO CLEANSE THE WORLD...
IT TAKES INTO ITS BODY THE POLLUTION LEFT IN THE SOIL BY THE OLD CIVILIZATIONS, TURNS IT INTO HARMLESS CRYSTALS, THEN DIES AND TURNS TO SAND.
THAT'S WHAT MADE THIS CAVITY HERE AT THE ROOTS OF THE FOREST.
BUT... IF THAT'S TRUE, THEN WE HUMANS ARE DOOMED...
MAYBE IT'S BEAUTIFUL DOWN HERE, BUT WHAT GOOD IS A LIFELESS WORLD WHERE EVEN THE INSECTS CAN'T LIVE?
IF WE HUMANS ARE THE REAL POLLUTION...

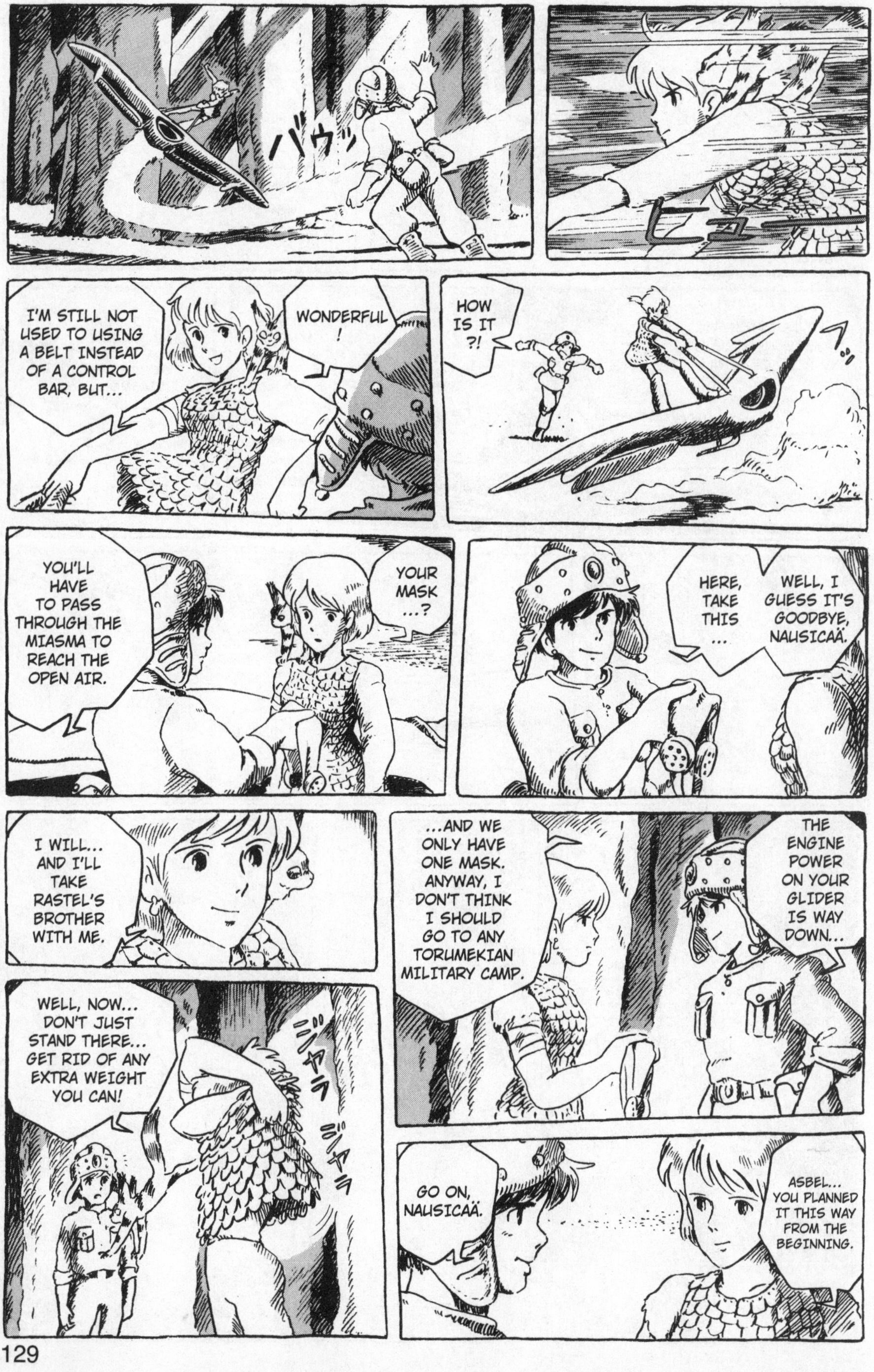
ヒュー
バウッ
HOW IS IT ?!
WONDERFUL !
I'M STILL NOT USED TO USING A BELT INSTEAD OF A CONTROL BAR, BUT...
WELL, I GUESS IT'S GOODBYE, NAUSICAÄ.
HERE, TAKE THIS ...
YOUR MASK ...?
YOU'LL HAVE TO PASS THROUGH THE MIASMA TO REACH THE OPEN AIR.
THE ENGINE POWER ON YOUR GLIDER IS WAY DOWN...
...AND WE ONLY HAVE ONE MASK. ANYWAY, I DON'T THINK I SHOULD GO TO ANY TORUMEKIAN MILITARY CAMP.
I WILL... AND I'LL TAKE RASTEL'S BROTHER WITH ME.
ジャラ
ジャラ
WELL, NOW... DON'T JUST STAND THERE... GET RID OF ANY EXTRA WEIGHT YOU CAN!
ASBEL... YOU PLANNED IT THIS WAY FROM THE BEGINNING.
GO ON, NAUSICAÄ.

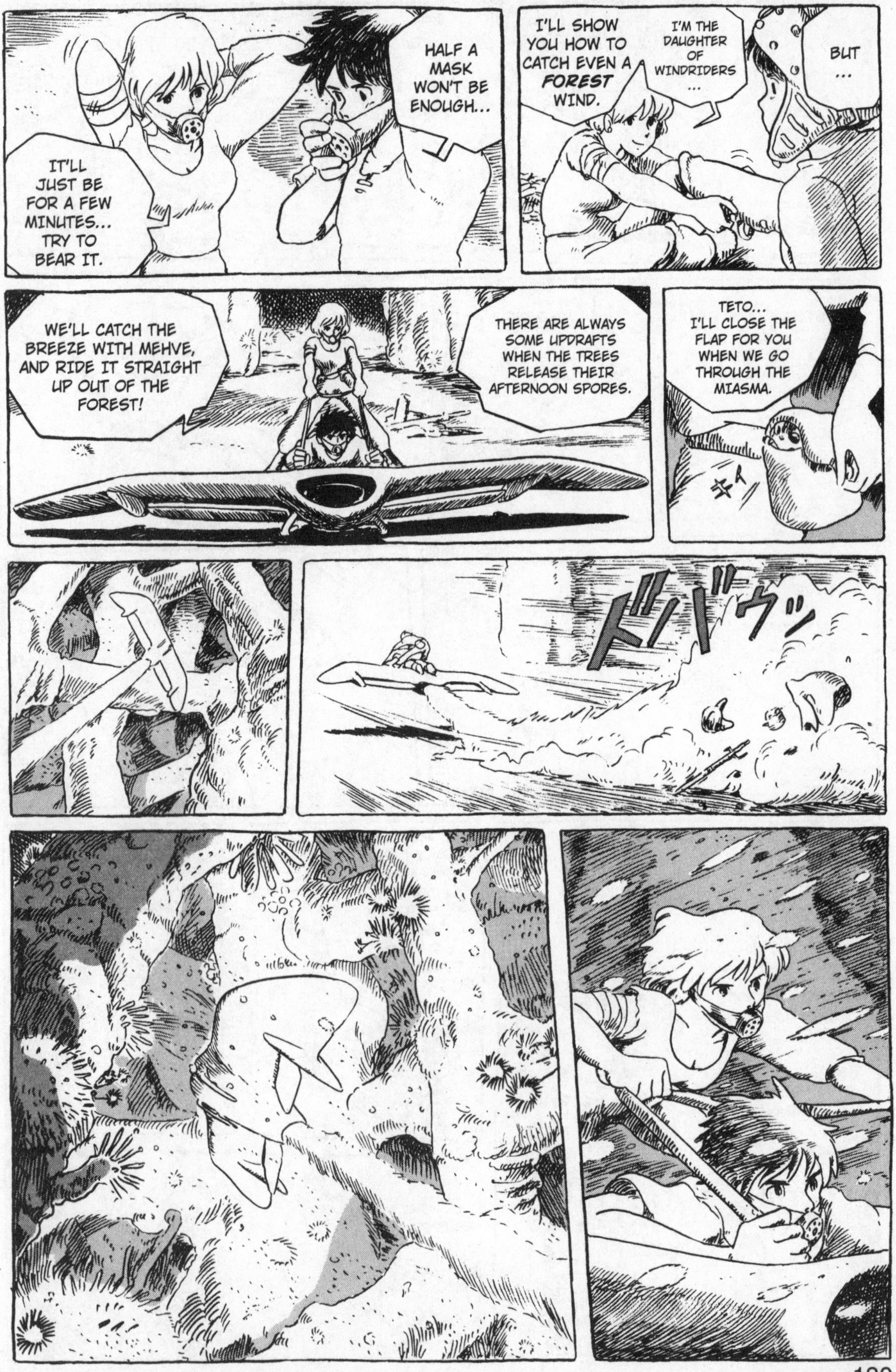
BUT ...
I'M THE DAUGHTER OF WINDRIDERS ...
I'LL SHOW YOU HOW TO CATCH EVEN A **FOREST** WIND.
HALF A MASK WON'T BE ENOUGH...
IT'LL JUST BE FOR A FEW MINUTES... TRY TO BEAR IT.
TETO... I'LL CLOSE THE FLAP FOR YOU WHEN WE GO THROUGH THE MIASMA.
THERE ARE ALWAYS SOME UPDRAFTS WHEN THE TREES RELEASE THEIR AFTERNOON SPORES.
WE'LL CATCH THE BREEZE WITH MEHVE, AND RIDE IT STRAIGHT UP OUT OF THE FOREST!
ドバウッ

# Nausicaä of the Valley of the Wind Guide to Sound Effects

VIZ has left the sound effects in *Nausicaä of the Valley of the Wind* as Hayao Miyazaki originally created them — in Japanese. Use this glossary to decipher, page-by-page and panel-by-panel, what all those foreign words and background noises mean. The glossary lists the page number then panel. For example, 6.1 indicates page 6, panel 1.

| | | |
|---|---|---|
| 31.8 —FX: Guoooooooon (vroooom) | 18.7 —FX: Fuuuu (hiss) | 5.5 —FX: Kooon (kong) |
| 32.1 —FX: Uiiiiin (vwoosh) | 18.9 —FX: Fuuu (hiss) | 6.1 —FX: Kiiin (klaaang) |
| 32.5 —FX: Zaaaa (shaaaaah) | 18.10 —FX: Gi (chomp) | 6.2 —FX: Jiiin (zing) |
| 32.7 —FX: Gigi kichi kichi (kch chk chk) | 19.4 —FX: Kii (kree) | 6.7 —FX: Ton ton (tap tap) |
| 32.8 —FX: Kichi kichi kichi kichi kichi kichi kichi gi gichi (chk chk chk chk chk chk kch kch) | 19.5 —FX: Kuuu kuuu (coo coo) | 6.9 —FX: Kachi (click) |
| 32.9 —FX: Kichikichi kichi kichi ki (chk chk chk ki) | 19.6 —FX: Kuuu kuuu (coo coo) | —FX: Bomu (pwoof) |
| 32.10 —FX: Gi (screech) | 19.11 —FX: Hyuuu (hwoooh) | 6.10 —FX: Kaan kaan (kang kang) |
| 33.1 —FX: Bali bali bali (crunch crunch crunch) | 20.6 —FX: Ta (hop) | 7.1 —FX: Kon (poof) |
| —FX: Pali pali (crunch crunch) | 21.10 —FX: Hahahaha (ha ha ha ha) | 7.5 —FX: Puchi puchi puchi (poof pop pop) |
| —FX: Uooooooon (vwoooom) | 22.3 —FX: Zawa zawa (chatter chatter) | 7.6 —FX: Pita (stop) |
| —FX: Meli meli (crumble crumble) | —FX: Hahahaha ahahaha (ha ha ha ha aha ha ha) | 7.9 —FX: Za (zwoosh) |
| —FX: Mishi mishi (creak creak) | 22.9 —FX: Hahahaha (ha ha ha ha) | 8.5 —FX: Kiiiin (vweeeen) |
| —FX: Bibiiii (screech) | 22.12 —FX: Hahahaha (ha ha ha ha) | 8.6 —FX: Kyululululu (bwatatata) |
| —FX: Bali baki baki baki (snap crumble crumble crumble) | —FX: Hahahaha (ha ha ha ha) | 8.8 —FX: Kyuuun (kweeeen) |
| 33.3 —FX: Pau Pau (blam blam) | —FX: Hahahaha (ha ha ha ha) | 8.9 —FX: Za (zwoosh) |
| 33.4 —FX: Pa (fwap) | 23.2 —FX: Jyuuu (whir) | 8.10 —FX: Lululu (tatata) |
| 33.6 —FX: Dou (dwoom) | 23.4 —FX: Hahahaha (ha ha ha ha) | 9.1 —FX: Gaaan (kick) |
| 33.7 —FX: Gyuuun (zoom) | 24.1 —FX: Dowa (vhooom) | 9.4 —FX: Kyuuun (kabooom) |
| 34.3 —FX: Uooooooon (vwooom) | 25.1 —FX: Vuoo (vwooosh) | 9.7 —FX: Zaza (crash) |
| —FX: Zuuun (boom) | 25.2 —FX: Hyuu (hwoosh) | 10.2 —FX: Kashi (click) |
| 34.6 —FX: Beki (crack) | 25.4 —FX: Kiiiin (vweeeeen) | 10.4 —FX: Pau (blam) |
| —FX: Zuwa (vwah) | 25.8 —FX: Dou (vhoom) | —FX: Shuwa (swoosh) |
| 35.1 —FX: Zuzuun (crash) | 26.5 —FX: Shuuu (shhh) | 10.5 —FX: Vuiiii (vwooosh) |
| 35.3 —FX: Bouuuuuun (kaboom) | 27.6 —FX: Ki (kree) | 10.6 —FX: Pau (blam) |
| 35.4 —FX: Za (whoosh) | 27.9 —FX: Hyuu (sheee) | 10.9 —FX: Su (zhoop) |
| 35.5 —FX: Zaaa (skreee) | 27.11 —FX: Dou (zwash) | 10.10 —FX: Gui (tug) |
| 35.6 —FX: Gooo gooo goo (gwooh gwooh gwooh) | 28.1 —FX: Gyaaa (sheeee) | 11.1 —FX: Fu (fwoosh) |
| —FX: Ta (tump) | 28.2 —FX: Vuuuun (vwooosh) | 11.2 —FX: Dou (shoom) |
| 36.5 —FX: Galagala (skrank) | 28.5 —FX: Biiiii (vweeeeh) | 11.3 —FX: Shuuu (vwoosh) |
| 36.8 —FX: Ha ha (huff huff) | 28.6 —FX: Shiii (sheeee) | 12.2 —FX: Dodo (crash) |
| 37.3 —FX: Zei zei (wheeze wheeze) | 29.3 —FX: Gii (screech) | 13.1 —FX: Shuwa (swoosh) |
| 39.1 —FX: Gongongon (hum hum hum) | 30.1 —FX: Uiiiin (vweeeen) | 13.2 —FX: Uiiii (vwooosh) |
| 39.2 —FX: Golon golon golon (hum hum hum) | —FX: Baki bak (crumble crumble) | 14.1 —FX: Kui (yank) |
| —FX: Uooooooon (vroom) | —FX: Mishi mishi (groan groan) | 14.2 —FX: Bo (ploof) |
| 39.4 —FX: Gooo (vrnnn) | —FX: Meki meki (crumble crumble) | 14.8 —FX: Ka (flash) |
| 39.7 —FX: Zaza (skeesh) | —FX: Bali bali (crunch crunch) | 15.1 —FX: Zun zun zun (boom boom boom) |
| 39.8 —FX: Wala wala (shuffle shuffle) | 30.2 —FX: Meki meki (crumble crumble) | 15.2 —FX: Pachi pachi pachi chichi (popopopop) |
| 40.3 —FX: Hiku hiku (twitch twitch) | —FX: Beli (rip) | 15.7 —FX: Gigigigi (whistle) |
| —FX: Kasa (rustle) | —FX: Baki baki (crack crack) | 15.8 —FX: Gigi (whistle) |
| —FX: Hiku hiku (twitch twitch) | 30.3 —FX: Gaaaan (boom) | 16.1 —FX: Gigigigigigigi (whistle) |
| 40.8 —FX: Hiku hiku (twitch twitch) | 30.5 —FX: Uiiiin (crack) | 16.2 —FX: Ba (bwaf) |
| 40.9 —FX: Gasa gasa (rustle rustle) | —FX: Zuuun gaaan (zaboom boom) | 16.3 —FX: Gigigigi (gheeee) |
| —FX: Picha picha (squish squish) | —FX: Bala bala (crumble crumble) | 16.6 —FX: Zazaaaan (crash) |
| 41.5 —FX: Hyuu hyuuun hyuuun hyuuu (kashoom kashoom kashoom) | —FX: Meki meki (crumble crumble) | 17.1 —FX: Hyuuuu (hwoooh) |
| 41.6 —FX: Uooooon (vrnnn) | —FX: Mishi (groan groan) | 17.3 —FX: Za (zoosh) |
| 41.7 —FX: Hyuuu hyuuu (hwooosh hwooosh) | 30.6 —FX: Saaa (shaa) | 17.5 —FX: Hyuuu (hwoooh) |
| 42.1 —FX: Shuu (fshhhaa) | 31.2 —FX: Meki meki (crumble crumble) | 18.3 —FX: Kiii (kree) |
| | 31.3 —FX: Bali bali (crunch crunch) | 18.4 —FX: Kaaa (hiss) |
| | | 18.5 —FX: Hyuuu (hwoooh) |

81.2 ——FX: Kueeee (coo)
81.3 ——FX: Wahahaha (wa ha ha ha)
——FX: Gulali (wobble)
81.4 ——FX: Ha ha ha ha he he he (ha ha ha hee hee hee)
81.8 ——FX: Bololololo (bwoom)
82.1 ——FX: Bolololo (bwoom)
82.2 ——FX: Oooooon (vrnnn)
82.5 ——FX: Goon goon (kank kank)
82.6 ——FX: Saa (fwoosh)
82.8 ——FX: Dou (vwoom)
83.1 ——FX: Hiiiin (hweeeeen)
83.4 ——FX: Oooon ooon (vrooom vrooom)
83.6 ——FX: Ooooo (vwoooh)
84.1 ——FX: Uoooooon (vrnnn)
——FX: Golon golon (rumble rumble)
84.2 ——FX: Uuuu uun (whir whir)
84.7 ——FX: Chi (tweet)
84.10 ——FX: Uoooooon (vwrooooom)
85.1 ——FX: Gooo (goosh)
85.2 ——FX: Hyuuu hyuuu (hwooooh hwooh)
87.10 ——FX: Gooooo (goosh)
88.2 ——FX: Kii (kree)
88.3 ——FX: Uooooon (vroom)
88.9 ——FX: Gooo gooo (vwoosh vwoosh)
88.12 ——FX: Gooo (vwoosh)
89.1 ——FX: Kiiiin (vweeeen)
89.3 ——FX: Pau (blam)
89.4 ——FX: Do (koom)
——FX: Ba (boom)
89.5 ——FX: Gyaaaaan (shree)
90.1 ——FX: Baum (boom)
——FX: Beki (snap)
91.1 ——FX: Basha ba basha bishi (blam scrunch blam)
91.2 ——FX: Ga (splat)
91.3 ——FX: Jaaaaa (splorsh)
92.2 ——FX: Dou (shoom)
92.3 ——FX: Biiin (snap)
92.4 ——FX: Gyaaaaaan (shree)
92.5 ——FX: Kiiin (shreee)
92.8 ——FX: Uiiiiin (vwish)
93.1 ——FX: Oooo (vroom)
93.3 ——FX: Hyuu (hwoooh)
93.8 ——FX: Ba (yank)
94.5 ——FX: Niko (grin)
94.6 ——FX: Bau (zoom)
94.8 ——FX: Ha ha (huff huff)
94.9 ——FX: Ha ha (huff huff)
95.1 ——FX: Gau gau (bang bang)
——FX: Dou dou (boom boom)
95.2 ——FX: Gagagagagagaga (bwatatatatatata)
——FX: Gangan (boom boom)
——FX: Dou dou (boom boom)
95.3 ——FX: Gagagang (ba-bam)
——FX: Zun zun (boom boom)
——FX: Gagagagaga (bwatatatata)
——FX: Dododododo (baboom)

54.4 ——FX: Dododo (thud thud)
54.5 ——FX: Dodododo (thud thud thud)
55.4 ——FX: Da (dash)
56.2 ——FX: Za (pounce)
56.3 ——FX: Giiiin (klang)
56.4 ——FX: Buun (whiz)
57.1 ——FX: Ka (crunch)
57.5 ——FX: Za (oomph)
——FX: Fu (hmph)
57.8 ——FX: Zun (zash)
58.8 ——FX: Bulu bulu (tremble tremble)
59.1 ——FX: Hahahaha (ha ha ha ha)
59.2 ——FX: Gula (wobble)
59.9 ——FX: Za (fling)
59.10 ——FX: Kiiin (kang)
60.4 ——FX: Vuoooooon (shoom)
60.5 ——FX: Ulaa ulaa ulaa (hurrah hurrah hurrah)
60.8 ——FX: Hahaha hahaha (ha ha ha ha ha ha)
60.10 ——FX: Hahahaha hahahaha (ha ha ha ha ha ha)
61.1 ——FX: Hahaha (ha ha ha)
61.5 ——FX: Uiiiiiin (vween)
61.6 ——FX: Uoooooon (vrnnn)
61.7 ——FX: Uuun (vwreen)
62.1 ——FX: Gooo gooo goo goo goo goo goo (gooo gooo goo goo goo goo goo)
——FX: Pachi pachi pachi pachi (crackle crackle crackle crackle)
64.1 ——FX: Ka (chack)
64.8 ——FX: Goo goo goo goo (goo goo goo goo)
——FX: Boo boo (spray spray)
——FX: Pachi pachi (crackle crackle)
——FX: Meki (crack)
69.8 ——FX: Gala gala (skreek skreek)
70.2 ——FX: Bo (pof)
70.4 ——FX: Dokun dokun (kathump thump)
70.5 ——FX: Piku piku (twitch twitch)
——FX: Doku doku (kathump thump)
70.9 ——FX: Waaa (aaaaugh)
71.1 ——FX: Gusha (splat)
71.4 ——FX: Jiji (sputter)
71.5 ——FX: Dokun dokun (kathump thump)
71.10 ——FX: Hyuu hyuu (hwooh hwooh)
72.1 ——FX: Gan gan (bam bam)
——FX: Uiii uiii (zhir zhir)
73.1 ——FX: Pasa (paft)
73.3 ——FX: Jala (kachank)
75.1 ——FX: Ki (kree)
77.6 ——FX: Gooo (whoosh)
77.7 ——FX: Hiiin hiiiin (vweeeen vweeen)
78.4 ——FX: Shuuu (fshhh)
78.5 ——FX: Bau (vwip)
78.6 ——FX: Hiiiiin (hweeeeeeh)
79.2 ——FX: Hiiiin (hweeeen)
79.4 ——FX: Lululululu (vrnnn)
80.3 ——FX: Fu (fwash)
80.8 ——FX: Uooooooon (Vrnnn)
80.9 ——FX: Kukuku (hee hee)

42.5 ——FX: Bo (pwof)
——FX: Ki (kree)
——FX: Po (plop)
——FX: Tonton (thump thump)
42.6 ——FX: Po (plop)
42.8 ——FX: Shuuu (fshhh)
43.2 ——FX: Don (bump)
43.3 ——FX: Ba (bam)
44.9 ——FX: Golon golon (rumble rumble)
45.1 ——FX: Uoooooon (vrnnn)
45.2 ——FX: Gooo (zwoosh)
45.4 ——FX: Vuooo (shoom)
46.4 ——FX: Zaza (skeesh)
——FX: Dodododo (vrnnn)
46.9 ——FX: Gaya gaya (yammer yammer)
47.3 ——FX: Bau (zoom)
47.4 ——FX: Fu (fwoosh)
47.5 ——FX: Vuoooo (shoom)
47.7 ——FX: Shaaa (whoosh)
48.1 ——FX: Za za (thump thump)
——FX: Doya doya (scurry scurry)
48.3 ——FX: Uiiiin (vweeeen)
48.5 ——FX: Pau (blam)
48.6 ——FX: Doba (zing)
48.7 ——FX: Ga (whud)
48.8 ——FX: Bau (vwoosh)
49.1 ——FX: Bou (vwoom)
——FX: Waa waa waa (yammer yammer yammer)
49.4 ——FX: Gooo (vwoosh)
49.5 ——FX: Saa (shwaaa)
49.6 ——FX: Goooo (vwoosh)
50.2 ——FX: Za (skeesh)
50.3 ——FX: Gyuuuun (vwooooosh)
50.4 ——FX: Za (zash)
51.4 ——FX: Moso moso (shuffle shuffle)
51.6 ——FX: Hiso hiso (whisper whisper)
51.10 ——FX: Kii (kree)
51.11 ——FX: Picha picha (squish squish)
——FX: Hiku hiku (twitch twitch)
——FX: Pita pita (slink slink)
52.1 ——FX: Hiku hiku (twitch twitch)
——FX: Hiku hiku (twitch twitch)
——FX: Hiku hiku (twitch twitch)
——FX: Pitcha (squish)
——FX: Hiku hiku (twitch twitch)
52.3 ——FX: Hiku hiku (twitch twitch)
52.4 ——FX: Zulu zulu (slink slink)
——FX: Hiku (twitch)
——FX: Picha picha (squish squish)
52.6 ——FX: Bishi (vwip)
53.1 ——FX: Ba (zap)
53.2 ——FX: Kii (kree)
53.3 ——FX: Peta peta (slink slink)
53.5 ——FX: Suta suta (stomp stomp)
53.8 ——FX: Basa (swoosh)
54.1 ——FX: Su (shoosh)

115.6——FX: Dou (shoom)

115.7——FX: Fu (fwoosh)

116.1——FX: Shuuu (swoosh)

————FX: Bau (vwoosh)

116.2——FX: Buiii (vwoosh)

116.3——FX: Bibibibi biii biii (buzz buzz buzz)

————FX: Kasa kasa (scuttle scuttle)

116.4——FX: Shii (swoosh)

116.5——FX: Buoooo oooo uoooo (buzz buzz buzz)

116.6——FX: Kachi kachi kachi (click click click)

————FX: Kchi kchi kchi (click click click)

————FX: Gigigigi (chk chk)

116.7——FX: Giiii (chk)

116.8——FX: Kiiiin (vweeen)

117.2——FX: Shaaa (vwoosh)

117.3——FX: Zugaan (crash)

118.2——FX: Zaaaa (vwash)

————FX: Bau (vwoom)

118.3——FX: Shuuu (shoom)

118.4——FX: Zu (slip)

118.6——FX: Don (whud)

118.8——FX: Ooooo (buzz)

————FX: Bou (vwoom)

119.1——FX: Gashi (crunch)

119.4——FX: Gili gili (chik chik)

119.6——FX: Zazaza (zwoosh)

119.7——FX: Zaaaa (sploosh)

119.9——FX: Kaaaan (klang)

119.10——FX: Ba (bwah)

120.3——FX: Shululululu (swirl)

————FX: Tosa (whump)

120.9——FX: Sawasawa (sha sha)

120.10——FX: Su (shu)

120.11——FX: Pa (fling)

121.1——FX: Za (zhoosh)

121.2——FX: Bali (yank)

121.6——FX: Yoro (wobble)

122.1——FX: Zawa zawa sala (sha sha sha)

122.2——FX: Hena hena (slump slump)

122.3——FX: Kii (kee)

122.4——FX: Fuuu (yawn)

122.8——FX: Hahaha (ha ha ha)

————FX: Fuuu (hiss)

125.6——FX: Tata (dash)

126.6——FX: Za (zhush)

127.9——FX: Saaaa (shhhaa)

127.10——FX: Sala sala (sprinkle sprinkle)

128.1——FX: Koli (crunch)

128.11——FX: Kuuu (zzzz)

129.1——FX: Huuuu (hwooosh)

129.2——FX: Bau (vroom)

129.3——FX: Fu (click)

129.10——FX: Jala jala (kashank kashank)

130.3——FX: Kee (kee)

130.5——FX: Dobau (kashoom)

————FX: Zawa zawa (sha sha)

106.8——FX: Zazaaan (sploosh)

107.2——FX: Yoro (wobble)

107.4——FX: Gata gata (tremble tremble)

107.7——FX: Yurari (stagger)

107.11——FX: Bibibi (buzz)

108.1——FX: Uooo (buzz)

108.2——FX: Ooo (buzzzz)

108.3——FX: Uiiiin (buzzzz)

108.5——FX: Waaan waan waaan (buzz buzz buzz)

————FX: Doba (sploosh)

108.7——FX: Kaaa (flash)

108.8——FX: Zazaza (splorsh)

109.1——FX: Zaba (bloosh)

109.3——FX: Dododo (rumble)

————FX: Zazazaza (splosh)

109.5——FX: Gu (grip)

109.6——FX: Pau (shoom)

109.7——FX: Ki (kree)

110.1——FX: Ba (sploosh)

110.4——FX: Bali (rip)

110.5——FX: Ki (kree)

110.7——FX: Shuuu (vwoosh)

110.9——FX: Doba (vroom)

111.2——FX: Kasa kasa (rustle rustle)

111.3——FX: Ha ha (huff huff)

111.4——FX: Ha ha (huff huff)

————FX: Zawazawa (chkchkchk)

————FX: Zoro zoro (scuttle scuttle)

————FX: Sawa sawa (chk chk)

111.5——FX: Hau (whoosh)

111.6——FX: Gan gan (bang bang)

111.7——FX: Ha ha (huff huff)

111.8——FX: Zazaaa (zhoosh)

111.9——FX: Zuba (chock)

111.11——FX: Ba (pounce)

112.1——FX: Sa (zhoop)

112.2——FX: Ka (fash)

112.3——FX: Pika (flash)

112.4——FX: Boto boto (thud thud)

112.5——FX: Bala bala (tumble tumble)

112.8——FX: Kasa kasa (scuttle scuttle)

112.9——FX: Ka ka (grip grip)

————FX: Shu (fwoosh)

112.10——FX: Bya (fling)

112.11——FX: Peta (stick)

112.12——FX: Palin (shatter)

113.1——FX: Zazaa (swoosh)

113.2——FX: Zubo (skoosh)

113.3——FX: Zaaa (sssttt)

114.2——FX: Shiiii (sheeee)

114.3——FX: Shaaa (swoosh)

114.4——FX: Shuuu (swoosh)

115.2——FX: Gaaaan (blam)

115.3——FX: Gan gan (blam blam)

————FX: Giii (chk)

115.4——FX: Ga (whack)

————FX: Zuzuzun (boom)

————FX: Gooo (gwhoooh)

————FX: Uooooooon (vwroooon)

95.5——FX: Oooo (wrooooh)

————FX: Zun (boom)

95.7——FX: Gagan Gan (bwatata)

————FX: Zuzun (boom)

95.8——FX: Ka (flash)

96.1——FX: Dobau (kabooom)

96.2——FX: Gooo (vwoosh)

96.7——FX: Ni (sneer)

96.9——FX: Guooo (vwroooh)

97.1——FX: Gyaaaaan (shree)

97.2——FX: Waaa (waaaugh)

97.3——FX: Uooon (vrmmmm)

97.4——FX: Oooo (vwooh)

97.5——FX: Goooo (gwooh)

97.6——FX: Gan (crank)

97.7——FX: Buaaa (vwoosh)

97.8——FX: Dou (voom)

98.1——FX: Uiiiiin (vween)

98.2——FX: Bau (blam)

98.3——FX: Ga (blam)

————FX: Uiii (shaboom)

98.4——FX: Hii (shree)

————FX: Pafu pafu (bwatata)

98.8——FX: Kiiin (shree)

98.9——FX: Kiiiin (shree)

————FX: Dodododo (brakabraka)

99.1——FX: Gooo (fwoom)

99.2——FX: Bala bala bala (tumble tumble tumble)

99.9——FX: Bouuuuuun (kaboom)

100.2——FX: Zaaaa (shoom)

100.5——FX: Doba doba doba (bang bang bang)

100.6——FX: Kiiiiin (shree)

100.7——FX: Uiii (shree)

101.7——FX: Shuuu (fwoosh)

101.9——FX: Kiiin (shree)

101.10——FX: Zuzuuun (ba-boom)

102.1——FX: Baum (boom)

102.3——FX: Gooo (fwoom)

102.4——FX: Oooon (vwroooom)

102.12——FX: Uoooon (vwroooom)

103.1——FX: Shuuu (fwooosh)

103.7——FX: Shaaa (fshaaa)

104.1——FX: Zaza (sploosh)

104.3——FX: Zaa (sploosh)

105.1——FX: Gula (wobble)

105.3——FX: Zazaa (kwoosh)

106.1——FX: Sawasawa sawasawa (shasha shasha)

————FX: Piku (twitch)

106.2——FX: Piku (twitch)

————FX: Sawa (sha)

106.3——FX: Zawa zawa (sha sha)

————FX: Katsun (konk)

106.4——FX: Kikiii (screech)

106.7——FX: Sawa sawa (sha sha)

# *Profile*

## Hayao Miyazaki

Animation film director Miyazaki was born in Tokyo, Jan. 5, 1941. He joined Toei Doga after graduating Gakushuin University's School of Political Economy. After designing the characters and scenery for *Prince of the Sun: The Great Adventure of Horus* (1968), Miyazaki joined A Production and wrote the original concept, script, and designed the scenery for *Panda! Go Panda!* (1972). In 1973, with Isao Takahata, he joined Zuiyo Films. After stints with Nippon Animation and Telecom, he helped the founding of Studio Ghibli. During that time, Miyazaki worked on scenery design and screen composition for *Heidi: Girl of the Alps* (1974), directed *Conan, The Boy of the Future* (1978), and directed his first feature film, *Lupin the Third, The Castle of Cagliostro* (1979). In 1984, based on his comic published in *Animage*, Miyazaki wrote and directed *Nausicaä of the Valley of the Wind*.

As a director for Studio Ghibli, Miyazaki has since released *Castle in the Sky* (1986), *My Neighbor Totoro* (1988), *Kiki's Delivery Service* (1989), *Porco Rosso* (1992), *Princess Mononoke* (1997), *Spirited Away* (2001), *Howl's Moving Castle* (2004), *Ponyo* (2008), and other feature animation films.

*Spirited Away* won the 52nd Berlin Film Festival's Golden Berlin Bear for Best Film and the Best Animated Feature at the 75th Academy Awards.

Some of Miyazaki's literary works include *Houses Where Totoro Lives*, *Shuna's Journey*, *What is a Movie?* (conversation with Akira Kurosawa), *Princess Mononoke*, and *Starting Point: 1979–1996*, a collection of essays, interviews, and memoirs that chronicle his early career and the development of his theories of animation.